EXPOSING LIFESTYLE TELEVISION

For my father – there, just ahead of me.

Exposing Lifestyle Television
The Big Reveal

Edited by

GARETH PALMER
University of Salford, UK

ASHGATE

Published by
Ashgate Publishing Limited
Gower House
Croft Road
Aldershot
Hampshire GU11 3HR
England

Ashgate Publishing Company
Suite 420
101 Cherry Street
Burlington, VT 05401-4405
USA

www.ashgate.com

British Library Cataloguing in Publication Data
Exposing lifestyle television : the big reveal
  1. Television program genres 2. Lifestyles
  I. Palmer, Gareth
  791.4'5655

Library of Congress Cataloging-in-Publication Data
Exposing lifestyle television : the big reveal / edited by Gareth Palmer.
  p. cm.
  Includes index.
  ISBN 978-0-7546-7430-6
  1. Television program genres. 2. Lifestyles. 3. Interpersonal relations on television. I. Palmer, Gareth.

  PN1992.55E97 2008
  791.45'6--dc22

                                                                    2008013460

ISBN 978-0-7546-7430-6

Mixed Sources
Product group from well-managed
forests and other controlled sources
www.fsc.org Cert no. SA-COC-1565
© 1996 Forest Stewardship Council
FSC

Printed and bound in Great Britain by
MPG Books Ltd, Bodmin, Cornwall.

Contents

Notes on Contributors

Maggie Andrews teaches Television Studies at Staffordshire University. In 1997 she published *The Acceptable Face of Feminism* (London: Lawrence and Wishart). She has since published widely on feminism and popular culture.

Anita Biressi is Reader in Media Cultures at Roehampton University. Her publications include *Crime, Fear and the Law in True Crime Stories* (Palgrave 2001), *Reality TV* (Wallflower 2005) and *The Tabloid Culture Reader* (McGraw Hill 2007).

Frances Bonner is a Reader in Television and Popular Culture in the English, Media Studies and Art History School at the University of Queensland. She is the author of *Ordinary Television* (Sage 2003) and is currently engaged in an extended study of British and Australian television presenters.

Fan Carter teaches Media and Cultural Studies at Kingston University. She is currently researching commercial constructions of parenting in popular media.

Buck Clifford Rosenberg is a PhD candidate in the Anthropology Program at the University of Melbourne. His thesis explores the relationship between home and lifestyle, examining concerns over home lifestyle television, DIY renovation and domestic décor. He has previously published on IKEA, and the connection between home lifestyle and the risk society.

Julie Doyle is a Principal Lecturer in Media Studies at the University of Brighton, UK. Her research interests include surgery and (gendered) embodiment, and media and the environment. She has published in journals such as *Body and Society*, *Science as Culture* and *Social Semiotics*, and she is currently working on a book project examining the mediation of climate change.

Laurel Forster is a Senior Lecturer in Cultural Studies and Literature at Portsmouth University. Her interests are in women's culture, history and writing. She is currently involved in an AHRC project on 1970s visual culture at Portsmouth, with a particular research focus on television and magazines of the period. Her publications include articles on women's magazines, film, the early modernist writer May Sinclair, and an edited collection, *The Recipe Reader* (Ashgate 2003). She is currently working on a longer project on feminism, women's magazines and the media.

Irmi Karl is Principal Lecturer in Media and Communications at the University of Brighton, UK. Her work engages with questions of sexuality and gender identities in relation to the consumption of (new) information and communication technologies. Other research areas include mobile technologies and space as well as the sexual and class politics of popular media forms. In this context she is concerned with consumerism, audience agency and the role of technology in the processes of mediation and lived experiences. E-mail: I.Karl@Brighton.ac.uk.

Heather Nunn is Head of Film, Media and Cultural Studies at Roehampton University and co-director of the Centre for Research in Film and Audiovisual Cultures. Her publications include *Thatcher, Politics and Fantasy* (Lawrence and Wishart 2002), *Reality TV* (Wallflower 2005) and *The Tabloid Culture Reader* (McGraw Hill 2007).

Gareth Palmer is an Associate Head of School at the School of Media, Music and Performance at the University of Salford. He has published widely on television and governance. At present his practical and theoretical work are focused on lifestyle and in particular health issues.

Deborah Philips is Professor of Literature and Cultural History in the School of Languages, Literature and Communication at the University of Brighton. She has written on women's writing, feminist theory and television; her publications include *Brave New Causes* (with Ian Haywood, Cassell 1998) and *Women's Fiction 1945–2005* (Continuum 2006). She is currently working on the narratives of the carnival site.

Guy Redden is a lecturer in the Department of Gender and Cultural Studies at the University of Sydney. He has previously taught at universities in Thailand and the UK, and has published widely in the areas of consumer culture, alternative lifestyles and contemporary media.

Yael D. Sherman is a doctoral candidate in Women's Studies at Emory University. Her dissertation is on femininity and normalization in personal makeover shows. She is the author of 'Tracing the Carnival Spirit in Buffy the Vampire Slayer: Feminist Reworkings of the Grotesque', published in *Thirdspace*.

Madeleine Shufeldt Esch is a doctoral candidate in the School of Journalism and Mass Communication at the University of Colorado in Boulder. Her dissertation research addresses the evolution of domestic advice and home improvement television in the US throughout the 1990s.

Isabelle de Solier is a PhD candidate in the School of Culture and Communication at the University of Melbourne. Her thesis is on the contemporary lifestyle of 'foodies', and examines lifestyle media such as cookbooks, TV shows, and food blogs. She has previously published on food television and class distinction, and the lifestyle politics of the Slow Food movement.

Lyn Thomas is the Deputy Director of the Institute for European Transformations at London Metropolitan University where she has taught on the French degree since 1989. She is the author of *Annie Ernaux: An Introduction to the Writer and her Audience* (Berg 1999), *Fans, Feminisms and 'Quality' Media* (Routledge 2002) and *Annie Ernaux: A la première personne* (Editions Stock 2005). She is currently editing a book for Palgrave with Martin Ryle and Kate Soper: *Better than Shopping: Counter-consumerism and its Pleasures*. She is a member of the Feminist Review Editorial Collective.

Chapter 1

Introduction – The Habit of Scrutiny

Gareth Palmer

Lifestyle television is at once one of the oldest of the medium's genres and the newest. Cookery shows, DIY programmes and various other celebrations of the domestic have long been part of television's deep structure. However, the last 20 years have seen the development of programmes that broaden lifestyle's brief by offering to change a person's home, appearance and indeed sense of self. This expanded remit has met with a mixed critical reception. For some lifestyle television's excesses are yet another sign of the medium's inexorable decline. Its emotional frameworks, quick results and freakish extremes often make the sub-genre look like the more flamboyant cousin of reality tv.

The writers in this book argue that lifestyle's perspective on class, gender, and sexuality illustrate significant shifts in contemporary culture. While cultural transformation underscored the injunction to 'inform, educate and entertain' that helped define public service television, new and more aggressive programmes foreground the possibilities of transformation to address questions of identity, the place of the family and the role of government. Lifestyle's images, stories and themes comprise a genre that offers emotional connection to the hopes and aspirations of audiences worldwide. This book considers the claims of this genre to empower its audiences in a neoliberal climate.

If lifestyle television offers an education in the consumer arts it may be valuable to consider the factors that have informed the curriculum. This introduction begins by considering changes in television produced by the rise of the market both as an economic force and as an ideal. This is followed with a discussion of the role of surveillance and the new stress on appearances given prominence in lifestyle television. The last section puts the genre in a wider context by connecting its promises to the world beyond its ornate borders.

To the market

At the heart of neoliberalism as it emerged in the 1980s was the ideal of the market. Popular culture presented the market as a natural phenomenon whose simple logic of exchange between goods, services and customers was a more natural, purer model than those envisaged by state mechanisms. As commentators and policy-makers warmed to the theme their rhetoric pictured the state as a body whose misguided interventions meddled in everyday affairs. Neoliberalism entails government taking place at a distance through the measures, techniques, procedures and discourses that shape subject populations. In this new orientation to government we are to prioritize our relationship to the market.

One of the first sectors to benefit from the promotion of market economics in the 1980s was the broadcast industry. Right-wing governments encouraged by global corporations challenged the primacy of public service broadcasting and opened up the old monopolies to the forces of the market. Within a few years the ways in which television was made and consumed had changed radically. The introduction of satellite and cable technologies meant that old systems faced new competition. The model of citizens watching a few channels was replaced by demographic analyses in which viewers were now customers and programme-makers were in a market. This new conceptualization is central to lifestyle television where the market model – the idea that one can create oneself from a supply of commodities – is fundamental.

As a commercial ethos gained ground the old notion of public service was increasingly exposed as patrician, patronizing and outdated. In order to maintain its status and justify its funding model lifestyle television became one site where public service blended responsible citizenship with enlightened consumerism. Public service broadcasters sought to retain their historical legitimacy in the new media marketplace as honest brokers offering their endorsements with the inherited sheen of respectability. But this new mode of address led to concerns about the dumbing down of public service television.

The rise of television's independent sector entailed radical changes in the way programmes were made. A system dominated by large broadcasters or networks was now challenged by a much more responsive and dynamic sector. New producers brought the mentality of commerce to broadcasting in their drive to 'keep to the bottom line', cut costs, and develop formats for export. By the 1990s the new production sector was responsible for creating efficient new strands for the home market. For example six 30-minute cookery programmes can be shot in less than a week using the same set, the same presenter and the same crew all working on short-term contracts. Ingredients for the shows can be brought to the location and the material 'topped and tailed' by a reality segment in the edit to suggest the passage of time and give the material a lifestyle flavour. This new industrial product would then gain an airing at times that maximized its audience share. Furthermore the focus on something as timeless as cooking means that the producer could continue to derive income as the shows were repeatable. Whether any changes took place in the eating habits of the audience is quite another issue. The point is that a new market model inspired and enabled lifestyle formats. Public service broadcasters responded to this challenge in two ways – by changing the ways in which their programmes were made by setting up an internal market and by marrying the pedagogic impulse to inform, educate and entertain to bright jazzy strands of consumer advice. In the new age of broadcasting both private and public sectors scanned the 'overnights' to check their ratings for these determined the market value of the product and their future prospects.

The last 25 years have seen labour in the broadcast industries increasingly casualized. As networks had to cut costs, training declined and a service industry ethos began to replace the last vestiges of a craft tradition. An awareness of changing economic circumstances brought together programme-makers, contestants and audiences. Thus when making a room over for $500 or sending competing teams out to buy antiques with £300 in their collective pocket, a need to keep within acceptable low-risk limits informs decision making on all sides of the camera. Not only are the contestants to be canny the producer demonstrates a praiseworthy cost-consciousness. Part of lifestyle's reflexivity is that no costs appear to be hidden, a strategy which recommends it as modern open enterprise. A frugal 'waste not, want not' approach is revealed when even the credits contain amusing out-takes from the show which once again stress the transparency of the process.

Advertising remains fundamental to commercial television but the expanded opportunities offered to the industry through the expansion of cable and satellite stations come at a time when research suggests audiences are less attentive to its messages. One consequence of this is that sponsorship now finds its way into programmes. This is crucial for lifestyle television because of the way it works to endorse a way of living with the right products. Advertising informs the sorts of programmes being made by favouring ABC1 groups with the most disposable income. Those living in more difficult circumstances are featured as subjects for treatment rather than ideal viewers. Some of the popular American formats depend for their existence on sponsorship while broadcasters leave onscreen expressions of gratitude by participants for all that they have done to transform their lives. Corporate benevolence and the need to please advertisers combine to produce lifestyle programming with maximum emotional impact on families.

Outside television the credit boom and the increase in home ownership meant that a premium was placed on quality advice. This new need to style the home was met by the rise of large self-assembly furniture stores and DIY centres such as IKEA in Europe and Home Depot in the US. For a new class, insecure about how they decorated their home, advice from television was perfect – discreet enough to be hidden yet bland enough to offer style-safety in an area where – as lifestyle television warned us – a decorative *faux pas* lurked just around the corner. As Bourdieu famously said 'Taste classifies as it classifies the classifier' (Bourdieu 1989) and lifestyle feeds on the insecurities and uncertainties of its audiences who may have wished to obscure their class origins. The 1980s and 1990s saw lifestyle television expand into new places in the schedule as it offered domestic skills such as cooking and gardening, as well as grooming and deportment advice – all questions of taste it was best to acquire discreetly so they did not seem 'learnt'. Even the humble garden migrated from being a space for the growing of vegetables to being a further space for the expression of the self. Lifestyle seemed to have an opinion on all aspects of contemporary culture which was rapidly becoming one in which one's taste was always on display. But lifestyle placated social anxieties by offering its advice in a breezy light tone in order to dispel any deeper concerns.

However, advice on home and garden is only part of lifestyle's story. In order to truly engage the viewer and maximize an emotional connection to the genre, producers developed programming which featured those struggling with the new world, those trying to reach beyond themselves or trapped by their own indolence. At the heart of this is the return of class.

The introduction of the market was supposed to have created a clearer, fairer picture of social relations in which class had only historical significance as a marker of outmoded and inefficient worker–management relations. But despite its glamorous sheen capitalism has helped deepen structural inequalities whose most enduring motif is the persistence of class. In the genre all classes have specific roles to play – from those in the upper middle class signifying prestige and bearing cultural capital to the lower working class – those in need of treatment. In between the two are the new and enterprising fractions of the middle class. Crucially it is the signs of class that lifestyle programming dwells upon because the social, economic and political determinants are beyond the genre's brief (Skeggs 2004). For lifestyle all that matters is the look for it is on the surface that it can make its most striking interventions. In the guise of re-education the working class can be made to see their problems from the perspective of objective expert/consultants who will stress performance and character rather than anything else. The aim thus becomes the trying if elementary one of erasing the unacceptable signs of lower class origins and making them respectable merely by looking respectable. The magic of lifestyle is that this transformation brings the grateful individual or family to a momentary understanding that the surface really is all that matters. In lifestyle frantic work on taste and deportment erase the determinants of class and turn life into a performance – a metaphor that perfectly expresses the genre's rationale.

The symbolic capital of the traditional middle class is foregrounded in their accents, dress sense and ease with a range of people. It is the 'natural' property of its owners. Regular television consumption makes it clear to the viewer that these codes are much respected in public life. Yet this demeanour is also deconstructed by its bearers as a type of performance and in doing so the 'democratic' potential of lifestyle is revealed – *viz*, if this is a performance then anyone can do it. Several British lifestyle programmes display the middle class advising the lower orders in deportment, dress sense, cooking, etc. to enable a long-standing class-based fantasy of escape or at the very least the frisson of 'blending in' with respectable (i.e. upper middle class) company. The problem for the middle class (and the guilty pleasure for the viewers) is that these well-meaning emissaries from the world of good taste are faced with the recalcitrant nature of the lower orders. Thus lifestyle offers on the one hand the democratic potential of 'passing' as a member of another class and at the same time essentializes class differences by vilifying those who fail to make it.

It need hardly be said that class differences are far more complex than lifestyle allows. In *Distinction* Bourdieu considers the role of the habitus, that structuring matrix of dispositions in the deep structure of the psyche (Bourdieu 1989). For example, the working classes live in a 'culture of necessity' that determines all of their life choices. What lifestyle takes from this is simply the principle of choice. It is quite elementary – we should choose to live differently.

Lifestyle depends for its emotional effects upon our familiarity with class markers. It exploits our fear of seeming to belong to a lower class by promoting class mobility. The horror of international formats like *Wife Swap* and *Honey We're Killing the Kids* is that those individuals may not be able to escape their class when the whole drive of consumer culture is to move upward. In lifestyle, class is like a return of the repressed as intimate technologies threaten to reveal the subject's true class and destabilize the carefully groomed surface of its aspirational owner. The good taste recommended by the genre becomes a badge of belonging for those feeling uncertain of their place in our social order. But in maintaining this performance some signs of class have to be submerged for they threaten to rise to the surface and hint at some of the great unsaids of lifestyle like economic plight. A concern with the surface is also a concern with disguise and what has to be disguised in public life is any sort of crisis.

Talk shows have long depended upon and even encouraged a carnivalesque perspective on signs of working class excess (Shattuc 1997). It is lifestyle's role to treat them. In lifestyle the fat person stands in for the working class in that he or she represents excess, indulgence of the wrong kind. Their very presence advertises all manner of exclusion. As such the format has to perform the work of getting him or her to 'fit in'. In the logic of the genre to be fat is either the choice of the profoundly deluded or the lazy. As a result the individual has no need of agency. After triggering the tv-consensus via a panel of experts or concerned friends, the charitable folks of lifestyle transform the victim who must learn to play the game of appearances and see him or herself as others do.

When faced with dysfunctional families of any kind lifestyle provides its own images of perfection in the form of effective teams in which everyone knows their place. The 'race against time' so fundamental to the genre is always successful because the teams cohere so well. What lifestyle foregrounds is process. By putting teams in front of the camera they add an extra pressure to their work but this also champions transparency; if they can do it then so can we. Selecting a range of individuals and putting them in all manner of testing scenarios, from surviving a week on minimal wages to rebuilding a shattered life, the genre illustrates that 'it can be done'. In one simplistic sense lifestyle celebrates a new world in which the old restrictions no longer apply. This is enterprise writ large, an enterprise that depends for its drive on the love of families and exults in its distance from the state and any other old-fashioned authorities. In place of a welfare state and notions of state dependency with its concomitant 'weakness' are networks of expertise in newly privatized realms all working to the same transparent managerial ethos.

But as we see day after day and week after week there is much work to be done. The West is home to millions of lost, overweight and deluded souls all in need of rescue. The challenge of engineering culture change cannot be left solely to those bearing the symbolic and cultural capital of the traditional middle class. To make effective up-to-date changes lifestyle has recruited another team of experts – a class described by Bourdieu as the new *petite-bourgeois*. As Featherstone comments

> They are perfect audience and transmitters, intermediaries for the new intellectual popularization of bodies of knowledge but a popularization of intellectual lifestyle too … They also act as cultural entrepreneurs in their own right in seeking to legitimate the intellectualization of new areas of expertise such as popular music, fashion, design, holidays, sport, etc. (Featherstone 2000, 100)

Bourdieu listed several new professions such as hairdressers, interior decorators, journalists and television producers in this new class (Bourdieu 1987, 387). Lifestyle television is the space *par excellence* for the celebration of this expertise tested and qualified in the marketplace. The experts have proved themselves in this sacred realm and are living breathing advertisements for their claims. The significance is that their qualification for being on television advising the rest of us comes from their successes outside it thus once again validating the importance of the market as a pure mechanism. Who better to teach us the lessons of consumerism than those validated by the only system that counts – the market? If we are to use them as models as we are encouraged to do then their expertise (coupled with their products) are essential tools. Perhaps there can be no greater validation for the triumph of the marketplace than our investment in lifestyle experts. And, in the commercial world that is lifestyle, we are asked to place our faith in their wisdom as well as being encouraged to make investment in the products they recommend. Perhaps the reason why various classes happily take lessons from these experts is that they are not coded as the interfering welfare workers of old but products of the marketplace operating as consultants. The fact that their advice tallies with government strictures is less significant than the fact that it seems to have emerged from the market and is thus 'pre-approved'.

It may also be worth noting that those responsible for producing lifestyle television have come to the medium through a relatively new route. Certainly for much of its history in the UK television was the province of Oxbridge graduates who dominated in producer/managerial roles. Broadcasting in its newest incarnation is the work of a generation of media students who graduated in the 1980s and 1990s. This group have a different understanding of how the medium operates. Rather than moving into relatively secure positions in large corporations a new generation of media workers make programmes within a market-led model of how television works – on short-term contracts – and live by the mantra that 'you're only as good as your last show'. For this generation the notion of the public service worked differently. Perhaps significantly for lifestyle television formats this generation may be socially closer to the rising *petite bourgeoisie* who constitute the class of experts. Lifestyle genres may be closer to collaborative models of what new producers and their associates believe the medium should do.

Lifestyle television is an agent of consumerism at the heart of which is a belief in the market and the importance of positive change. The principal target for the genre is nuclear families whose representation in the genre may be out of step with their declining numbers but who predominate for reasons that have to be connected to advertising and the quest for those with the right sort of disposable income. The family has to bear a burden of representation. They are empowered as agents of change and encouraged to work together to achieve the universal dream of class mobility while struggling under neoliberalism's strictures. Nevertheless striving, discretion and good taste are key themes of the genre whose dedication to maintaining a type of performance helps us forget what lies beneath the surface.

Who's watching?

The politics of the self as a phenomenon arising out of the 1980s signals the rise of a narcissistic and self-reflexive culture in which individual crises, family histories and personal complexities provide an anchor for contemporary insecurities in the affluent culture of advanced technocratic society. (Biressi and Nunn 2005, 100)

Inspired by a mix of factors involving public security and the changing shape of policing over the last 20 years, surveillance has played an increasingly important role in public space. This spread of surveillance technology has had significant impacts in both the materials used in television in general but in factual formats in particular. This development plays an important if overlooked part in helping to construct a culture where the look is so important.

Reality television is a key precursor of modern lifestyle formats and has to a large extent been formed by surveillance culture. Its dependence on 'real people' and its eye on the bottom line are two key elements it shares with lifestyle television. But the significance of reality television lies less in formats than in how it has integrated the surveillance ethic into television's grammar. It has done this in three ways: police programmes such as *Cops* helped us come to terms with the fact that we were now under increasing amounts of surveillance. While these formats' rationale was the much-vaunted one of security we were able to overlook the infringement of personal liberties it represented. Secondly, the development of international brand formats such as ... *from Hell* prepared us for a new type of television in which people, neighbours and others, were seen training cameras on each other. Various disorders and acts of incivility now went public in the name of infotainment. Keeping an eye on order became partly the responsibility of the public enabled by camcorder technologies and informed by communitarian discourses such as Neighbourhood Watch. The third aspect of lifestyle sired by reality tv is the use of camcorders as diaries. Here we see revelations of the self in what Dovey has called 'first person television' (Dovey 2000). Since *Video Diaries* in the early 1990s, lifestyle has used the camcorder confessional as a crucial technology for maximum emotional impact while also reminding us that self-scrutiny is a responsibility to the self.

The imposition of surveillance in the cities and workplaces has rendered up material for debate on questions of behaviour and the standards people live by. The rhetorics of reality television help us envision the urban environment as a disordered one in need of stronger policing backed up with our participation. Lifestyle television cannot countenance anything as complex as civic engagement and so it leads a retreat into the home, a stable place for cocooning the family and the acting out of classic role models. Licensed by the myth of its effectivity on the streets, surveillance now has to be welcomed into the home where it can open the question of behaviour.

Surveillance as a means of interrogating behaviour has become an important tool in helping lifestyle fight off competition from other media such as the internet. Rather than acting as a commentary on social phenomena, television now proves its own added value by changing lives through a variety of formats. In this way the medium now offers itself as a resource for self-achievement, a consumption technology offering individuals new ways to order their lives in line with their own ambitions and those of designated psy-experts licensed to make these intrusions into the domestic. While the experts in taste and decorum come from the new *petite bourgeoisie* and might even be taken issue with, the psy-experts come with more ruthless tools to carve an actualized self in which exterior and interior have to match for the subject to feel 'whole'. In earlier incarnations these experts of the psy made frequent appearances on talk shows where their counsel was sought by hosts convinced that their therapeutic discourses had transformative value. But since those stages have been evacuated to give participants more space to fight, the experts have migrated to the cleaner veneers of lifestyle television where their pronouncements get respectful attention. The expertise on offer here has three important components – it must be simple, demonstrable in television's frames and have no connection to class. Those offering their expertise will have gained their distinction principally in the marketplace. Indeed it is the practical visible evidence of their efficacy in training dogs, hoodlums and unruly children that takes pride over any paper qualifications. Simplicity is a key theme. The model of the self to be treated is stripped down to one in which personal responsibility overrides any social, economic or political factors. Everything is seen through the prism of the responsibilized self. Lifestyle articulates a peculiar view of a pliable subject reaching out for definition, an unstable subject no longer placed in the fixed hierarchies of class and sex but now floating free. The self is an object for contemplation, a project to be moulded. While magazines and advice columns in various media have colonized this subject in the past, this model of the endlessly improvable self is ideal for television. In lifestyle's model of the self there is no limit to what the individual can do. Lifestyle programming rewrites the legacy of identity politics as a series of consumer choices. The person you want to be is down to you.

As we have seen, lifestyle formats open up the home in the name of class re-education but shaming need not be restricted to any class. Shaming can be used to make any individual aware of the message their appearance sends out to their community. The 'other' is now used to confirm our existence, to remind us that what we are is partly what others think of us. For example, in *What Not to Wear*, a successful transatlantic format discussed by Philips and Sherman here, surveillance footage taken by friends is used to license a transformation in the subjects 'best interests'. The shame that we see on-screen, felt by those seeing footage of themselves from the perspective of friendly spy-cameras, is deserved for they are not living up to this ideal that we should look good and presentable at all times. To be badly 'turned out' seems like a wilful refusal to play the lifestyle game and as such it deserves tele-punishment. Similarly, in *10 Years Younger*, vox pop judgements become a 'consensus' while surveillance footage becomes proof (Doyle and Irmi, this volume). When the two are combined they offer evidence that extreme measures can now be deployed to create change. In the face of these facts resistance is futile: conformity is king and queen. As the changes get under way, being cruel to be kind motivates the trainers, dieticians and other new experts of the self at the core of lifestyle. But the genre always offers happy endings. When the big reveal takes place before friends and family the object of all this attention is revealed to herself as a perfected product of the surgeon's art/the stylist's taste/a new diet and her own determination. She surveys herself through the eyes of others and finds herself complete. Now at least she is what she seems to be. Furthermore by admitting herself flawed and undergoing the makeover she has won the approval of those who had previously engineered her surveillance. Transformation is achieved by marrying surveillance to nervous narcissism thus producing fragmented insecure and unstable identities. Subjection to a model of normative femininity is presented as the acme of empowerment, a perfect expression of the choice maxim that defines lifestyle television.

It should become clear that television that can exploit this new structure of feeling might be likely to succeed in a time of risk and anxiety. The threat of exposure that lies behind the apparently random nature of those chosen for tele-treatment underlines the importance of always maintaining a 'front'. The panopticon is at work here in the name of entertainment. Behind the jolly banter and ironic commentaries, lifestyle offers platforms for appraisal systems, popularizing managerial perspectives on daily life to be lived as efficiently as possible. When the private space of the home is opened out for inspection and treatment it serves as lesson and example for all citizens as well as justifying the intrusion. But it also helps spread the surveillance ethic. When a transformation is effected the message is clear – surveillance works both in terms of a reformed family/subject and as a technology that helps us to monitor ourselves. Now we appreciate the value of being transparent subject-citizens comfortable with discipline. The bright and cheery tones of lifestyle deflect us from considering this a regime of normalization. Instead we focus on the transformed – a happy bundle of consumers making their own choices, choices that happily coincide with those of the experts. Class, economics, politics are all part of a dread legacy to be avoided in the bright future. The new and endlessly flexible subject has only to pick and choose from options created by market-approved psy-experts. The complexities created by dynamic psychological models of yore can be dismissed as too time-intensive. In its place are market-tested models such as Cognitive Behavioural Therapy (CBT) whose techniques fit television's frames and whose results can be easily tracked week-by-week. Never was a model of the self so media-friendly, never did the psychological seem so persuasive. The drive behind consumer culture to make us all flexible, malleable selves finds a natural home in the genre.

But of course identities rooted in consumer culture are by their very nature unstable and subject to the vagaries of fashion. The result is anxiety, an anxiety that is conjured up only to be resolved and then rekindled afresh for the next episode. Whatever challenge we see or encounter can be overcome but never quite permanently. Lifestyle is about the never-quite-completed subject, the consumer with a still lingering itch of doubt about his or her decisions and open to change.

One significant source of lifestyle's philosophy can be found in the personal development movement (PDM). This loose coalition of self-help entrepreneurs and assorted therapists has developed significant economic and symbolic power over the last 20 years. Appearing at first on talk shows in their more liberal incarnations in the 1980s, self-help gurus like Anthony Robbins, Dr Phil, and NLP-spokespeople such as Paul McKenna all offer a model of the psychological that floats free of any social, political or economic determinants. Their beliefs can be expressed in short pithy sound-bites while their many products in the forms of DVDs, books, seminars and courses all elaborate the same message that you can 'be all you can be'. The problem that they identify is fundamental to all people – a faulty or ineffective belief system. Once this is corrected through one of the programmes on offer then the individual is free to realize their potential. This rather mechanical model of the self is perfect for lifestyle as it discards the past and leaves the individual free for any form of shaping – ideally that offered by other PDM merchants.

Behind the all-important formulation 'empowerment = choice' that informs lifestyle is the return of normative femininity. Bolstered by the rise of evolutionary psychology that informs PDM multi-million sellers like *Men Are from Mars and Women Are from Venus* lifestyle producers indulge in the most reactionary fantasies. Some American makeover shows spend millions on technological transformations but its narratives depend on the oldest possible formulation of boy-meets-girl. It is almost as if the revolutionary potential of technology itself has to be constrained by the ideological demands of the nuclear family. Those who need rescuing by the medical-industrial complex (here presented as the beauty business) are for the most part seeking romance, seeking to rekindle the flames of passion with hubby or struggling to get out there dating again. Classic gender divides are set up by lifestyle – the single woman is to be pitied, the married woman has 'let herself go'. Lifestyle rescue comes via surgery and shopping; surgery offers not freedom but the opportunity to regain a place in the stable family. Such transformations present an ideal that will please advertisers as well as those already prepared for such fantasies by consumer culture. Retail therapy is a fun name for a disciplinary process in which woman puts herself back in the gaze and is asked to value it. Lifestyle parades the return of a normative femininity as a kind of 'back-to-nature' move of the kind Faludi discovered in popular American media after 9/11 (Faludi 2007). The big reveal is not just a visual celebration of unity (with extended family/with mirror) but a climax that validates the transformation into core femininity. The most important element here is that the way the subject feels about herself as 'finished' is endorsed by all these significant others. She 'fits' her role perfectly. It is simply a good coincidence that her sense of herself fits with a normative femininity.

How does lifestyle get away with selling such stories? The first response must be to point to the continuing dominance of patriarchal models promoted elsewhere in consumer culture, the prevalence of which may be informed by the reactionary politics of evolutionary psychology. But for lifestyle the trick of selling such traditional goals as a form of feminism-lite is to use irony. The quest for a man/partner is sometimes undergone in an ironic manner, as if we were just playing. This strategy enables presenter, contestant and viewer to gain a critical distance on the chase while at the same time being seduced by it. This dual aspect is lifestyle having its cake and eating it – playing at traditional romance while adopting a postmodern critical distance. It may not be honest but it is a good way of building audiences. And as we have seen it is the market that dominates in all ways.

Although women still make up the majority of subjects for treatment in lifestyle, two new versions of masculinity have come to prominence in the genre – the metrosexual and the camp. Lifestyle is proud to foreground a newly feminized male or, more recently, 'metrosexual' comfortable with a discussion of interiors and concerned with his appearance. Sophistication and self-awareness are crucial qualities in the lifestyled male for he is the new aesthete, addressed as a knowing subject in these entertainments. Meeting his concern for house and home are a generation of new presenters who exhibit a high degree of camp, a campness that raises the spectre of their difference in the same moment it extinguishes it – it's only a 'Queer Eye' after all. This new representation of masculinity comes at a time when men are also subject to new pressures at work as various surveys indicate that judgements on health and appearance are considered more important for career progression than ever before. In lifestyle we see hints of the new man becoming subject to the same psy-complexes as women. He could yet find himself susceptible to the ideals and body-dysmorphia that have affected women. But for the most part this is not so much a new man as a neutered man shopping side by side with his partner with little else but suburban bliss on his mind. Then again, how satisfying can such a mate be for women urged elsewhere in the genre to pursue a manly ideal whose failure to get in touch with his feelings is a guarantee of his difference and thus essential masculinity?

Fortunately lifestyle can provide answers. In the first place suburban men are encouraged to pursue manual labour around the home which helps reinforce their masculinity. They are presented with ideals such as Ty Pennington or Scott Cam whose handiness sets them apart from the feminized hubby (Rosenberg here). Secondly, manly heterosexuality is illustrated by his bemusement or embarrassment when confronted with the camp or gay men offering advice; the very fact that these men are in need of domestic surgery from such experts illustrates that they are essentially different. Thirdly, men are often shown not quite understanding basic domestic devices like washing machines. This inability can be read as a form of calculated ignorance but lifestyle uses it to suggest their class location – it is often the working class male for whom the inability to function in the domestic sphere is proof positive of his manliness. Makeovers might place an egalitarian sheen on the surface but men's essential difference from their womenfolk is never endangered for long – indeed it cannot be or the lifestyle-nexus would collapse.

Beyond lifestyle's borders

As the writers in this book make clear, lifestyle television offers a distinct series of pleasures. Its marriage of old-fashioned stories to the very latest techniques makes for emotionally persuasive television. Although it is inspired by the need to attract advertisers, maintain and build audiences and please sponsors, this should not detract us from acknowledging the power of the genre. Lifestyle offers viewers a sense of completion through restoration narratives. At the end of the operation/swap/ diet the changed individual comes home both to him or herself as well as a loving, usually nuclear family, in turn supported by a warm community of self-sacrificing empathic neighbours. Formerly unattainable dreams and ideals have come to these families through the good graces of television and we are all encouraged to share their tearful gratitude. But what would be wrong would be to confuse this emotional excess and the passion of the rhetoric with actual effects. Annette Hill's empirical work on lifestyle's audiences reminds us that viewers feel a great deal of scepticism when viewing these programmes. Some feel that those taking part have made pacts with producers or that they deserve the treatment they get (Hill 2007). Furthermore Hill records viewers' reluctance to learn from lifestyle which, given its pedagogical drive, is interesting. For some it may be the case that the production values that surround the enterprise devalue the message rather than enhance it.

A second significant consideration underscored by some writers here is that lifestyle's discourses are mediated on a variety of websites and other spaces, thus contesting the expertise, however confidently delivered. More than ever before programmes no longer end but have a half-life not simply as repeats but on websites and other locations where they engender further debate. The programme's message may be clear but it is worked through by communities armed with their own knowledge and expertise.

It is also important to acknowledge that lifestyle's rationale is to reach the first generation of children to drift away from television towards online. The make-believe of transformation will have particular appeal for children particularly if it comes bundled up with advertisements for other magical places. Winning the hearts and minds of this generation is one of the crucial battles broadcasters must win if they are to attract advertisers. Chasing this audience might also explain an investment in fairy-tales.

One of the fascinations of lifestyle is what we catch sight of in its shadows, the background to the endless progress the programmes celebrate. In *Extreme Makeover: Home Edition*, for example, each week begins with a videotape of another shattered American family reaching out for help in a country where the gaps between rich and poor are wider than at any time in living memory. If these moments were stripped from their narratives of progress and put into an hour long 'special' providing glimpses of the real conditions of existence for millions of Americans it would be a revelation aeons away from lifestyle's brief. But one struggles to imagine ABC endorsing such a brutal uncoupling! Lifestyle television is deeply indebted to the myth of progress and can-do enthusiasm's ability to leave the past behind. Likewise the miraculous multi-million-dollar transformation of ugly ducklings into swans helps distract us from the need elsewhere in the world for other extreme makeovers such as restoring basic facilities, food and shelter to the thousands of war victims around the world. But again this is marked way beyond the realm of lifestyle. Lifestyle's work begins where charity always does – at home.

Sixty years after it first entered the home as a provider of information and entertainment, lifestyle television has become a portal to transformation. Television offers itself as a tool kit to a new you. The only consistent theme in this perfect televisual complement of consumer culture is that change is good and that the past can and indeed should be disregarded in order to buy oneself a better life. Change is a duty for the individual working on the project of the self. But one question lifestyle's pedagogy inspires is the simple one: does it work? One would have thought that in a harder market, after spending so much time and energy selling the potential for change, someone should consider the results. There is of course a wonderful well-established irony that those who are considered most in need of help are castigated for watching television and often described by experts as couch potatoes – poor family interaction is partly defined by excessive telly-watching. So lifestyle hasn't worked its magic here. Yet. But how else are the 'problem families' identified by the state to be reached? Despite the determined exhortation to rise above circumstances, economic factors persist. In 2008, in the UK, home repossessions look set to increase significantly. The development of obesogenic environments throughout deprived urban areas makes lifestyle's inspirations rather challenging. But the good news is that in such an economic climate the genre will never run out of potential subjects to sell its jolly narratives of progress.

Bibliography

Biressi, A. and Nunn, H. (2005), *Reality TV: Realism and Revelation* (London: Wallflower).

Bourdieu, P. (1989), *Distinction* (London: Routledge).

Dovey, J. (2000), *Freakshow: First Person Media and Factual Television* (London: Pluto Press).

Faludi, S. (2007), *The Terror Dream: Fear and Fantasy in Post 9/11 America* (New York: Metropolitan Books).

Featherstone, M. (2000), 'Lifestyle and Consumer Culture', in M.J. Lee (ed.), *The Consumer Society Reader* (Oxford: Blackwell).

Flanders, J. (2003), *The Victorian House* (London: HarperCollins).

Heller, D. (ed.) (2006), *The Great American Makeover: Television, History, Nation* (New York: Palgrave-Macmillan).

Hill, A. (2007), *Restyling Factual TV* (London: Routledge).

Kavka, M. (2006), 'The Makeover Show Crosses the Atlantic', in D. Heller (ed.), *The Great American Makeover: Television, History, Nation* (New York: Palgrave Macmillan).

Shattuc, J. (1997), *The Talking Cure* (London: Routledge).

Skeggs, B. (2004), *Class, Self, Culture* (London: Routledge).

Chapter 2

Bad Citizens: The Class Politics of Lifestyle Television

Anita Biressi and Heather Nunn

This chapter explores the ways in which lifestyle makeover programming identifies, frames and isolates the 'bad citizen'; that is the citizen who fails to conduct their life according to the idealized 'middle class' norms (see Palmer 2004) which are repeatedly articulated through political and consumer culture and via the competencies of taste and social skills. Taken as a corpus, makeover programmes offer audiences a range of declensions of class positions, exploring the relatively fixed or transitional potential of those subjects who take part. As such they allow audiences to explore the hierarchies of social difference and to review their own relative position within them. Following recent Economic and Social Research Council funded investigations on inequality trends in Britain, it was observed that when people make social comparisons they do so explicitly in terms of lifestyle, material consumption and individual achievement, voicing few sentiments of solidarity either with their peers or with anyone else. Outside of their own social context respondents expressed little resentment of the rich but were extremely critical of certain poorer categories such as benefit holders and refugees from whom they 'actively distance themselves' (Paul 2008, 76). These programmes arguably intersect well with these modes of understanding both social inequalities and individual aspiration and the ways in which citizens understand their social position in relation to others.

In other words, lifestyle programmes culturally underpin the broader social understanding of class position as determined by lifestyle 'choices' and individual aspiration. Lifestyle programmes adopt a pedagogical posture; devising a curriculum with rules to be followed in order for participants to achieve satisfactory progression in terms of family dynamics, personal grooming, financial management and so on. In the example we mainly focus on here, *Honey We're Killing the Kids* (BBC3 2005 onwards) (abrev. *HWKK*), the show's resident expert Kris Murrin is trailed as 'the teacher of parents' who facilitates the family's rise through levels of competency in terms of eating, socializing, mutual respect, exercise and activity and so on. In doing so she also makes patently clear what is out of bounds in terms of attitudes, behaviour and lifestyle for the aspirant well-socialized family. We want to argue that if television works to delineate or map or direct citizenship in the twenty-first century then it is partly doing so by invoking, exposing, shaming and instructing the bad subject; a figure against which we – the idealized viewing public – might measure ourselves and our own progress (see Moseley 2000, 314) as self-determining individuals in the privatized public sphere.[1]

In this last sense these programmes work to promote 'core national values' which they convey by implication and in contrast to the stereotyped morals of certain social classes and the non-conformist ways of living ascribed to them (see Berlant 1997, 310). We contend that as cultural artefacts they nicely encapsulate the post-1980s ascendancy of the political values of consumerism, choice and individual self-reliance over the older ethos of cradle-to-grave universal care and the notion of the state as the final bulwark against serious mental or physical decline, social or pecuniary distress. These ascendant values have found expression most evidently in popular reality genres that champion social mobility as an achievable personal goal which can be reached by virtue of individual merit in both the private and public spheres (closely fused as they are). Whether TV subjects are moving from *Ladette to Lady* (ITV 2005 onwards), *From Asbo Teen to Beauty Queen* (C5 2006), from council estate, single mother origins to high-flying entrepreneur in *The Apprentice* (BBC1 2005 onwards), or simply sorting out their *Life Laundry* (BBC 2002) along with their emotional baggage, it seems that the 'rules for life' played out there conform to increasingly nationally articulated values of choice, personal merit and to notions of how that merit should be measured.[2]

In this chapter we intend to focus on lifestyle programmes involving food, nutrition and family conduct in order to explore three related topics against the backdrop outlined above. Firstly, that those who are unwilling or unable to fully take on board the mechanisms of self-improvement are 'bad' (i.e. irresponsible) subjects who undermine the core national value of and imperative to social mobility. Secondly, that these subjects are marked out as bad by a spectacle of embarrassment and sometimes even humiliation. Finally, that the programmes paradoxically both inflate and at the same time suppress the social differences that subtend the class politics of food, consumption and personal conduct. They inflate social difference through stereotypes of lower class lifeworlds (see Habermas 1981) and middle class achievement and via scenarios of social failure which are depicted as extreme and marginal to mainstream society. At the same time they suppress the economics of social difference by suggesting that anyone can escape social failure should they choose to make the effort and by closing down any discussion about the resources needed to achieve this.

HWKK explicitly formulates these equations between lifestyle, moral conduct and class – often linking issues of food consumption to an explicitly lower class

---

1   The definition of citizenship which we keep in mind when addressing these issues is as outlined in Nick Stevenson's glossary (2003, 155): 'the common rights, responsibilities and symbols of membership that define the political community. Can also include practices of deliberation and public engagement that are drawn upon in deciding matters of public importance'.

2   See also the British series *Faking It*, which trains the subject in the acquisition of cultural capital, correct deportment and lifestyle in order to temporarily 'pass off' successfully in an entirely different social and work milieu (see Bonner 2003, 165).

lifeworld of unarticulated experience. The BBC website[3] sums up each family who takes part quite nicely. Here, we reproduce the synopsis of the McDowell family:

> Single mum Paula McDowell and her four children, Ashlay (aged five), Elena (eight), Connor (ten) and Stacy (thirteen), live in north Wales. Paula's house acts as a drop-in centre for the whole estate but, while it may offer her some emotional support as a single parent, it means the household lacks any sense of routine and structure. The kids rule the roost and live for sweets and fights. They're additive addicts and their sugar highs, fatty fry-ups and salted ready meals are having a terrible effect on their behaviour and long-term health. Five-year-old Ashlay has already lost nine teeth, Connor has behavioural problems and Stacy has a 10-a-day cigarette habit. Expert Kris Murrin says the McDowells are one of the most difficult families she has had to work with.

The overall implication is that behavioural laxity or incontinence, lack of structure and/or discipline, in other words, the 'indisciplinarity' of the 'difficult' family, is the terrain to be struggled over, rather than food and healthiness *per se* and each show illustrates the family home as a battleground between generations, between couples and between siblings. Murrin, it is announced, is qualified to take on the family in her capacity as a mother of three, a child psychologist and a government consultant on child welfare.

Each show begins with snapshots of the family's chaotic behaviour explained via a voiceover: the family overeating, children swearing, fighting, and so on. Then the scene shifts to Murrin who is shown working with her high-powered technical team to process and analyse the results of a battery of medical and psychological tests taken by the family. The whole scene is evocative of forensic crime and police procedurals and its dramaturgy of expert knowledge makes plain the incontrovertible culpability of parents who are 'literally' killing their children. It also contributes to the internal logic of the show which is (like much reality TV) a pseudo-social science experiment and which consequently represses random, uncontrolled factors such as family history, income, social networks, education and so on from its narrative.

At this point the parents or parent are then summoned into an intimidating whitewashed bare-brick chamber where they come face-to-face with Murrin: well-groomed, authoritative and unsmiling. Murrin explains the damage done to the family, the risks they currently run and then shows them manipulated photo-imagery projecting what their children will look like when they reach 40 years of age, should they continue with their present habits. Using the 'latest police digital morphing technology' we watch with them as their children transmute into pallid, slack-jawed obese or underweight adults who appear older than their projected years. Suspense is heightened through rhythmic heartbeat music and Murrin's exchange of looks with the parents. Frequently the parents shake, look grief stricken and even cry, invoking what John Langer (1992) has called a 'reflex of tears' which he suggests is emblematic of tabloid television. They are informed that if they carry on in this manner their children will be 'at risk' of colon cancer or eating disorders, of morbid obesity and heart disease, of impaired intelligence, mental ill health and

---

3   <http://www.bbc.co.uk/health/tvandradio/honey/series3honeyfamilies.shtml>, accessed 4 April 2007.

so on. In short, and to borrow a phrase from Gareth Palmer (2003, 145 and 156), shows such as these can facilitate a 'spectacle of shame', exposing and ridiculing the subject's moral character, making links, which may be unfounded and certainly can be damaging, between one's conduct and one's character and between one's character and one's social class. At the end of the programme, having followed the recommended regime, successful parents are rewarded with new digital projections which forecast the children growing into healthy, *attractive* adults. Unsuccessful parents are still shown these alternative futures but warned that they have not done enough to make them happen.

These forecasts are always shot through with class imagery and the symbolism of social difference. In the second set of projections subtle differences in clothes and hairstyles (the substitution of an open-necked shirt for grubby sportswear, a blouse for a t-shirt with exposed bra straps, or a neat modern haircut instead of a shaven head, a broad smile instead of a frown, good grooming rather than an aura of self-neglect) suggest that improving one's behaviour and changing one's lifestyle will also spur social or class mobility. Both Murrin and the parents seem aware of these connotations. In episode 5 of series 4 (2007), for example, Murrin asks single mother Nadine Feeney for her initial reaction to the projections of her daughter Kelsea: 'Married, kids, nice house?' 'I don't think so', replies Feeney, 'sad, she just looks sad.' In the previous episode the following exchange takes place between Murrin and Laura Ali concerning her daughter.

> Murrin: What did you want for her?
>
> Laura Ali: College, university, a career.
>
> Murrin: And I'm assuming that's not what you see there?
>
> Laura Ali: No.

The central section of the programme follows the family as they struggle to adhere to Murrin's new rules, especially tailored to fit their situation of being overly housebound, TV-addicted and so on. Footage frequently shows the families lazing about, eating fatty take-out food, smoking and arguing as well as struggling to shop for or cook healthy food or going on a family outing. Parents also talk to camera about the trials of the new regime. At several stages they are called back into the chamber to be reprimanded or commended and to be given additional rules. At the end of the show parents have their children's new futures revealed to them. Feeney is shown Kelsea's alternative future – she appears fashionable, well-groomed, smiling and wearing a smart jacket. Feeney observes, 'she looks happy, career woman, anything she wants to be'. The opportunity for social mobility is recognized by the parent when the new, improved future is revealed to them. But Murrin replies severely 'Have you done enough?' Feeney believes she has, having stuck to eight of the nine rules (she could not give up smoking) but she looks crestfallen as Murrin declares 'I can't tell you at the moment that you are there, that's not the future I can guarantee.' Finally she declares 'my job is done' and leaves Feeney with the message that she needs to persist with the rules for her family's well-being.

Television, parenting and the expert

The intervention of the expert into family life, both privately and on television, is far from recent and the criteria used by the expert in these programmes bears the traces of earlier class-based judgements about respectability and self-management.[4] Here the expert may function as a contemporary version of the health visitor or housing officer who judged the effort of the working class subject and who was so critically depicted in docudramas such as *Cathy Come Home* (1966) and *Ladybird, Ladybird* (1994) and in Carolyn Steedman's (1986, 38) memoir *Landscape for a Good Woman*. However, in examples such as *HWKK* and related programmes such as *Supernanny* (C4 2004 onwards), which is devoted to more middle class families, this intervention appears to be welcome – the Ali family declare after the show that they are grateful despite finding the experience difficult and embarrassing. Perhaps this is because, as Ron Becker (2006, 186) notes of *Supernanny* and its type, although the family appears to need professional help, at least the help is 'privatized rather than socialized' and thus avoids the stigma of state interventionist family support. While these programmes seem to undermine romantic notions of the self-sufficient family, in fact the families featured function 'as dysfunctional exceptions that demonstrate the importance of functional "normal" families' (176). So whereas ingrained suspicion of the state means that a programme such as *Supersocialworker* is literally inconceivable, the emphasis in these programmes on self-sufficiency and their 'internal logic about what needs to be changed in order to make these families better' is in keeping with a broader neoliberal politics of the family (Becker, 185–6) and thus rendered acceptable. As Becker notes, in these scenarios trouble starts and ends with the family unit and self-improvement is both necessary and manageable. Social or health worker intervention is highly undesirable, rendered unpalatable by its classed connotations and outmoded by post-welfarist notions of the role of the state. But self-help supported by other kinds of experts (counsellors, therapists, nutritionists, financial advisors, etc.) bears no such associations, as these are often privately paid for by the more affluent in the medical, therapy and lifestyle marketplace. Murrin's intervention is tolerable to participants and viewers firstly because she is positioned in this field and also because the regime, although severe, is smuggled in as a life-changing, transformative *experience* which is in keeping with a broader cultural ethos of unmaking and remaking the self (see Hawkins 2001, 414) and with short-term solutions to long-term problems.

There is of course a longer history of television that has overtly striven to impart parenting skills through instructional programming, often despite viewers' resistance to didactic television and to the connotations of state-supported social intervention. In 1980 Christopher Jones, writing as deputy head of Educational Programme Services at the Independent Broadcasting Authority, argued that although research showed that the public would rather have programmes on home improvement than good parenting, these preferences should be put to one side in the interests

---

4   For discussions of the roles of experts and/or ordinary people in early British family-oriented factual programmes see, for example, Booth (1980); Thumim (2004, 102–10); Biressi and Nunn (2005, 63–9).

of the public good. The challenge, of course, was to persuade viewers to watch television that was good for them. For example, reviewing provision during the previous decade, he described a failed attempt to move beyond simple magazine formats to a more 'downmarket approach' aimed at childminders (an unsuccessful programme called *Other People's Children*) and the far more popular *All About Babies* and *All About Toddlers* which were lively and fast moving, aiming to engage 'unmotivated audiences' with minimal formal education (Jones 1980, 20–21). All of these programmes invited audiences to write in for leaflets supplied by the Health Education Authority and were in some senses regarded as social interventionist projects. But as Jones also noted, the difficulty inherent in this kind of provision lies in negotiating the fine line between information and politics, between explaining to a teenager how to overcome educational deficiencies and get a job and explaining the socio-economic and political reasons why he or she might be poorly educated and ill-equipped for life in the first place (24). Jones was writing at the cusp of the new Conservative regime when Thatcherite values of the consumer-parent and the idea of the family as the space where 'commerce comes home' (Nunn 2002, 110) came to the fore. The child in Thatcherite discourse was increasingly drawn on to naturalize 'the market as the impetus to self-improvement and exchange' (Nunn, 105). Family television inevitably adopted some of these values even while shying away from overt politics with, for example, Jones's suggesting that programmes should help parents take an 'active consumer role' in pursuit of their children's education. This last suggestion was in itself indicative of the ways in which prevailing political philosophy can creep into family programming even while programme and policy makers actively disavow its influence.

The Conservative emphasis on responsible individualism, consumerism and self-improvement touched on here was later reconfigured in the self-consciously meritocratic ideology of New Labour in which education was promoted as the key to 'valued social participation' and social mobility was regarded as 'the best index of overall social health' (Dench 2006, 8). In a sense these lifestyle programmes are the (un)natural offspring of Thatcherite family-oriented consumer values and New Labour's interventionist meritocracy which, argues Geoff Dench (11), has focused on the 'state management of personal social capital', the political exploitation of the concept of meritocracy and the ongoing sponsorship of public social mobility. In Dench's words, 'The open model of meritocracy has shifted into an imperative form' (12) and those who fail to be directed by this imperative may fall by the wayside.

So, as Irmi Karl (2008, 2) has argued, 'reality TV appears to have developed a major role in what could be deemed a public class re-education project through body politics'. Via lifestyle programming in particular it undertakes a bio-political disciplinarity which aims to redirect bad citizens towards the socially approved goals of a slim, healthy and well-groomed body, a well-managed, well-socialized family and an aspirant future trajectory. Perhaps these parenting programmes are more palatable to audiences than their predecessors because they combine the disciplinarian directive with highly pleasing and *culturally relevant* discourses of social aspiration, social mobility and self-improvement. The overall ethos here is of attributing blame to the individual subject but at the same time allowing that change is possible through individual submission to the expert's rules of behaviour. As Nick Stevenson (2003) explains in his discussion of Ulrich Beck's work on individualization 'life is increasingly lived as an individual project. Through the decline of class loyalties and bonds (along with growing income inequalities) human beings are increasingly thrown back on their own biographies' and in a sense 'individuals are "condemned" to become authors of their own lives' (30).

Class politics and food politics

Beck's proposal that the industrial society's plea of 'I am hungry', which was based on want, has been replaced in the context of the post-industrial consumer society by the phrase 'I am afraid' (Stevenson ibid.) is also salient here. In the post-industrial society we work hard to reduce risk and endangerment and the politics of food – what we buy, what we eat, what we feed our children, what we waste – is arguably part and parcel of this new orientation. In lifestyle programming, being financially and/or educationally and/or time poor are not regarded as mitigating circumstances – as Murrin makes plain to her subjects, 'you are literally killing your kids'; your children are at risk and you are choosing to do nothing about it. Dominant political and cultural discourses insist that we are the architects of our own futures; we are our own route to personal safety, health and security and we are individually to blame should we fail. In shows like *HWKK* and *You Are What You Eat* (C4 2004 onwards) (abrev. *YAWYE*) subjects are confronted with endless risks: of stroke, cancers, diabetes, depression and infertility and admonished for bringing them down on themselves. Food is frequently associated with disgust (sometimes but not always based in classed associations), incontinence, endangerment and, as we have shown, even social failure.

In lifestyle programming the subject is not necessarily keen to confess to bad habits and they are shown to be blind, dismissive or downright negligent of the attendant risks. Murrin asks Mr and Mrs Ali: 'Would you like to see them [your children] at 70?' They nod cautiously. 'None of your kids will make it to 70', she replies. Often participants are subjected to shock tactics such as this, confronted without warning by friends or family, the evidence of hidden cameras and the diet expert or psychologist/guru. The individual subjected to these revelations is criticized and exposed as a bad citizen who must reform. The idea that the subject might choose not to or simply be unable to conform to these injunctions is not be countenanced.[5] Gillian McKeith, the host of *YAWYE*, offers a frank and plain-spoken challenge to her subjects. The series epitomizes a contemporary preoccupation with

---

5   Carolyn Steedman (1986, 88) observes in her family memoir/cultural critique about working class aspiration that 'accounts of mothering need to recognise not-mothering, and recognising it, would have to deal in economic circumstances and the social understanding that arises out of such circumstances'. There is no scope in these shows for this perspective on 'difficult families' and those whose lives are judged to be failing. Other reality shows, such as observational documentaries, can be far less judgemental and as a result at least allow their subjects to articulate the often elaborate complexities of surviving on the breadline. See for example the BBC1 series *Skint* (2007).

the dangers and risks of unhealthy food to the extent that in one episode an overweight policeman is actually confronted with a body bag brimming full of processed meat representing his weekly consumption. As McKeith herself notes, she is determined to wipe the embarrassed smile off his face. In ways such as this *YAWYE* adopts reality TV techniques to explore consumption through abject imagery of the sick, grotesque body and an emphasis on confession to camera about overindulgence. It takes the route of individualizing responsibility for health and 'good' food consumption rather than politicizing food and critiquing industrialized food culture as very few programmes have tried to do. It is some small irony that reality television's gory or pseudo-scientific revelations of the effects of wrongly-directed and unhealthy consumption are frequently followed on by TV adverts featuring cheerful mums and satisfied families shopping for ready meals and eating fast food; promotions often aimed at economically or time-impoverished consumers.

Britain is a late-modern industrialized nation in which principles of choice, affordability, convenience and lifestyle thread through the production, distribution and consumption of mass-produced food. Britain is also relatively affluent. For sizeable sections of the population, a sense of food as a source of basic nurturance and survival has been supplanted by powerful notions of food as a form of pleasure and indulgence, a treat, and for some a signifier of social position or cultural capital or a threat to well-being through over-consumption. However, for some families low or inconsistent income, poor transport infrastructures, pressures of single parenthood and modern superstore marketing which targets cheap processed food at poorer consumers have resulted in 'food poverty'. Hence the often invisible face of food culture in Britain is the social exclusion that denies people the ability to select a nutritious diet (Hitchman et al. 2002). Indeed as Beck argues, older, more established inequalities of wealth and social class now intersect with contemporary risks and decision-making about how to (or attempt to) ward them off: 'risks seem to strengthen, not abolish the class society. Poverty attracts an unfortunate abundance of risks; by contrast, the wealthy (in income, power or education) can *purchase* safety and freedom from risk' (Beck 1992, 34). Beck adds with a certain irony that, 'A sufficiently well filled wallet puts one in a position to dine on eggs from "contented hens" and salads from "pampered heads of lettuce"' (ibid.).

Here we can only sketch a little of the context of food politics and rhetoric of personal responsibility that intersects with these programmes. But it is clear that the politics of food is fused with the moral issues that attend the politics of class. The media representations we have selected crystallize the ways in which engagement with food consumption involves an individualixed politics of responsibility, individual merit and social progress. In both series cited here there is an *aggressive* exposure of, variously, underachievement, low self-esteem, chaotic lifestyles and risk in order to mark out ways in which the subject's behaviour is dysfunctional, not to say dangerous, as well as socially irresponsible and nonconformist. And the moral issues underscored by these programmes concern personal culpability, moral laxity and an all-round failure to adhere to core national values. When Gillian McKeith condemns the contents of a single mother's fridge as 'toxic' or Kris Murrin confronts a family of chaotic eaters, judgements are made not only about lifestyle but life conduct and the lifeworld of the subjects involved; that is the texture of social experience, habits and associations which always remain unspoken and unexamined. Lifestyle television consistently seeks to confront subjects and make over their lives but in such a way that the politics of food and its relationship to the politics of class and social difference, although firmly present, is submerged in the rhetoric of individual transformation. The phrase 'you are what you eat' is doubly loaded for the bad citizen who is identified with and symbolically associated with the food they consume: the food is not only unhealthy, salty and full of fat – it is also cheap, disgusting, downmarket, tasteless and even toxic. Its message is not just 'you are what you eat', but as Palmer has observed in relation to fashion makeover shows – 'you are what you appear to be' (Palmer 2004, 184).

In lifestyle programming the most compelling moment is perhaps when the subject is obliged to self-disclose, to own up to their secret vices and bad habits, to confess to their ongoing failure to stick to the rules. In *HWKK* there are many scenarios of embarrassment and self-disclosure to camera but the overall message is that the surrender of this private space of the self to the scrutiny of the expert, the programme and to viewers will be worth while in the longer term, which indeed it may well be for the individuals concerned . But it is also the case that, as Nick Couldry (2003, 116) notes, 'the price of this expansion of private experience [through self-disclosure] ... is to submit that experience to the power dimensions of the mediation process. The symbolic landscape in which people's mediated confessions occur is neither simple nor even' and, we would add, there is little space within some of these TV texts for subjects to express the complexity of their lived experience.

Bibliography

Beck, U. (1992), *Risk Society: Towards a New Modernity* (London: Sage).

Becker, R. (2006), '"Help is On the Way!": *Supernanny, Nanny 911*, and the Neoliberal Politics of the Family', in D. Heller (ed.), *Great American Makeover: Television, History, Nation* (London: Palgrave), pp. 175–191.

Berlant, L. (1997), 'The Political is Personal', in R. Guins and O.Z. Cruz (eds) (2005), *Popular Culture: A Reader* (London: Sage), pp. 309–323.

Biressi, A. and Nunn, H. (2005), *Reality TV: Realism and Revelation* (London: Wallflower Press).

Bonner, F. (2003), *Ordinary Television* (London: Sage).

Booth, J. (1980), 'Watching the Family', in H. Baehr (ed.), *Women and Media* (Oxford: Pergamon Press).

Couldry, N. (2003), *Media Rituals: A Critical Approach* (London: Routledge).

Dench, G. (2006), 'Introduction: Reviewing Meritocracy', in G. Dench (ed.), *The Rise and Rise of Meritocracy*, special issue of *The Political Quarterly* (Oxford: Blackwell), pp. 1–14.

Habermas, J. (1981/1989), *Theory of Communicative Action: Critique of Functionalist Reason Vol 2* (Cambridge: Polity Press).

Hawkins, G. (2001), 'The Ethics of Television', *International Journal of Cultural Studies* 4:4, 412–42.

Hitchman, C., Christie, I., Harrison, M. and Lang, T. (eds) (2002), *Inconvenience Food: The Struggle to Eat Well on a Low Income* (London: Demos).

Jones, C. (1980), 'Parent Programmes', in R. Rogers (ed.), *Television and the Family* (London: UK Association for the Year of the Child and University of London), pp. 17–25.

Karl, I. (2008), 'Class Observations: "Intimate" Technologies and the Poetics of Reality TV', in *Fast Capitalism 2.2.*, at <http://www.uta.edu/huma/agger/fast capitalism/2_2/karl.html>, accessed 23 January 2008.

Langer, J. (1992), 'Truly Awful News on Television', in P. Dahlgren and C. Sparks (eds), *Journalism and Popular Culture* (London: Sage), pp. 113–29.

Moseley, R. (2000), 'Makeover Takeover on British Television', *Screen* 41:3, 299–314.

Nunn, H. (2002), *Thatcher, Politics and Fantasy: The Political Culture of Gender and Nation* (London: Lawrence and Wishart).

Palmer, G. (2003), *Discipline and Liberty: Television and Governance* (Manchester: Manchester University Press).

Palmer, G. (2004), '"The New You": Class and Transformation in Lifestyle Television', in S. Holmes and D. Jermyn (eds), *Understanding Reality Television* (London: Routledge), pp. 173–190.

Paul, R. (2008), 'Growing Inequality: Do People Know What is Going On?', in J. Clake (ed.), *Britain in 2008: The State of the Nation* (Swindon and London: Economic and Social Research Council), p. 76.

Steedman, C. (1986), *Landscape for a Good Woman: A Story of Two Lives* (London: Virago).

Stevenson, N. (2003), *Cultural Citizenship: Cosmopolitan Questions* (Maidenhead: Open University Press).

Thumim, J. (2004), *Inventing Television Culture: Men, Women, and the Box* (Oxford: Oxford University Press).

Chapter 3

Digging for Difference: British and Australian Television Gardening Programmes

Frances Bonner

While most types of lifestyle programmes are concerned with portable objects like food, clothes and soft furnishings, or increasingly modifiable and readily relocatable bodies, those looking at houses, and more definitively gardens, are subject to fixed conditions less under the control of individual practices and preferences. It seemed valuable therefore, to examine the neglected area of television garden programming through the prism of a comparison of British and Australian programmes. The two countries provide very different geographic and climatic conditions for gardening, with Australia a largely dry continent ranging from the cool temperate south to the tropical north, while the smaller, wetter UK is for the most part considered temperate marine. Acting contrary to this though is the history of white colonization of Australia, under which plants, gardening practices and beliefs were brought to the colonies in the eighteenth and nineteenth centuries by settlers primarily from the United Kingdom. The material terms of Australian gardening, then, provide causes both for difference from and similarity to British practice and the television programmes which speak to and of it.

Gardening programmes have been part of television output almost from the beginning, first as instructional programmes and then moving very smoothly into the lifestyle category once that developed in the late 1980s. The studio based format of most early television was easier for programmes about cooking or other interior domestic arts than for gardening programmes. *Gardening Club*, one of the earliest BBC programmes, had involved trucking a ton of earth and plants into a Birmingham studio each week, then removing it only to bring more back for the following week's programme (Search 2003, 8). This was very much instructional programming, and Charlotte Brunsdon's comparison of 1972 episodes of the BBC's *Gardener's World* with 1990s makeover programmes like *Ground Force* makes this clear. She comments on the 'editing and commentary governed by the logic of exposition' (Brunsdon 2001, 55), describing the earlier show as characterized by a prevalence of close-ups of plants and flowers and then of a human hand, with humans kept in mid or long shot until the very end.

Writing in 1972 about *Gardeners' World*, Raymond Williams approvingly notes its 'simple honest visual instruction' and Percy Thrower's comfort with the necessary repetition of simple seasonal tasks (1989, 173). Thrower was the original lead presenter of *Gardeners' World*, which began with colour television in 1968, but he was already a familiar figure, since prior to that, as well as radio shows, he had hosted the aforementioned *Gardening Club* (Search 2003, 8). *Gardeners' World* used outside broadcast facilities to shoot on location from Thrower's own garden as well as that of his fellow presenter Arthur Billit, interspersed with visits to other gardens large enough to accommodate the equipment and its many operators, as well as generate the two 30-minute programmes required by the investment in getting them all there (Search 2003, 9–11). Barrie Edgar, producer from 1972 to 1979, recalls Thrower complaining about the repetition admired by Williams, and how he, Edgar, reminded him of the necessity of catering to newcomers to the programmes as well as the reassurance even experienced gardeners felt about being reminded of seasonal tasks (Search 2003, 11). The introduction of portable single cameras at the end of the 1980s meant smaller gardens could be visited and ended the need to shoot two programmes from the same site. The programme changed to a magazine format in 1990.

The current situation in both countries is that there is a small range of dedicated garden programmes, mainly screening over the weekend, as well as occasional gardening items on daytime shows like ITV's *This Morning*, but only the prime time free-to-air shows will be considered here, drawing mainly on the last 10–15 years, but focusing on 2006–7. Both public service broadcasters have flagship magazine shows: *Gardeners' World* in Britain; and the Australian Broadcasting Corporation's (ABC) *Gardening Australia*, which was explicitly modelled on the British programme and replaced individual state programmes in 1991. On a per capita basis, they have similar audience numbers – *Gardening Australia* one million and *Gardeners' World* three million. The total number of gardening programmes was reduced in both countries in 2006–7 and standalone garden makeovers disappeared. Makeovers had been instances of great similarity between the two countries, to the extent that the massive growth of outdoor entertainment areas in British gardens was talked of as a makeover-driven Australian influence.

A number of other types of gardening programmes have been developed on both public and commercial channels. Arguably the most significant Australian gardening programme was *Burke's Backyard*, an hour-long prime time show which screened on the commercial Nine Network from 1987 until 2004. Its host and producer, Don Burke, has long asserted that it was the first lifestyle television programme in the world. As the title indicates, it eschewed the term 'garden' and looked at all the activities conducted in the typical Australian backyard – growing flowers and vegetables, keeping pets and building barbecues and children's play areas. Screened nationally, it nonetheless considered itself a community programme and, as well as celebrities, Burke visited various ordinary people across the country to talk about their gardens and neighbourhoods. The target audience and the ordinary people portrayed were primarily working and lower middle class. Although it did the occasional makeover, as is often the case with generic 'firsts', it is rather anomalous.

The only regular prime time company for *Gardening Australia* now is *Better Homes and Gardens*, launched in 1995 on the commercial Seven Network. It is now an hour-long Friday night show with interior design, house renovation and cooking segments, as well as gardening items. Occasionally it includes makeover segments.

Two relevant short series appeared in 2007: *Australia's Best Backyards* also on the Seven Network; and *Vasili's Garden* on the public multicultural broadcaster, the Special Broadcasting Service (SBS). Unlike the UK where short gardening series, like *Christine's Garden*, are common, this was an unusual move in Australia.

Lisa Taylor's observation about the particular popularity of British garden lifestyle programmes since the 1990s (2002, 484), seems no longer accurate. Indeed, judging from the 12 months to September 2007, garden shows of any kind can now only be found on BBC2. ITV has only the occasional items as mentioned in daytime general magazine shows. Channel 4, once the location of quite a number of significant garden programmes, no longer even lists gardens as a category under lifestyle on its website. Channel 5 similarly has no mention of gardens under 'Homes and Property'. Both countries include garden programmes among their lifestyle pay options, most of these being repeats of previously screened free-to-air shows, but there are occasionally new programmes like the Australian gardening magazine *Moar Gardening*.

As is usual when doing British/Australian television comparisons, there are more British than Australian programmes to consider, but here British programmes rarely appear on Australian television. Garden programmes other than documentaries are not often internationally traded directly (other than for pay channels which carry quite a lot), though obviously *Ground Force* provides an instance of a format trade. In an unusual instance of a presenter trade, Jamie Durie, Australian presenter of the axed makeover *Backyard Blitz* and the new *Australia's Best Backyards*, now works also in the US as the host of the long-running PBS gardening show, *The Victory Garden*.

Makeover programmes

Starting in the late 1990s, both countries screened stand-alone makeover shows, in particular the *Ground Force* format, which began on the BBC in 1998, hosted by Alan Titchmarsh, also at that time the lead presenter on *Gardeners' World*. Both public and commercial channels screened these in the UK, but in Australia they have only been on commercial channels. Another highly popular British makeover, the BBC's *Home Front*, ran from 1998 to 2003 combining an interior refit with work on the garden, in which designers Laurence Llewellyn-Bowen and Diarmuid Gavin worked to a customer's brief rather than producing the makeover as a surprise gift. In Australia, two reasonably similar programmes ran on commercial networks, varied not only by that location, but also by a more 'bloke-y' style of presenter. There is no Australian equivalent of the dandy aesthete, Llewellyn-Bowen. Women were involved in the Australian presenting teams though, with *DIY Rescue* even having a female lead, Leah McLeod. *Renovation Rescue* combined interior and exterior makeovers into an hour-long programme, and *DIY Rescue* saw incomplete and incompetent house renovations rectified while a garden was transformed and the marital problems caused by the husband's misplaced confidence or enthusiasm were also fixed. Both countries also have real estate shows which, to a greater extent in Australia than in the UK, involve sprucing up the gardens to improve sales prospects.

The Australian version of *Ground Force* ceased in 2004 and with the demise of its more popular near-clone *Backyard Blitz* in 2006, there are now no standalone garden makeovers left. British *Ground Force* also ceased in 2006. The last British makeover was *Digging Deep*, screened late in 2006, which added something of a new age twist through the attempt to suit the new garden design to the owner's psychological needs, but there are no plans to produce a second series. There have been no British garden makeovers during 2007.

I will investigate the makeovers separately from the other shows, since they are quintessentially lifestyle television. Not that other garden shows necessarily escape the label. I think it is now very difficult to consider any programmes that deal with the sites where lifestyle is addressed as non-lifestyle, it is so very much the dominant contemporary frame. A garden cannot help but speak of its owner's identity, since that is now how it is read. The initial distinction operating here is between the untrammelled lifestyle programmes of the makeovers and the less lifestyle dominated ones, primarily the garden magazine shows. The latter are sometimes called 'hobby' gardening shows. The term seems rather dismissive and will not be used here, though it signals an instructive division. Brunsdon's investigation of the melodramatic and realist approaches to lifestyle television clearly and usefully places makeovers in the melodramatic and shows like Channel 4's *Real Gardens* or *Gardeners' World* in the instructive and realist (2003, 11, 18–19).

The strongest distinction between garden makeover programmes and others is in the extent to which in both countries, the former are about design and how little this involves actual gardening. In lifestyle terms, this could be ascribed to the imperative of display; the garden has become not an area for pleasurable or productive work, nor a place to send the children. Real estate agents even warn against vegetable gardens when selling houses, since they signify work. The contemporary garden is instead a place for the display of the self, and the appurtenances of the desired lifestyle. Australian garden historian, Peter Timms, dates the rise of garden design from the 1950s, with a slow progressive shift of display from the front garden to the back. He notes how the backyard now is 'no longer a strictly private area, nor is it, very often, a functional one; it is one we use to impress our friends with our economic standing and civilised tastes' (Timms 2006, 73). In other words lifestyle has triumphed. Makeover advice is predicated on there being a mismatch between the garden owner and the garden which can be rectified by producing a new garden which is both fashionable and tailored to some aspect of the owner's personality (for more on this and the centrality of fashionability, see Bonner 2003, 105–8, 130–136). Feona Attwood's analysis of *Home Front* argues that the client's desire 'for somewhere in the garden to entertain friends is represented as a quest for self-expression, knowledge and style', but that they need to be guided in this by the presenters (2005, 96). Lifestyle, and the lifestyle media, have been vectors for an expansion of the new view of a garden's function across a much larger proportion of the population that was previously the case, and even though makeovers seem to have ceased, this view continues to be evident.

Before examining this though, it is worth considering the difference between British and Australian makeovers. Although Australian programmes have included occasional instances where houses and gardens have been renovated for charitable causes, and *DIY Rescue* addressed problems in the makeover recipients' relationships, the range of programmes is narrower than in the UK, almost certainly as a result of their only appearing on commercial channels. None operated to a client's brief as *Home Front* did and so owner agency in the transformations is occluded. Makeovers only appeared as gifts from television networks and programme sponsors following the suggestions of family and friends of the garden owners. The only Australian site where garden makeovers can currently be found is in real estate shows where they are a standard component, perhaps compensating for a less diverse field than is the case in the UK. People are rarely seen searching for properties on- or offshore, as is the case with *Location, Location* (shown as an import on Australian pay-TV). Even including real estate segments, the places visited lack the wealthier homes of *Home Front*, or the more complex briefs *Digging Deep* addressed. Australian gardens were most commonly transformed into a single highly groomed zone dedicated to entertaining, unless they were particularly large. Some things are common. Despite considerably different proportions of the year in which they could reasonably be utilized, both British and Australian gardens regularly gained the addition of a wooden 'deck', at times replacing a concrete or brick patio. In both countries this was explained as being to facilitate entertaining, the core activity catered to by contemporary garden design and the key way in which one's lifestyle indicators can be shown off.

Class issues

Timms argues that in Australia the highly designed but simple gardens considered as spaces to impress, actually characterize only 'a certain social stratum' and that immigrant and older gardeners still grow produce, while many working class backyards 'are given over to car maintenance, hobbies and light engineering' (Timms 2006, 73). He blames the media (magazines and books as well as television) for the emphasis on style and theme without consideration of location or climate. He argues that they lead to people wanting striking gardens, but not wanting to do the work, so contractors are used, but with people's media-driven aspirations outstripping their financial resources, only quite simple gardens can be afforded, so cottage gardens or bush ones are displaced by large areas of decking and tidy contained beds (Timms 2006, 95). His valuable and engaging, but rather popular, study with its rather sweeping observations is supported by Lisa Taylor's observations on class in British gardening media, since she finds that 'the garden lifestyle media sanctions the symbolic power of the middle-class as the primary arbiter of symbolic capital' (Taylor 2005, 121). Drawing on Bourdieu, she does not see this as homogenous since 'Garden lifestyle texts not only showcase different kinds of (middle-) class aesthetics which demonstrate the internal divisions within class groups, but also testify to the contiguous friction between different fractions of a social class' (2005, 119).

Somewhat of a caricature of an Australian version of this can be found in Andrew West's populist polemic, *Inside the Lifestyles of the Rich and Tasteful*. West's argument is built around his seeing a division in the upper middle class between materialists and culturalists based on the former's only being interested in spending money on status-giving possessions, while the latter evince their status differently, being greener, pro-refugee and more likely to downshift. He identifies the culturalists' guru as food writer Stephanie Alexander and remarks on their possession of country getaways and their interest in gardening, while characterizing the materialists as under the sway of Jamie Durie and his directions on landscaping (2006). There are many problems with using the book beyond its status as reportage, not least its implicit connections to Australian inflections of the neoconservative 'new class' rhetoric (on this see, e.g., Dymond 2004), yet there is something useful there if it is taken cautiously.

Taylor's division of the middle class is between the traditional educated patrician and the postmodern new *petite bourgeoisie*, with the lifestyle approach characterizing the latter. While her characterization of the new *petite bourgeoisie* is more precise than West's perception of his materialists as upper middle class, these are much the same social fraction. The culturalists though do not map well onto Taylor's patrician traditionalists and it is not just a national difference. Taylor's main example of the patrician is the current *Gardeners' World* presenter Monty Don, but she considers him through his pronouncements as the gardening writer for the *Observer* during the late 1990s, rather than through his television work. Don's class position, his aesthetic practices and his education are as Taylor describes, but his television work, starting on *This Morning* in 1990 and covering several short-run series on Channel 4, has been different. At *Gardeners' World* he continued the work of the far more plebian Alan Titchmarsh and the continuities of the programme – instructive, practical advice shaped as common sense – diminish his social distance from viewers somewhat. Taylor's own earlier evaluation of Don's work on *Real Gardens* remarks on his downplaying of the role of experts and his gardening in company with the ordinary person whose actual garden has been visited (Taylor 2002, 490–91). At times that programme emphasized lifestyle concerns, with repeat visits to the same garden to observe progress with the implementation of a new design, but the actual regular work of creating and maintaining a garden was always at the forefront.

A further sign of the greater range of British garden programmes comes from Don's later television programme, *Growing Out of Trouble*, where he attempted a Jamie Oliver-like redemption of damaged youth by encouraging young drug addicts to establish and work in a market garden. The aesthetic here was very much in keeping with that of West's refugee-supporting green culturalists. Reluctant though I am to continue to call on West's work by using the term culturalists, there is a major presence among televisual gardeners in accord with elements of his characterization. In the UK, an even clearer member is Don's subordinate *Gardeners' World* presenter and chief presenter of *Grow Your Own Veg!*, Carol Klein, a vegetarian concerned with economic, as well as environmentally sound, gardening. Perhaps I could call this position the composters, since it involves a practical and usually green approach. That Don can be both patrician and composter (though more often the latter) and Titchmarsh all three (though most convincingly a materialist) is an indication that the groupings are contingent on the programme's ethos, and are not necessarily personal.

In Australia the composting perspective is represented unequivocally by Peter Cundall and his junior *Gardening Australia* presenters: sustainable gardening advocate, Jerry Coleby-Williams; and permaculturalist, Josh Byrne. Manchester-born Cundall is one of the most recognizable faces and voices on Australian television, well known for his active support for environmental issues, refugees and his opposition to the Iraq war. Commercial programmes and their presenters unsurprisingly represent the materialist position.

A three way split does not negate Taylor's arguments about middle class dominance but it helps to explain where the national difference is located. There is something about gardening and visiting gardens and having hero gardeners that is more emphatic in the British situation or psyche and the patrician term may be its best enunciator. Televisually the patrician perspective is most evident in documentary series about gardens, a common British category. Feeding into this position is the constant presence in the less lifestyle-oriented programmes of the touchstone of the Royal Horticultural Society and especially their gardens at Wisley, as well, though to a lesser extent, as the Chelsea Physic Garden, and of course the annual ritual of the Chelsea Flower Show. They provide a national focus of peak practice that is absent in Australia where climatic variation is complicated by separate state bodies. Although *Burke's Backyard* used to have items visiting the Chelsea Flower Show and *Better Homes and Gardens* still does, this is within the garden magazine format; there really are no Australian garden documentaries. The closest to a patrician perspective are moments in *Gardening Australia*, when large established gardens are visited. These segments, like similar British ones, are presented in an aspirational garden lifestyle frame; the British garden documentaries, like those set at Kew or the Eden Project, are closer to tourism advice.

Australia's Best Backyards, screened on the commercial Seven Network, cannot be placed under the patrician rubric even though its format involves visits to five gardens each episode (at the conclusion of each show, the three presenters agree on which one is the best and their choices are put up for public vote at the series' end). The traces of reality television, the dominant presence of Jamie Durie and the emphasis on garden design is too strong. This is emphatically lifestyle television from a materialist perspective. At least four of the week's five gardens are described as having been designed for ease of maintenance and to facilitate entertaining. That gardening itself might be a continuous, and at times arduous, activity enjoyed for its own sake, or for the sake of the produce it provides – the composter perspective – never appears.

Ethical garden advice

Television gardening provides an opportunity to consider how programmes and presenters act as conduits for ethical information, in this instance especially about organic and waterwise gardening. For the purposes of this section, I will not consider garden documentaries, since they rarely operate in this way. The difference between the two areas of ethical advice here is striking and they need to be considered separately. As far as makeovers are concerned, waterwise gardening, inasmuch as it involves plant selection, especially of striking xerophytic examples, and the use of aesthetically valued mulch, was much discussed in Australian makeover shows prior to their disappearance. I even recall one instance of *DIY Rescue*, where the gardening expert refused to lay that staple of the makeover genre – instant turf – because the garden concerned was located beyond piped/town water. The disappearance of garden makeover programmes during a period of drought might be thought to be related to their dependence on instant turf and water features to produce the all but instantaneous dramatic transformation were it not that the same timing applies in the UK where drought has been much less extensive.

All Australian gardening programmes address the issue of reducing water dependence. Indeed after seven years of inadequate rainfall across most of the country, it would be impossible for any programme concerned with gardening in Australia to ignore the need to inform people about dealing with drought in the garden. Commercial programmes are very fond of hard surfaces and far more likely to see them as solutions, so *Better Homes and Gardens* instructed viewers to make a waterwise garden by producing a chequerboard of paving and succulents. The programme stays closer to lifestyle practices in focusing on plant selection, but has included items on installing rainwater tanks (British 'butts'). The lifestyle imperative of visible signs of distinctive consumption continues with the range of signifiers expanding to include tanks, the design and aesthetic appeal of which often attracts more attention than their storage capacity.

Few recent episodes of *Gardening Australia* have gone to air without some advice on keeping gardens alive under drought conditions; entire episodes are devoted to waterwise practices. The programme follows one of two usual patterns: the first visits large, often public, gardens to recommend plants and practices for home use; the other involves items shot in the homes of the two presenters who have been demonstrating waterwise sustainable and permaculture gardens for the last year or so. Because they have been shown the development and installation of these gardens, viewers are aware of their significant installation costs. Technically, they too could be considered makeovers, but they are far slower and more thorough-going for the term to be useful.

The real difference comes with the newest of the Australian gardening shows: *Vasili's Garden*. This ex-community television show, still defiantly showing its origins in its cheap production values and focus on mainly Greek and Italian migrant gardeners, is comprised overwhelmingly of garden visits. It looks particularly different because unlike most garden shows, aesthetics is not the major consideration. It is not just a *different* aesthetic in operation, but a different valuation. Regardless of pleasing appearances, good gardening here produces fruit and vegetables, especially tomatoes. Only occasionally and very much in passing does the camera show any part of a garden other than the productive patch; flowers are an irrelevance. The consequence of this, and of the types of gardeners visited, is to represent on Australian television a type of gardening heretofore little represented though much practised. Regardless of the actual class of the people visited, the impression the show gives is of working class gardening, of people making do rather than spending up big on an outdoor room. (*Christine's Garden* would be the nearest British equivalent, but that combines the presenter's care for her working class neighbours' gardens with her visits to wealthier people for whom she acts as consultant.)

Water use is central. The programme is shot in Melbourne, where severe water restrictions apply, so the gardeners must have developed ways of coping if they are to have the requisite fruit and vegetables. The presenter, Vasili Kanidiadis, regularly asks how his guests keep their gardens watered. The programme is not afraid of repetition, so even when the same response is forthcoming most weeks, the gardeners are asked what they are doing and they persistently answer: storing rainwater. But this is all very rough and ready – 44 gallon drums and wheelie bins full of water are located throughout the sections of the gardens we see. There are no drip irrigation systems or designer tanks here, indeed rarely any purpose-made tanks of any kind.

The Australian pattern is established. Commercial shows unsurprisingly promote consumption. Water wisdom involves buying new tanks, more pavers or other hard surfaces and new plants. The ABC is less concerned with consumption, though its persistent display of the installation of systems to reuse grey water endorses the lifestyle of the green consumer. SBS, although it now carries some advertising, bought the community television ethos along with the programme, and here is anti-consumption; people recycle in ways reminiscent of the 1950s rather than today.

I had never noticed any reference to waterwise gardening in my British television watching prior to 2006 and the term is not in common use. However, in that year, sections of the UK were experiencing a drought and living under water restrictions involving hosepipe bans and in consequence waterwise gardening featured intermittently on *Gardeners' World*. One episode talked about the use of grey water; another had included an item on installing a water butt and announced the team's commitment to using only grey water and rainwater on the long borders at their main site; but most weeks passed with no mention of such practices. No other programme dealt with the matter. The first half of 2007 continued similarly, but the mid-year floods may have altered this approach.

Organic practices are very rarely seen in either country's makeover programmes. There is no rapid lifestyle benefit from soil conditioning, for example, so makeovers do not install compost heaps, nor even tidy worm farms, nor employ used carpet or underlay as mulch. Less lifestyle-dominated programmes can consider these, since their concern is with gardening as an ongoing process, something which involves growing things, including the necessary soil preparation and conditioning. Concerns with the overuse of chemicals were evident in the UK before lifestyle television came into existence, although the removal of Percy Thrower as lead presenter of *Gardeners' World* was the result of his appearance in ICI commercials, rather than his use of the company's products (Search 2003, 11). Geoff Hamilton, chief presenter of *Gardeners' World* from 1979 to 1995 was very different, being credited with 'almost single-handedly taking organic gardening out of the realm of the cranky and into the mainstream' (Search 2003, 71). Another figure of early British organic gardening was Bob Flowerdew, presenter of the *All Muck and Magic* sequence of organic gardening shows on Channel 4 from 1987 until 1990.

The varying ABC state gardening programmes prior to 1991 make identifying early references in Australia close to impossible, but the first organic gardening special on *Gardening Australia* occurred in 1992, within its first year of production. Cundall has spoken for a very long time of the importance of organic gardening, so it seems likely that *Landscape*, the (Tasmanian) state programme he had previously presented, also espoused companion planting, compost and avoiding harmful chemicals. As far as commercial channels are concerned, it is similarly difficult to be sure. Organic gardening was not a major concern of Don Burke, though he certainly advocated compost, and resident insect specialist, Desley Clyne, proselytized on the usefulness of beneficial insects rather than chemical sprays.

To some extent, organic gardening has become the default position for British garden shows, so very much unspoken common sense that it is possible to watch a month or so of gardening programmes and never hear the word mentioned. A viewer would in the same period not hear chemical sprays or artificial fertilizers mentioned either.

Grow Your Own Veg! was able to use the word organic and present organic practices because it was a short series which started from scratch. The explicit organic comments however all related to one of the three segments of the show – that with first time gardener Louise, who was being instructed by presenter Carol Klein. Louise spoke at the beginning about wanting to grow her own vegetables for her family, because she wanted to be secure about what had gone into growing them. This nicely demonstrates the way organic practices in the UK are driven by food concerns, so much a part of everyday middle class life.

In Australia, with a much less established organic culture generally, the heavy reiteration of being organic and what that entails that characterizes *Gardening Australia* is foundational. Peter Cundall's own garden and his vegetable plot in the Hobart Botanical Gardens provide the basis, but are now accompanied, as previously mentioned, by a sustainable garden in Brisbane and permaculture one in Perth. The programme has followed the establishment of both, giving different refinements on contemporary organic practices and providing a narrative framework that allows repetition of advice within a novel framework.

Both sustainability and its more hardcore fellow, permaculture, operate from a position antithetical to lifestyle culture. They are marked by a strong environmental consciousness which climate change and drought have made more salient. The incompatibility may not be immediately apparent however. It is quite obvious from consumer magazines and newspapers supplements that 'green' is very fashionable at the moment, and that organic foods are central components of certain lifestyle practices, especially those of middle class urban parents. The continuing presence of the once counter-cultural activities on the flagship Australian show represents more than a merely fashionable green move. The key words 'sustainable' and 'permanent' mark a refusal to adopt the ideology of fashionability and the rapid turnover of identity indicators which underpin lifestyle.

Timms commented that the presence of permaculture on *Gardening Australia* in company with items on pruning roses, 'is thought to be less contradictory than admirably tolerant of difference' (Timms 2006, 186). This is in accord with the way in which lifestyle culture subsumes difference under the banner of choice: options are available and choice between them should be made to best express the individuality of the chooser. One of the consequences of the drought though is that, with the exception of those set in the tropics, a much greater cohesion can be seen between the different items on the programme, and for that matter across Australian gardening programmes. While their organic advocacy may vary, programmes need always to remark on the water demands of whatever elements of a garden they are discussing. A reciprocal effect though is that when environmentally conscious gardening of one kind (i.e. waterwisdom) is prevalent, it produces a more thoughtful climate encouraging other ethical gardening practices.

Taste, trust and sincerity

In any lifestyle programme, but especially in those dispensing ethical advice, the presenter's persona is an important analytic variable, albeit a difficult one to interrogate. Again I need briefly to deal with makeover programmes to bring out the distinctions. Because makeovers focus on design, i.e. appearance and style, the key quality a presenter needs to exhibit, after a televisually transmissible personality, is taste. In her consideration of gardening makeover presenters, Taylor sees them as 'presenter-interpreters' making 'elite artistic garden design knowledge readable for the ordinary would-be gardener' (2002, 488–9). Attwood is more forthright, seeing Llewellyn-Bowen and Gavin in *Home Front* acting 'as arbiters of taste and guides for the consumer' (2005, 96). Knowledgeability here involves both an awareness of what products are available and a level of training by which to judge their suitability for the situation in question. It is in the latter that taste resides.

In a consideration of the British ex-*Changing Rooms* presenter, Linda Barker, as a taste-maker, Helen Powell and Sylvie Prasad argue that the public lost trust in her privileged claim to 'good taste' after her appearance in *I'm a Celebrity ... Get Me Out of Here!* and her commercials for the electrical goods chain, Curry's (2007, 60–1). Although I believe that only a low level of trust would have been needed by so melodramatic a programme as *Changing Rooms*, the question of trust in a presenter's judgement is of much more moment when it comes to the ethical advice given on the more realist programmes.

Trust is something viewers give or withhold and best assessed through ethnographic or survey data. Presenters may attempt to project themselves as 'trustworthy' though and I will explore this aspect of gardening presenters and their advice through considering both the way knowledgeability is conveyed and the operation of the quality 'sincerity'.

While in many lifestyle fields (like motoring programmes) presenters seem to have gained their expertise primarily through being specialist journalists, gardening presenters have formal horticultural training which viewers are told about, sometimes in the programmes themselves, but always on the associated websites. Knowledgeability then relates to quite traditional assessments of expertise, involving data that can (unlike taste) be subject to truth claims. Yet presenters operate in a social field where intangible qualities make some more able than others to convince viewers of their right to pronounce. Makeover presenters demonstrate their taste week after week and viewers can decide whether it suits them or whether they will continue to watch for other aspects like the entertainment of the reveal. With the more instructional shows and ethical advice, assessments of both the knowledgeability and the sincerity of the presenter become relevant.

I have previously discussed sincerity as characterizing Don Burke (Bonner 2003, 77, 207), but think it is central to the *Gardening Australia* presenters too. Paddy Scannell's study of this quality as one of his 'conditions of intelligibility' of broadcasting (Scannell 1996, 3) suggests that, among other things, it requires that there be a congruence of the public and private life (1996, 73). It might be that Linda Barker's revelation of what was seen more as the 'real' private self in the celebrity reality programme showed as much a lack of congruence with her role as taste-maker, as her endorsement of downmarket white goods. Most garden presenters try explicitly to show us congruence. Carol Klein used her own garden as one of the three sites for *Grow Your Own Veg!* Most *Gardeners' World* series have come in part from the lead presenter's own garden, and while currently it does not, viewers are aware of Monty Don's garden from its being the site for his earlier programme *Fork to Fork* and from his books, including the 2005 *Organic Gardening*. Even Jason Hodges on *Better Homes* showed viewers the water tank he had installed at home. We know from extratextual material that Peter Cundall's organic gardening is part of a thoroughly engaged political life. The sincerity with which he passes on organic advice is unquestioned.

Balancing the seriousness, with which advice in the non-makeover programmes needs to be delivered, with the humour, which the sociability required by a broadcast medium finds desirable, requires fine judgement. Humour is more necessary in the makeover shows and that is why Alan Titchmarsh, working simultaneously in both, was such a remarkable performer and has subsequently been able to operate successfully on shows with no link to gardening. While primarily appearing as a gardener though, he was careful to balance the makeover shows not just with *Gardeners' World* but also with the instructional *How to be a Gardener* and *The Gardener's Year*. Yet even he did not always succeed, as the reprimand over his excessively 'laddish' commentary with Dairmuid Gavin from the Chelsea Flower Show in 2005 indicates. To take advice from television presenters on an area of such salience as gardens are to so many of their owners, viewers need to trust the speakers. Sincerity sets up the precondition for that trust.

Conclusion

The similarity of television format, lifestyle imperatives and the shared consequences of global chemical use both in agribusiness and in domestic situations bring garden programmes in the UK and Australia closer together regardless of geographical and climatic variation. The overall diminution of gardening shows on television in conjunction with the particular loss of makeover ones, means that proportionally the representation of gardening in hardcore lifestyle terms has been reduced. Television gardens are once again the sites of gardening, not just of entertaining. The continued presence of gardening programmes on Australian commercial television provides something of a difference here since they are still based in strong lifestyle premises. Lifestyle approaches themselves have by no means disappeared elsewhere, but their dominance is in question.

And it is the material of gardening itself, in its requisite encounters with the environment of which it forms a part, that has made this change evident. Until recently it would not have been easy to demonstrate. While much is similar in the more instructive and realist British and Australian garden shows, it is in material environmental aspects that difference is found. The climate means British gardening shows must pay regular attention to glasshouses, which Australian shows hardly ever address. While watering has always been given more attention in Australia, the inescapability for Australian gardeners of dealing with the day to day consequences of the current severe drought, which every type of garden programme must deal with, has led to a more visible divergence. The overriding question in Australian gardening shows is now: can this plant or design element be recommended given limited water availability? This really does restrict the free flow of lifestyle advice since it limits choice in ways not dependent on fashionability and the desire to express an individualized vision of the self. Climate change may result in similar restrictions to more types of lifestyle programmes in both countries (and the extent to which the Australian drought is a consequence of such a change is not yet clear), but it is certainly possible already to see in the difference between the two countries' garden programmes a closing down in the ability of lifestyle television to advocate unfettered consumption.

Bibliography

Attwood, F. (2005), 'Inside Out: Men on the *Home Front*', *Journal of Consumer Culture* 5:1, 87–107.

Bell, D. and Hollows, J. (eds) (2005), *Ordinary Lifestyles: Popular Media, Consumption and Taste* (Maidenhead, UK: Open University Press).

Bonner, F. (2003), *Ordinary Television: Analysing Popular TV* (London: Sage).

Brunsdon, C. (2001), 'Once More on the Insignificant', in C. Brunsdon, C. Johnson, R. Moseley and H. Wheatley, 'Factual Entertainment on British Television: The Midlands TV Research Group's 8–9 Project', *European Journal of Cultural Studies* 4:1, 29–62.

Brunsdon, C. (2003), 'Lifestyling Britain: The 8–9 Slot on British Television', *International Journal of Cultural Studies* 6:5, 5–23.

Dymond, T. (2004), 'A History of the "New Class" Concept in Australian Public Discourse', in M. Sawer and B. Hindess (eds), *Us and Them: Anti-elitism in Australia* (Perth: APT Network).

Heller, D. (ed.) (2007), *Makeover Television: Realities Remodelled* (London and New York: I.B.Tauris).

O'Connor, A. (ed.) (1989), *Raymond Williams on Television: Selected Writings* (London and New York: Routledge).

Powell, H. and Prasad, S. (2007), 'Life Swap: Celebrity Expert as Lifestyle Adviser', in D. Heller (ed.), *Makeover Television: Realities Remodelled* (London and New York: I.B.Tauris).

Sawer, M. and Hindess, B. (eds) (2004), *Us and Them: Anti-elitism in Australia* (Perth: APT Network).

Scannell, P. (1996), *Radio, Television and Modern Life* (Oxford: Blackwell).

Search, G. (2003), *Gardeners' World: Through the Years* (London: Carlton Books).

Taylor, L. (2002), 'From Ways of Life to Lifestyle: The 'Ordinari-ization of British Gardening Lifestyle Television', *European Journal of Communication* 17:4, 479–93.

Taylor, L. (2005), 'It was Beautiful before You Changed it All: Class, Taste and the Transformative Aesthetics of the Garden Lifestyle Media', in D. Bell and J. Hollows (eds), *Ordinary Lifestyles: Popular Media, Consumption and Taste* (Maidenhead, UK: Open University Press).

Timms, P. (2006), *Australia's Quarter Acre: The Story of the Ordinary Suburban Garden* (Melbourne: The Miegunyah Press).

West, A. (2006), *Now Australia: Inside the Lifestyles of the Rich and Tasteful* (Melbourne: Pluto Press).

Williams, R. (1989), 'Hardy Annuals', in A. O'Connor (ed.), *Raymond Williams on Television: Selected Writings* (London and New York: Routledge).

Chapter 4

'Who Let the Dogs Out?'
Pets, Parenting and the Ethics
of Lifestyle Programming

Maggie Andrews and Fan Carter

In an episode of the cartoon *South Park*, Eric Cartman's mum, desperate to find the techniques to control her over-indulged son, summons the professional expertise of *Nanny 911*, *Supernanny* and then finally, and with more success, Cesar Millan, *The Dog Whisperer*. *South Park*'s parody highlights not only the abundance of programming within the lifestyle format that has emerged in the last five years, but also one starting point for this chapter, namely the parallels between parenting programmes and dog training ones. They each focus on family units as sites of concern and expert intervention and are devoted to improving the skills of participants to tackle problem children and pets. Franklin (1999) notes that animals are increasingly viewed as part of the family, a move which is linked to the growing numbers of smaller families and childless households in post-industrial countries (Nast 2006, 900). Dogs in particular are increasingly viewed as objects of 'pet love' (Nast 2006, 896) and often referred to as a child substitute or alternative. Indeed, within commercial sectors the term 'pet parent' has replace 'pet owner' in common parlance (Nettle 2007, 14). Such trends might not only help to account for the recent rise in dog training programmes on British television but also point to their popularity and appeal.

As Hawkins notes, '*ethics* have become *entertainment* ... growing amounts of television programming now involve examinations of *ways to live*' (Hawkins 2001, 412) [emphasis in the original]. Parenting and dog training formats organize their ethical dilemmas along similar trajectories, with comparable terminology and techniques. References to 'tough love' occur in both; shouting is frowned upon, while physical violence and overt bribery, the techniques of control and discipline of the past, are taboo. In their place, a rational approach to management through controlled and consistent discipline is introduced, modelled and learnt.

The commercial logics of multi-channel television have produced a glut of programming organized around the 'makeover', articulating fantasies of self-actualization within the logic of consumer capitalism. The material we focus on here marks a shift from stylistic transformations to ones that purport, at least in the words of the programme-makers, to 'change lives' (Ricochet 2005) as unruly children and dogs are made over in pursuit of ideal domesticity. In particular we draw comparisons between *Supernanny* (Channel 4 2004 onwards) and *Honey, We're Killing the Kids*

(BBC3 2005 onwards) and *Dog Borstal* (BBC 2006 onwards) together with *Help!
My Dog's as Fat as Me* (BBC 2006) and *It's Me or the Dog!* (ITV 2005 onwards).
These lifestyle programmes, however, need to be seen within a wider political and
cultural context.

In this chapter we suggest that the ethical dilemmas of parenting/dog ownership
articulate New Labour discourses of parental responsibility and self-discipline
fostered by the intercession of experts. The narrative of *Supernanny* is structured
around a transformative visit from a modern day Mary Poppins whose advice turns
a household of unruly children and ineffectual parents into a harmonious family.
Alternatively, in *Honey We're Killing the Kids* the aberrant family's transformation
is pivoted upon weekly visits to an expert in clinically sterile surroundings where
they receive weekly 'rules for living' along with dire warnings of the horrendous
future their children face if these are not followed. In *It's Me or the Dog!*, dogs
and their owners are visited at home by the expert Victoria Sitwell who prescribes
a series of modifications to diet, routine and behaviour and returns to monitor and
admonish where necessary, whereas *Dog Borstal* and *Help! My Dog's as Fat as Me*
rely on removing the participants from their homes and placing them in alienating
institutional environments to effect change. *Dog Borstal* offers dogs and owners a
short sharp shock in a quasi-military camp complete with secure fencing, army issue
tents and surveillance towers while *Help! My Dog's as Fat as Me* involves a series
of visits over several weeks to a country house style 'club' where a team of experts
work to produce slimmer, well behaved dogs and equally trim owners.

As Hill (2005) illustrates, domestic animals have been a staple feature of reality
scheduling throughout the 1990s in programmes such as *Animal Hospital* (BBC
1994–2004) where they were positioned as sentimentalized victims of illness, abuse
or death. According to Hill, such programmes explored a particular ethic of care,
serving to re-educate the 'fundamentally female' (2005, 115) carers and 'encourage
viewers to apply ethics of care in their everyday lives' (2005, 133). In contrast,
this new sub-genre of dog *transformation* show operates within a very different
representational paradigm. Here dogs are not doe-eyed victims of a lack of care, but
rather victims of too much feminized caring and in need of discipline. These dogs
symbolically invoke the out-of-control inner city youth or the sedentary and obese
child that feature so prominently in the alarmist rhetoric of tabloid journalism and
contemporary political campaigns. Thus the following language of criminality and
threat is used to describe a new entrant to *Dog Borstal*, 'Sam's tried everything to
get Lily under control … now she's being sent down for theft and vandalism' (*Dog
Borstal*, series 2, 2006). These dog training programmes offer ways of treating, and
at the same time making light of, the new anxieties around parenting.

New Labour and domestic labour

The family has been a central theme in New Labour's reworking of the welfare
state, identified in Blair's 1994 leadership campaign as the cornerstone to
effective government when he argued that 'the values of a decent society are in
many ways the values of the family unit' (cited in Fairclough 2000, 43). Arguably,

the priority given to family life has been one of the strategies employed to build alliances between Labour's traditional core voters and the middle classes; although, within New Labour discourse, the family and domestic sphere are not an alternative, but rather an add-on to paid work and have been positioned as both economically and emotionally significant.

New Labour's approach to family life can be seen as an example of what Fairclough terms 'cultural governance', 'governing by shaping and changing the cultures of the public services, claimants, the socially excluded and the general population' (2000, 12). Central here is the concept of 'parenting' as a set of discursive skills, techniques and dispositions conceived as fundamental to the construction and maintenance of family life. These skills have been directly targeted at vulnerable families in the form of early learning centres and parenting workshops under the 'Sure Start' programme which aims to 'improve the lives of families, parents and communities' (Sure Start 2007).

Family life more generally is increasingly subject to the same culture of performance as the public service industries and caring professions. These areas have seen an increased blurring of professional and managerial roles with the result that systems of accountability and measurement are taken as indices of quality (Dent and Whitehead 2002, 12). As the journalist Maureen Freely remarks, parents are increasingly positioned as middle managers charged with delivering 'culture change' not only within their own family units but society at large (Freely 2006). Arguably, in today's performance-led culture, increased government funding and resources in areas such as nursery provision and after-school care are to be matched by improved performance and productivity by parents and externally verified through statistics on truancy and anti-social behaviour orders.

Historically private, domestic space has been subject to intervention by an army of experts, in the form of health visitors and social workers, surveying and regulating working class mothers throughout the course of the twentieth century. More recently, and facilitated in no small part by Thatcherism's dismantling of welfare provision and discursive emphasis on the 'welfare-consumer', self-reliance and the concept of enterprise, such strategies of population management have given way to 'governance at a distance' in which

> norms of conduct for the civilised are now disseminated by independent experts … They operate a regime of the self where … one is encouraged to understand one's life, actually or potentially, not in terms of fate or social status but in terms of one's success or failure acquiring skills and making the choices to actualise oneself. (Rose 1999, 87)

Contemporary discourses of parenting appeal directly to this model of subjecthood, prioritizing self-management through the acquisition, practice and self-monitoring of specific knowledges, techniques and skills. Given the pervasive discourse that parents/owners are unable to help themselves without expert advice, it is perhaps of little surprise that the charity 'Family and Parenting Institute' reports that parents are increasingly anxious and unsure of their role (Family and Parenting Institute 2005). This seems to be borne out in the postings on various parenting websites such as 'netmums' which frequently detail specifics of children's 'bad' behaviour along with pleas for advice and techniques to 'solve' these. Parenting is conceptualized as an ongoing process of learning, reflection and importantly self-appraisal; a domesticated model of the self-actualizing and enterprising subject of contemporary capitalism. At a moment when parenthood is increasingly understood in terms of personal choice and lifestyle option, rather than eventuality, it is perhaps not surprising that it has come to be reconfigured as a site of reflexivity and expertise.

The cultural focus on parenting and the domestic, as evidenced in lifestyle programming, is not merely a product of the New Labour political moment. It also converges first and second wave feminist demands for a re-evaluation of domestic labour (the wages for housework campaigns and mothers' strikes of the 1970s) with a post-feminist consumer feminism of the 1990s – whereby the domestic, the child and indeed the dog are new sites for female power, expertise and, perhaps more importantly, for spending. The appeal of the genre for various TV channels is therefore clear (see Medhurst 1999). Television 'our friend in the corner', the item which, in the latter half of the twentieth century, came to define the home and as Silverstone (1994) argues, links those within the home reassuringly with society beyond, provides the ideal space for a range of experts and professionals to facilitate cultural change, in line with UK television's public service ethos (just as the wireless was perceived to do in the interwar years). Indeed the National Children's Bureau's 1998 report, *Family Viewing*, on 'parents, children and the media' found that 82 per cent of parents surveyed wanted more TV programming on parenting and family issues (McCarthur 1998, 16) with some expressing it as the broadcasters' 'duty' to provide. Almost ten years later, the TV schedules are awash with programming addressing parenting and family issues. Addressing various stages from pre-birth to adolescence, parenting issues have provided a rich source of programming in recent years. However, these are increasingly giving way to symbolic parenting in the form of dog training and transformation shows. With, potentially, a wide audience base, and perhaps less likely to provoke the sort of moral concern and professional backlash which has recently beset programme-makers and presenters of parenting programmes (see Aitkinhead 2007), dog programmes have become regular additions to prime time schedules across the channels. Indeed dog training programmes arguably offer specific opportunities for genre development and creativity. With dogs as their object, 'tough love' is allowed to slip into physical restraint and control in ways that would be inadmissible in parenting programmes, as the furore over the ITV documentary *I Smack and I'm Proud* attests (NSPCC 2006). Moreover, direct competition between participants/contestants, a feature which is entirely absent from child-parenting programmes, is a common feature of dog training shows. These draw on the conflict and characterization motifs of reality game-doc formats (such as *Big Brother*, Endomol, C4) and it is to these generic structures that we now turn our attention.

Genre and structure

Structurally both parenting and dog-ownership programmes are formulaic: the unacceptability of the out of control child or dog is initially established as the participants subject themselves to the intrusive surveillance of video cameras in the domestic sphere. The audience watches families engaged in otherwise private and mundane activities such as getting ready for school, mealtimes or walking the dog. Importantly though, these are disrupted by the offending child or dog and the ensuing chaos and breakdown of everyday life is emphasized in these opening scenarios. This pervasive visual monitoring transfers power from ineffectual parents/owners to the expert under the appraising gaze of the audience. This is a point emphasized by props and *mise-en-scène*, for example in *Dog Borstal* where one trainer is repeatedly shot viewing the mayhem through his field glasses and in *Supernanny*, where Jo Frost gives the camera a knowing look. Editing, camera work, voice-over and non-diegetic music serve to build drama and construct expert intervention as the only possible route forward.

Surveillance, together with the expert's commentary, are key elements in ensuring that the cause and responsibility for children's and dog's errant behaviour is firmly placed with the parent/owner. As trainer Mic Martin reveals to camera, 'this dog's got all the problems and she's learnt them from the owners' (*Dog Borstal*, series 2, 2006). Remedy and transformation involve a combination of tutorials, acquisitions of skills and disciplining techniques underpinned by the enactment of the freely choosing and self-actualizing subject of contemporary culture who, to paraphrase Andrejevic (2002), willingly submits to surveillance as a means to self-knowledge. Parental responsibility is further reinforced in moments of 'revelation' which involve parents/owners pictured shame-faced while they view themselves on camera under the watchful and evaluative eye of expert and audience. As Palmer (2006) notes, 'shame' plays an important part in reality TV programming. These moments of revelation blend the typologies of 'authoritarian' and 'willing victim' shaming and 'work as a force of patrolling behaviour' (Palmer 2006).

These scenes of mundane domesticity further provide what Gledhill (1997) terms emotional realism, as they involve a version of parenting where children are disrespectful, ungrateful, ungovernable, cruel and at times abusive. Here, enacted on the screen for voyeuristic viewing, are the repressed and unseen of domestic culture, the misery of motherhood that would arguably be unpalatable without the pleasure offered by the narrative of transformation. The feminist project to acknowledge the significance of domestic labour has, arguably, converged with a post-Freudian discourse of parental – or as we suggest more specifically maternal – responsibility. The slippage from parents to a focus on mothering is problematic and we suggest that it diverges quite fundamentally from anything recognizable as a feminist project.

Although the narrative regularly includes resistance to the experts, children defy the nanny, parents and dog owners refuse to follow dietary and lifestyle 'rules', ignoring the experts is not, narratively speaking, an option. Lurking in the background as a structuring absence are images familiar from news and documentary genres, of ASBO children, dangerous dogs and negligent parents. At various points, these spectres punctuate the narrative with a mixture of fear and fascination. The dog behaviourist expert Rob Alleyne in *Dog Borstal* calmly explains to camera that the owners of one particularly difficult pet seem unaware of the seriousness of their dog's problem. At present, he suggests, the best future scenario for these owners, and furthermore expectant parents, is 'a bitten baby, at worst no baby at all', so emphasizing the imperative to 'regain control' in order to avoid the catastrophic domestic and social problems that lie ahead.

Performing self-improvement

These televised scenarios of governance are enacted through the language of performance management and appraisal. While more familiar in the contemporary workplace, these strategies are increasingly applied to areas of domestic life and labour which are reconfigured as sites, and forms, of work. The terminology of, and references to, work abounds: for example Lily's owner in an episode of *Dog Borstal* explains that she wants her to become a more 'productive member of the household' while the reward charts of *Supernanny* are 'incentives to reward good conduct and punish bad'. Transformation, however, does not come easily. It involves sacrifice and work with experts, ready to admonish errant parents or owners if they slack in their tasks. A key feature of *Dog Borstal* is that attendance is hard – the dogs appear to be placed in an army cooler, the owners in dreary and leaky army tents, devoid of luxury, whilst lack of work, or lateness, leads to ritualized punishments: press-ups on the training field or kennel cleaning duties. Parents and children in *Supernanny* and *Honey We're Killing the Kids* have key performance indicators, externally set, and individualized priorities and tasks allocated by the experts. Furthermore, in *Dog Borstal*, the graduating tests undertaken at the end of the programme are geared to dog's/owner's initial failings and are graded, mirroring management appraisal systems utilized and legitimated in many workplaces.

Arguably, these programmes promote the ideal subjectivity for contemporary capitalism, producing 'autonomous, self-regulating and self actualizing individual actors' (Du Gay 1995, 77) in the home as well as the workplace. Indeed the ritualistic narrative structure of the 'makeover' enacts a transformation into this enterprising and reflexive self. Importantly, participants, by virtue of their appearance on the show, are already coded as willing and wanting to change to take control of their lives, themselves, their children or their dogs. A conscious and authentic desire to rework the self is permissible, while a conniving performance can be heavily criticized by viewers. For example, a lively debate on the website *Dogsrule* (*Dogsrule* 2007) aired concerns about the perceived authenticity of specific participants. 'Reality show groupies', as they were termed, came in for rebuke. Such questioning of motivation is not permissible with parents, whose genuineness is guaranteed through performances of care and often signified in emotional excesses such a shouting and/or tears. Appeals to emotional authenticity are increasingly made within the contemporary workplace (Hochschild 1983); however, excesses have to be managed, disciplined and remade in terms of acceptable emotional literacy and effective caring.

Back to class: Consumption, taste and rules of improvement

These programmes' relationship with consumer culture is at times contradictory and problematic, as almost all experts are enterprising, commercial operators keen to extend their brand. They offer knowledge and skills for sale through their websites in terms of private consultations, books and DVDs and the *Supernanny* 'naughty step' retails for under £20. However, while the invitation to participate in the transformative processes offered through the purchase of associated consumer goods is a common theme of lifestyle television, within these formats owners and parents are expected to consume responsibly and with restraint. Excessive consumption is frowned upon; televisions in children's rooms, junk food and computer games are ritualistically purged in *Honey We're Killing the Kids*, while owners who overindulge their pets are lambasted on *My Dog's as Fat as Me*. And so at this point we too hit the discourse of taste, intrinsically linked to class, so familiar in lifestyle television.

Arguably, lifestyle TV genres promote fantasy narratives of social mobility and transformation while at the same time classifying and judging modes of classed behaviour and the taste cultures of participants in acts of 'symbolic violence' (McRobbie 2004 and also Biressi and Nunn 2002, 53). The domestic sphere has already been established as the site where competing class factions are constructed in terms of ethical debates in programmes such as *Wife Swap* (C4 2003 onwards) and *How Clean is your House?* (C4 2003 onwards), while talk shows such as *Jeremy Kyle* (ITV 2005 onwards) continue to explore moral boundaries around the parenting practices of working class participants. *Honey We're Killing the Kids* offers perhaps the most overt guide for parents on acquiring a middle class future for their children by engagement in a particularly middle England version of a middle class lifestyle – playing musical instruments, taking up sport and exercise (horse riding in one episode), the rituals of meal times and an efficiently regulated domestic life. Furthermore families are encouraged to undertake 'improving days out' – acquiring cultural capital and 'distinction' (Bourdieu 1986). In one episode the children are taken to learn how to eat, converse and behave appropriately in a restaurant, while mums and their eldest child are often sent off to enjoy quality time in the form of creative arts (pottery classes for example). At periodic intervals, the parents are invited to glimpse the potential futures of their children in the form of fast-morphing digital images; these invariably look like police mug shots on the one hand and corporate portraiture on the other as visual signifiers of hair, dress and body language effectively class their digital subjects. Indeed, in one episode, faced with the 'happy ending' shot, one mother comments 'he looks successful' – an ideal performance index in today's competitive culture of parenting.

Cleanliness also play a central role in the transformation, echoing the nineteenth century euphemism of 'the great unwashed', as discussed by Stedman Jones (1971). The ritualized moments of cleaning which punctuate these programmes enable, as Couldry suggests, the values which they represent 'to be successfully reproduced without being exposed to question' (Couldry 2004, 60). Notions of rational respectability and scientific regimes of household management which circulated in the early twentieth century are here reworked as opportunities for self-actualization. House rules to share domestic duties serve to establish boundaries for put-upon parents and teach self-reliance to errant, selfish children. Second wave feminism's critique of domestic labour is sidelined as housework is here recast as 'helping mum with the chores'. The theme of ritualized cleaning also occurs in *Dog Borstal*, evidenced in strict regimes of kennel care and hygiene, while the unruly and potentially dangerous dog which becomes a candidate for Borstal carries connotations of a mythologized working class, fighting and gangs as constructed in popular journalism. The term Borstal is itself a signifier of marginalized working class youth which *can* be transformed. As if to emphasize this point, the voice-over in one episode explains, 'Penny's ASBO tendencies have turned this once respectable couple into social lepers'. As with New Labour's discourse on education, which promotes equality of opportunity and meritocracy, the dogs and their owners can, through expert training, acquire access to a middle class lifestyle again.

Audiences: Pleasures and negotiations

The dog/owner relationships as conveyed in lifestyle programming not only represent child/parenting ones, but are also suggestive of many other potential relationships, from those with workplace colleagues to those with friends and other family members. The idealized dog is devoted, loyal, subservient to the owner's wishes, easily pleased and ready to defend its owner from harm – a fantasy relationship for the alienated and over-stressed individuals of contemporary society. Most importantly, in this idealized relation, the work put in to training (of self and dog) is directly related to the satisfaction obtained, another appealing fantasy at a moment of performance indices and audit culture. This fantasy of devoted reciprocity is a key element of the transformation in such programmes. The last moments of these shows include images of idealized domesticity but there is always something fleeting, temporary, and unstable in them. Parents and owners in some episodes seem to seek frantically to express a narrative of progression, to grasp a glimpse of the fantasy of parenting/ownership that contemporary commercial culture offers, but lived experience fails to provide. Fantasy, as Ang points out, is 'one dimension of life in which the distance between a (pleasurable) absent and an (un-pleasurable) present can be eradicated' (Ang 1985, 134). At one level, these programmes operate by offering a fantasy of an idyllically pleasurable, but all too often absent, vision of parenthood/ownership. Certainly it is suggested that an idealized version of parenting, and this is most often invested in the figure of the mother, is within grasp if only the right techniques are enacted. In attempting to unite strategies of governance and control with performances of emotional intimacy and literacy, the contemporary ethics of parenting, not to mention dog ownership, are fraught with contradictions and potential disappointments. It is, perhaps, these tensions and inconsistencies that some audiences find appealing and engaging.

While we have argued that these texts make claims for moral certainty and discursive authority, we also want to suggest that their appeal and meaning may be more complex than at first appears. For some enthusiastic members of the audience, these texts do indeed offer techniques and recommendations and provide authorization and validation which enable the viewer to imagine themselves in particular modes of subjecthood. Alternatively, for an audience rendered increasingly insecure by the spectacle of 'ordinary people' audited, appraised and found wanting in the contemporary political and cultural climate, the scrutiny and surveillance of others may offer particular compensatory pleasures. Significantly, on *YouTube*, the cultural space of the younger generation, video clips of errant dogs, badly behaved children and domestic tension predominate, an indication perhaps of the moments the audience find truly pleasurable.

Audiences have a range of investments and engagements in these texts which may provide a framework from which to work through and reassess the ethical problems of parenting/relationships. Arguably, for the active audience whose engagement with television is diffused (Abercrombie and Longhurst 1998) and no longer restricted to scheduled viewing slots (Sconce 2004), these texts serve as a starting point in the multiple and contested discourses which proliferate on programme linked websites and in chat rooms. These virtual communities offer spaces to engage critically with the 'ethics' of domestic childcare/dog ownership, and the role of parent/owner. Interestingly, in these spaces, alongside enthusiastic commendation of presenters, there is much irreverent dismissal of 'experts' and plenty of evidence of the 'urge to deconstruct and subvert all comforting ideologies, beliefs, heroes and myths' (Dent and Whitehead 2002, 1). Our scanning of viewers' chat room comments and website postings would suggest that readings of the text are as varied as the viewers who watch them. Indeed, the popularity of these programmes may perhaps lie in their ability to facilitate *ethical trouble* (cf. Butler 1991).

Bibliography

Abercrombie, N. and Longhurst, B. (1998), *Audiences: A Sociological Theory of Performance and Imagination* (London: Sage).

Aitkenhead, D. (2007), 'Playtime's Over', *The Guardian*, 8 September, 35.

Andrejevic, M. (2002), 'The Work of Being Watched: Interactive Media and the Exploitation of Self-disclosure', *Critical Studies in Mass Communication*, June, 230–48.

Ang, I. (1985), *Watching Dallas* (London: Methuen).

Biressi, A. and Nunn, H. (2002), *Reality TV: Realism and Revelation* (London: Wallflower Press).

Bourdieu, P. (1986), *Distinction: A Critique of Social Judgements of Taste* (London: Routledge).

Butler, J. (1991), *Gender Trouble* (London: Routledge).

Couldry, N. (2004), 'Teaching Us to Fake It: The Ritualized Norms of Television's "Reality" Games', in S. Murray and L. Ouellette (eds), *Reality TV: Remaking Television Culture* (New York: New York University Press), pp. 57–74.

Dent, M. and Whitehead, S. (eds) (2002), *Managing Professional Identities: Knowledge, Performivity and the 'New' Professional* (London: Routledge).

Dogsrule (2007) [website] <http://www.dogsrule.co.uk/blog/>, accessed 26 February 2007.

Du Gay, P. (1995) *Consumption and Identity at Work* (London: Sage).

Fairclough, N. (2000), *New Labour New Language?* (London: Routledge).

Family and Parenting Institute (2005) [website] <http://www.familyandparenting. org> (homepage), accessed 18 April 2007.

Franklin, A. (1999), *Animals and Modern Cultures: A Sociology of Human–Animal Relations in Modernity* (London: Sage).

Freely, M. (2006), 'Prime Suspect', *The Times Online* [website] (updated 5 November 2006) ,<http://www.timesonline.co.uk/article/0,,2099-2432133.html>, accessed 9 November 2006.

Gledhill, C. (1997), 'Genre and Gender: The Case of Soap Opera', in S. Hall (ed.), *Representation: Representations and Signifying Practices* (London: Sage), pp. 337–86.

Hawkins, G. (2001), 'The Ethics of Television', *International Journal of Cultural Studies* 4:94, 412–26.

Hill, A. (2005), *Reality TV: Audiences and Popular Factual Television* (London: Routledge).

Hochschild, A. (1983), *The Managed Heart: Commercialization of Human Feeling* (Berkeley: University of California Press).

McCarthur, L. (1998), *Family Viewing: A Report of the Research Project into Parents, Children and the Media* (London: National Children's Bureau).

McRobbie, A. (2005), 'Notes on "What Not to Wear" and Symbolic Violence', in L. Atkins and B. Skeggs (eds), *Feminism After Bourdieu* (Oxford: Blackwell), pp. 99–109.

Medhurst, A. (1999), 'Day for Night', *Sight and Sound* 9:6, 26–7.

Nast, H.J. (2006), 'Critical Pet Studies?', *Antipode*, 894–906.

Nettle, S. (2007), 'From President to Pet Parent', *Quad* (London: Queen Mary College), No. 16, 14–15.

NSPCC (2006) [website] (updated 21 September 2006), <http://www.nspcc.org.uk/whatwedo/mediacentre/pressreleases_wda33701.html>, accessed 21 April 2007.

Palmer, G. (2006) '*Video Vigilantes* and the Work of Shame', *Jump Cut* 48, Winter [online version], <http://www.ejumpcut.org/archive/jc.48.2006/shameTV/text.html>, accessed 27 April 2007.

Ricochet (2005) [website] <http://ricochet.co.uk> (home page), accessed 16 April 2007.

Rose, N. (1999), *Powers of Freedom* (Cambridge: Cambridge University Press).

Sconce, J. (2004), 'What If?: Charting Television's New Textual Boundaries', in L. Spigel and J. Olsson (eds), *Television after TV: Essays on a Medium in Transition* (Durham NC: Duke University Press), pp. 93–112.

Silverstone, R. (1994), *Television and Everyday Life* (London: Routledge).

Stedman Jones, G. (1971), *Outcast London: A Study in the Relationship Between Classes in Victorian Society* (Oxford: Clarendon).

Sure Start (2007) [website] <http://www.surestart.gov.uk/aboutsurestart/>, accessed 30 January 2008.

Chapter 5

Fashioning Femininity: Clothing the Body and the Self in *What Not to Wear*

Yael D. Sherman

In the final scene of an episode of *What Not to Wear* (*WNTW*), Sohni is shown modelling her new look, while in a voice-over she says:

> I noticed since the makeover I definitely feel a lot different in my clothes. I feel a lot more powerful. I can still be unique and different and look like somebody who's fun without all that mess. It's a lot more clean and it actually makes me feel more in control. I think in the past when I was dressing young I kind of felt young. I had thought about law school in the past and now it seems a lot more doable. (Sohni 2005)

Even as Sohni is objectified in the televisual grammar of glamour, she speaks as an empowered agent. Sohni is in fact doubled in representation, body and voice, literally split into subject and object. Yet in her speech, it is her appearance, her objectified self, which has made her feel empowered to go to law school. In becoming a feminine subject, Sohni has discovered a new sense of efficacy, agency, and upward-mobility.

In this chapter, I analyse the refiguration of normative femininity in the American version of the makeover show *WNTW*.[1] Femininity is the central project of the show, as participants are repetitively made over into aspirational feminine subjects. Like the older version of normative femininity described by Sandra Bartky and John Berger, that of *WNTW* is also tied to a split subjectivity of 'surveyor and surveyed' (Bartky 1990; Berger 1977, 40). However, in *WNTW*, this mode of feminine subjectification is put to new work under a neoliberal regime, as the discipline of femininity is used to form ambitious, enterprising, and 'empowered' feminine subjects.[2] Even as

---

1   The original version of this show is the British version, which airs on the BBC. As Martin Roberts points out, the BBC has a public-service mandate which, after deregulation, is translated into 'improving' the self. Paid for by taxpayers under the terms of public service, the British program could claim a 'license' to improve the participant for her own good (Roberts 2007). While the American version plays on the commercial television cable channel TLC, it too claims a kind of public service mandate for itself as 'The Learning Channel', promising viewers that it will teach and improve them.

2   Of all the makeover shows, *Queer Eye* is most like *WNTW*. As Toby Miller argues, *Queer Eye* relies on and extends neoliberalism in both its production and its metrosexual message (Miller 2006).

WNTW mandates and extends the reach of femininity, it challenges the links between femininity, female dependency, and the private sphere.

Neoliberalism

Neoliberalism is both an economic-social policy and, in a Foucauldian sense, a mode of government (Dean 1999; Foucault 1991). Rooted in the assumptions of classical economics, neoliberal policy champions the principles of the market as the solution to the 'problem' of government and what is portrayed as the ever-growing state (Burchell 1996, 27). As exemplified by Reagan and Thatcher, neoliberalism calls for privatization, deregulation, 'free' trade, the global expansion of markets, and the destruction of social safety nets (Duggan 2003). As Lisa Duggan argues, though these policies are undertaken under the masquerade of a value-neutral expertise that will 'promot[e] universally desirable forms of economic expansion and democratic government around the globe', they actually work to maximize profits and concentrate wealth (Duggan 2003, 10). For Duggan, the key terms of neoliberalism are *'privatization* and *personal responsibility'* (Duggan 2003, 14, emphasis in the original); as the state does less, citizen-subjects must do more.

As a mode of governmentality, neoliberalism 'governs at a distance' (Rose 1996, 43), 'through the regulated choices of individual citizens' (Rose 1996, 41). Neoliberalism seeks to 'actively create the conditions within which entrepreneurial and competitive conduct is possible' (Barry et al. 1996, 10), recasting the citizen as a rational consumer and enterprising agent (Gordon 1991, 44). As social services like schools or hospitals are turned into competitive markets, the citizen becomes a consumer whose choices shape those services. Consumer choice powers this mode of governmentality; the citizen must be made to make choices, as such newly-made markets depend on the consumer to act on their rational desires. Consumption is rendered central to personhood and citizenship. As Nikolas Rose writes:

> The enhancement of the powers of the client as customer – consumer of health services, of education, of training, of transport – specifies the subjects of rule in a new way: as active individuals seeking to 'enterprise themselves,' to maximize their quality of life through acts of choice ... (Rose 1996, 57)

The ideal citizen-subject of neoliberalism is the 'actively responsible individual' (Rose 1996, 57), who seeks self-mastery and self-fulfilment, rather than acting communally in the public sphere. The apparatus of neoliberalism rests on both self-esteem, which enables the citizen-subject to act on their own behalf, and on media and advertised lifestyles, which 'integrate subjects into a moral nexus of identifications and allegiances in the very processes in which they appear to act out their most personal choices' (Rose 1996, 57–8). Neoliberal governmentality works through indirectly shaping the choices and desires of the 'empowered' citizen-subject.

Femininity and dependency

Normative femininity is, traditionally, a kind of technology for producing non-citizen subjects. Separately Sandra Bartky and John Berger describe the structure of femininity in very similar terms: as a doubled subjectivity in which the feminine person is both watcher and watched, 'surveyor and surveyed,' subject and object (Bartky 1990, 38–41; Berger 1977, 40). Drawing on Simone de Beauvoir, Bartky argues that given women's 'life situation',

> Knowing that she is to be subjected to the cold appraisal of the male connoisseur and that her life prospects may depend on how she is seen, a woman learns to appraise herself first. The sexual objectification of women produces a duality in feminine consciousness. The gaze of the other is internalized so that I myself become seer and seen, appraiser and the thing appraised. (Bartky 1990, 38)

Similarly, Berger argues that women learn to 'survey' themselves because they know they are 'surveyed' by men and their future determined by men: 'ultimately how she appears to men, is of crucial importance for what is normally thought of as the success of her life [marriage]' (Berger 1977, 46). In order to control their fate, women must internalize the male gaze and evaluate themselves through it in order to manipulate men. This argument assumes that women are fundamentally dependent on men. This dependent woman is really a heterosexual middle class construct of a particular time and place, yet both Bartky and Berger place her at the center of their analyses. Problematically, they ignore class differences and efface the importance of women's labour. For both Bartky and Berger, this form of feminine subjectivity persists due to the objectification of women in popular culture; because women are valued as beautiful things, they value themselves as beautiful things. In asserting a dependent woman at the center of their theories, Bartky and Berger ignore changing social realities; in proclaiming the power of popular culture, they efface other sources of female identity.

In another version of this argument, Bartky details how and why a woman works on her body. Drawing from Foucault's work on the panopticon, Bartky argues that women are produced as disciplined docile bodies. For Foucault, discipline is a practice of power tied to modernity, in which the body is fragmented and made analysable, its most minute movements described and controlled (Foucault 1995). Under the panopticon, the subject watches, judges, and polices him/herself according to the disciplinary norm, because they never know when they are being watched and judged.[3] That is to say, the subject takes over the work of policing him/herself. Bartky applies the notion of discipline to femininity, arguing that women's bodies are fragmented and analysed in popular culture such that an entire range of products has been developed to 'help' women deal with their 'problem areas'. Women police their

---

3   Jeremy Bentham designed the panopticon as a kind of ideal prison, where the architecture itself would enable a new kind of policing. The panopticon is literally a ring of cells arrayed around a central tower, which may or may not be occupied by a guard. While the guard can see all of the prisoners, they cannot see him or each other. Not knowing if they may be watched, the prisoners watch themselves (Foucault 1995).

own bodies according to the 'panoptical male connoisseur [who] resides within the consciousness of most women' (Bartky 1990, 72). Women watch themselves from the perspective of the 'male connoisseur' because they are everywhere watched; discipline is 'institutionally unbound' (Bartky 1990, 75). A failure to perform femininity may result in being shamed, disciplined, or worse yet, 'the refusal of male patronage', which is 'a very severe sanction indeed in a world dominated by men' (Bartky 1990, 76). For Bartky, patriarchy both causes and benefits from women's obsessive self-surveillance, as 'This system aims at turning women into the docile and compliant companions of men' (Bartky 1990, 75). Indeed, 'this self-surveillance is a form of obedience to patriarchy' (Bartky 1990, 80). However, while Bartky argues femininity is required of women, she also maintains that for even successfully beautiful women, their efforts result in 'little real respect and rarely any social power' (Bartky 1990, 73). In this analysis, femininity is inevitable, oppressive, and once again, a product of women's fundamental dependence on men.[4]

Becoming feminine

In a world where women are no longer fundamentally dependent on men, *WNTW* responds to a seeming crisis in normative femininity by mandating femininity for women.[5] The participant is nominated for the show by friends and family, who contend that the participant does not know how to dress and needs to learn to dress well for her own good. Watching the secret footage of the participant in her daily life, Stacy and Clinton, the two hosts of the show, substantiate this accusation with their critiques of the participant's appearance. Stacy and Clinton criticize Amanda for dressing like a child in t-shirts and jeans; they critique Gina's tight, revealing, clothes for being too sexy and therefore not sexy at all; and they critique Laurie for dressing frumpily in tapered acid-washed jeans. They rail against the choice of comfort clothing on the part of Raina and Elizabeth, who respectively wear oversized t-shirts and sweatpants and shapeless dresses. The review of the participants is a kind of ritual humiliation, a shaming of the participants because they lack femininity. Stacy and Clinton's critiques fall into three categories: childish, overly sexy, and frumpy. Lurking behind these critiques is the norm that adult women should be 'sexy and sophisticated'. All of the women who appear on *WNTW* have failed or resisted this version of normative femininity and therefore must be made over.

Under the discourse of neoliberalism, the participant cannot be transformed against her will; her will and desire must be engaged. Even though the participant is

---

4   Susan Bordo offers a different reading of the role of the panopticon in women's self-normalization. Unlike Bartky, Bordo treats patriarchy as a system in which both men and women are embedded and shaped. Bordo points to the punishment and shaming of those who violate norms of appearance, but unlike Bartky, she does not lay the burden of this policing solely on men. Bordo also highlights women's participation in reproducing cultural norms and the fact that women are rewarded for doing so. For Bordo, patriarchy is a system in which both men and women participate. Drawing on Bordo, one might argue that the gaze is patriarchal, but it is not necessarily male (Bordo 1993).

5   Men make up only about 10 per cent of the participants on the show. Space constraints necessitate the exclusion of male participants from this chapter.

almost always resistant to the project of the show, she always agrees to participate. Why? Stacy and Clinton offer the participant a 5,000 dollar debit card to shop with if she promises to 'give yourself over to us, body, mind, and wardrobe' (Elizabeth 2003). The debit card is a bribe, a powerful promise of shopping dollars for those who could not otherwise afford a 5,000 dollar shopping spree. In accepting the debit card, the participant accepts Stacy and Clinton's authority and promises herself to them 'body, mind, and wardrobe'. This deal frames the relationship as an exchange to which both parties agree: a contractual relationship. In order to change the participant, the show must first get her to agree to participate. In other words, the condition of submission is the exercise of agency. The logic of neoliberalism requires the participant's agency to authorize her subjectification; indeed, as will be discussed below, she must be made to want to change.

The process of feminization begins with leading the participant to adapt the split subjectivity of femininity. She must be taught to survey and objectify herself from the perspective of the upper middle class hosts, who metaphorically occupy the guard tower of the panopticon. When the participant is first confronted by Stacy and Clinton she is told that she has been secretly filmed for two weeks by her family, friends, and/or co-workers. She is faced with the knowledge that she was being watched all along, objectified without her knowledge or permission. This revelation creates a *retroactive panopticon*: the participant tries to remember what she was wearing when, how she looked when she was watched. When Michelle was told of her secret footage, she said 'Now I'm reviewing everything I've worn in the last two weeks' (Michelle 2006). Despite the fact that she had picked out her outfits knowing that others would see her as she moved about her work, she had not apparently thought of how she would look to others or on camera. Simply hearing about the secret footages cues the participant to anxiously monitor herself, gaze at herself, and objectify herself. As Susan Murray and Laurie Ouellette argue, reality TV promotes a 'panoptic vision of society [which offers] protection from both outer and inner social threats' (Ouellette and Murray 2004, 6). Here, the threat of the unruly self is contained by surveillance. The panoptic public sphere is invoked in the revelation of the secret footage; the participant learns that others are watching and she should watch herself, because she is judged by her appearance.

When the participant actually watches her secret footage with Stacy and Clinton she is made to literally view herself from outside of herself. The participant watches herself as seen from the eye of the camera, from another. The participant is made simultaneously both subject (watcher) and object (watched), literalized in the visual doubling of the participant as both recorded and 'live' or present with Stacy and Clinton. The doubling of the participant is accomplished through the camera's ability to take an outside perspective and preserve it, enabling retroactive access to oneself as an object. By literalizing the split consciousness of femininity in this way, the show encourages the participant to adopt this split perspective and literally watch herself.[6]

The participant is made to see herself through the concrete perspective of Stacy and Clinton, even as she is made to see that other people are watching her. Watching

---

6   Gareth Palmer notes that self-surveillance is a key technology in the British version of *WNTW* (Palmer 2004).

the secret footage creates a panoptic effect; if the participant might be filmed or watched at any moment, perhaps she should watch herself. Yet at this point the participant does not yet know how to evaluate her image. Watching the footage with Stacy and Clinton is itself an exercise in training the gaze. Stacy and Clinton verbally break the clothed body of the participant into pieces to be analysed and discussed terms of fit, color, print, and style. For instance, when Misti covers her eyes as the 'secret footage' shows her from behind in a pair of tight Capri pants and asks 'do we have to look at that?' (Misti 2003), Stacy insists on it and tells her it looks like she has a 'wide load' because she is wearing tight capris. As Stacy and Clinton discuss her sartorial shortcomings with her, asking her to explain outfits or particular choices, the participant is led to see herself from their specific perspective, forced to reflect on her appearance through the mediation of the hosts. The secret footage serves the dual purpose of warning and instruction: because others watch and judge you, you should survey yourself first. Under the panoptic mode of objectification, the participant must learn how to see herself as the upper middle class experts see her. As in the 360 degree mirror, the criticism of the participant's appearance is tempered with the promise that if the participant learns to dress well, she too can become normatively feminine and beautiful.

In order to become a feminine subject, one must see oneself within the norm of femininity. Stacy and Clinton try to get the participant to care about the way she looks, to want to look good, and to believe that she can look good, so that she will *want* to dress well. Before her makeover, Camilla, a 22-year-old human resources manager, wore too-tight pants held together with safety pins and old button down shirts missing buttons. When Clinton confronts Camilla in the 360 degree mirror, he tells her 'You're telling the entire world that you've gained weight and that your buttons popped off. Rather than dressing your body as it is now, which is what we always recommend' (Camilla 2006). Clinton asks if she's not buying clothes because she wants to lose weight and she agrees that this is case. Clinton then tells her that she should 'buy new clothes because you're beautiful and you have a great body' (ibid.). Rather than holding Camilla to a particular body ideal – such as the extremely thin ideal she carries with her – Clinton tries to convince her that she is beautiful and deserves to look beautiful. In the logic of the show, she must see herself within the feminine ideal so that she will work on her appearance; if she feels excluded from the norm and disidentifies from it, she will not 'take care of herself'. Clinton suggests that dressing well will change how Camilla feels about herself; if she dresses correctly for her body, she will find herself within the feminine norm. Further, adopting a new perspective on herself and dressing to enable and express that new perspective will change how others see her; in order to be perceived as a professional, Camilla must look like she cares about her appearance. Camilla must learn to see herself as normatively feminine in order to invest in her image, manage her 'self' and manage the impressions that she gives off. In this scene, Clinton tries to engage Camilla's desire to be beautiful, so that she will (want to) dress well.

The ideal of beauty on *WNTW* is defined by a particular version of normative femininity, as noted earlier, where women should be sexy, sophisticated, and adult. This ideal is not a physical ideal that everyone must fit into such as 'blonde and busty', but a set of individual 'rules' for each participant that will help her maximize her good aspects and hide the bad ones (as defined by the show) while creating visual interest through sophisticated use of layering, color palettes, and accessories. Clothing is used to 'balance' the body and make it appear to be an hourglass. Lean participants are dressed in clothes that emphasize curves; curvy participants are dressed to appear long and lean. The ideal of 'sexy and sophisticated' is not a matter of having the perfect body, but of dressing for one's body, one's age, and the occasion, within a narrow range defined by upper middle class taste. Fabric choice is imbued with class implications: manmade materials like polyester are forbidden and branded as lower class on the show, while natural fibers like cotton are promoted. Clothing, hair, and make-up should not overshadow the participant, but rather should make her visible in a new way: she shouldn't hide behind frumpy long dresses, t-shirts and jeans, or overly sexy clothes and loud make-up. Paradoxically, the participant must see herself as someone to be looked at – she must embrace her status as object in order to dress well and be seen as herself. The ideal of beauty is both normalizing and individualizing as everyone is assigned a particular set of rules in order to look 'their best'. In the logic of the show, any body can be beautiful if it is dressed well, and every body must look beautiful.

Individualized rules for dressing are modelled by three clothed mannequins for each participant. Each mannequin displays a different kind of outfit: work wear, casual wear, and date or evening wear, exemplifying the contexts in which the 'sexy and sophisticated' woman will be found. Stacy and Clinton use the models to teach the participants what would look good on them. For instance, Stacy and Clinton directed Tish, a blue-eyed blonde who wore only wore black, to instead wear blue-toned reds, blues and greens, to bring out, as Stacy says, her 'beautiful blue eyes' (Tish 2004). As in the example above, while Stacy and Clinton describe the clothes they also talk about the positive physical characteristics of the participant; a tiny waist will be complemented as a wrap dress is recommended. Stacy and Clinton want the participant to feel attractive, to internalize their gaze and judge herself favourably. They always ask the participant how she feels about the outfit and they engage with her response. For instance, when Gina objected to the length of the pencil skirt, Stacy explained that it would make her look longer and leaner and advised her to try it on and decide for herself. If the participant refuses to accept the outfit as a potential model of dressing and claims not to like it, Stacy tells the participant that they've seen her taste and it is ugly. Outright resistance is met with dismissal; agency within the range of the norm is solicited. The participant learns how to dress through discussing the example of the mannequin, as she is seduced into seeing herself through the feminine ideal.

While shopping, the participant learns the pleasure of seeing herself through the lens of normative femininity. Laura, an accountant who dressed like a teenager in funny t-shirts and jeans, resisted wearing grown-up clothes, until she tried on a black and white tweed coat and discovered that she loved it. Staring into the mirror she announced that

> I love the coat! I love the coat! I love the coat! I'm so getting the coat ... I just feel wonderful. I'm so happy we came here. I'm so happy with what I picked out. I can't even ... it's undescribable [sic]. (Laura 2005)

Though initially resistant to dressing 'well', Laura does find, as Clinton predicts, the experience of being 'well-dressed' transformative. Laura stares at her mirror image with her newly-trained gaze; she looks at her image as from the outside and finds it satisfying. She has learned to survey herself and has learned the pleasure of seeing herself within the feminine norm. In her speech, Laura takes responsibility for her choice, marking her agency; she picked out the coat that made her so happy. Though she is the author of her actions, her actions were shaped by the show's authorities, Stacy and Clinton. As Nikolas Rose writes:

> The regulation of conduct becomes a matter of each individual's desire to govern their own conduct freely in the service of the maximization of a version of their happiness and fulfillment that they take to be their own, but such lifestyle maximization entails a relation to authority in the very moment as it pronounces itself the outcome of free choice. (Rose 1996, 58–9)

Even as Laura feels free, beautiful, and happy, she has learned from Stacy and Clinton how to shape herself and invest in her image.

Shopping is the privileged site of self-production, as it is in buying clothes that the participant shapes herself as a neoliberal feminine subject.[7] Given 5,000 dollars, a new perspective, and a list of stores, the participant is endowed with new capacities to shape herself. For instance, Katie, a legal assistant, absorbed the rules and correctly avoided 'flying squirrel sleeves' and polyester, but initially resisted spending a great deal of money on her clothes. After some reflection, she ended up buying four expensive items. This action was out of step with her previous frugal image of herself and her world and required recalibrating both. Katie commented that

> It just doesn't feel real. I'm walking around NYC on blocks I walk on often. But completely as if I'm in a different town because I feel like a different person. I would never have walked in Precision. But it's a store that I've stared inside millions of times, saw one price tag in the window and kept on walking. And today I bought a $450 jacket so … I'm pretty excited. (Katie 2006)

Learning how to dress changed her knowledge of her self and her place in the city; doors literally open for her. She attains a kind of consumer citizenship previously denied. Of course, this transformation is only possible because she had the money to spend as well as the knowledge of how to spend it; her movement into previously barred territory demands upper middle class resources, middle class taste, and consumer desire. Later in the episode, Stacy comments that Katie looks like a lawyer and not an assistant; her clothes affirm her new taste and class status. Middle class resources enable Katie to attain a upwardly mobile femininity previously denied to her by her lack of knowledge and money.

---

7   Shopping is also a panoptic experience for the participant, as she is filmed but does not know if or when Stacy and Clinton might watch. Surveillance leads to an anxious self-surveillance, as the participant tries to figure out what to buy in order to obtain cultural citizenship. In this scene, surveillance in everyday life is normalized and tied to citizenship.

Resistance on *WNTW* is very nearly futile. Nearly every participant resists during the episode and nearly every participant is gratefully transformed by the end of the show. Alana, a thrift-store shopper and a funky dresser, initially tried to resist the show's version of normative femininity. She even made a list of her own rules of what she would wear – 1980s style clothes, bright colors, and sparkly things – and read them to Stacy and Clinton. Unimpressed by Alana's display of resistance, Stacy and Clinton tell Alana to sit down and shut up. Nonetheless, in designing outfits for Alana, Stacy and Clinton reflect her 'funky' side in a metallic animal print, a purple sequin shrug, and fun, visually interesting high heels. When shopping, Alana selects expensive funky hats (spending $500 for two hats) and expensive funky glasses; though she initially felt that 'fancy clothes are for other people' and explained that she didn't like to pay full price, she learned to enjoy buying funky, expensive accessories (Alana 2005). Alana bought into her transformation at the hands of Stacy and Clinton; after shopping with them, she confessed 'I can't imagine going back because this looks more like me' (ibid.). Despite her initial resistance and awareness of the process of normalization, her image of herself and her desires shifted over the course of the episode. Despite resisting consumption and middle class style, Alana is transformed into a feminine subject whose funky style is reflected in her hats and glasses. As the example of Alana demonstrates, the show practices a kind of appropriation of countercultures, as participants who were too 'funky' are allowed to maintain their 'funky' style through accessories like shoes, purses, jewellery, and hats. Normative femininity is stretchy; it can include personally expressive or even subversive elements even as it brings the participant's desires in line with its ideals. Though the participant may try to resist, the show works on her desire and self-image, leading her to turn herself into a middle class feminine subject.

Reconstituting femininity

On *WNTW*, femininity is defined not as being a sex object, but as being a competent agent for the self. Laura initially objects to being made over, arguing that 'don't you think that women are judged, you're either one way or another, you're either pretty or intelligent?' (Laura 2005). Laura is afraid of being marked as someone who is only a beautiful body, someone only valued for her body. Her concern echoes Bartky's assertion that in identifying with the feminine body, a woman 'may well experience what is in effect a prohibition or a taboo on the development of her other human capacities' (Bartky 1990, 41–2). Yet Stacy rejects this model of femininity, responding 'Those aren't the categories that we're actually talking about, pretty or intelligent ... We're talking about somebody who is pretty *and* intelligent matching her inside to her outside. And that's what I think most women have a tendency not to do when they're as busy as you are' (Laura 2005). Here Stacy rejects the mind/body division that casts women as the (pretty) body to the male mind; women can be both beautiful and intelligent. Stacy argues that Laura should use her clothes instrumentally to display her intelligence, her 'inside'. Clinton adds 'I think that once you see yourself in clothes that fit you and clothes that give off a different image that you might come around to our side' (ibid.). Clinton implicitly suggests that Laura's fears are ungrounded, that dressing well will in fact convince other people (and herself) to take her seriously. Clothing is a resource for both working on the self and others; it is a site through which one demonstrates competency. For Stacy and Clinton, dressing well, that is, identifying with normative femininity, will help Laura be and be seen as both 'beautiful and intelligent'.

The show offers three rationales for why the participant must become normatively feminine. First, *self-esteem*; embracing normative femininity will make the participant feel better about herself and will enable her agency. Second, *romantic relationships*; the 'right' kind of femininity will attract the 'right' kind of man. Third, *work*; normative femininity will help the participant to be taken more seriously as a worker and will enable her upward mobility. Self-esteem undergirds the second two rationales; only with self-esteem can the participant be 'actively responsible' for herself. All participants are subjected to the rationale of empowerment, but the second two rationales are applied differentially, depending on whether the participant is married or not, young or beginning a career track, and of course, the participant's own concerns. Though participants enter into the show from different classes and to a lesser extent, different races, they are all told that in order to be all that they can be they must become middle class (white) feminine subjects. In the logic of the show, everyone is potentially middle class and upwardly mobile if they just 'dress the part'.

Normative femininity is portrayed as the route to empowerment and self-esteem on the show. When Elizabeth sees herself made over in the mirror with Stacy and Clinton, she says 'I have to say guys you really knew what you were talking about. I can't believe how empowered I feel' (Elizabeth 2003). Later, after she dresses up for her big reveal, recreating her new look, one friend comments that 'You can tell there's a change on the inside, she feels so much better about herself' (ibid.). Affirming that the inside is what really matters, the friend actually justifies the makeover as a way to manage the inner self. After her makeover, Misti says, 'I can't believe how much this appearance has changed me. I'm totally motivated to go home and go to school or get two jobs so I can shop and shop. It's totally changed my outlook, my perspective on myself and the way I want to be, the things I want to do with my life' (Misti 2003). Being made over changes how Misti feels about herself and her capacities for the better. She wants to shop and work so she can shop; her ambition is triggered by her new appearance. Investing in her feminine image leads Misti to become a neoliberal citizen. For Aysha, a young woman from Pakistan, the makeover leads her to embrace American individualism:

> All my life I've been doing stuff for my family, or my sister, or my brother. I'm too involved in family ... This is the first opportunity that I got that's all about me. This whole week made me realize what life's all about, it's not only job and home and there are a lot of things to do and I can move on with life. So I'm glad that I'm here. (Aysha 2004)

Becoming an object for oneself is shown to be a rewarding experience; as the participants shape their image through the feminine norm, they feel a sense of power and agency. Becoming feminine 'empowers' the participants to act *for themselves*.

Many participants have resisted normative femininity by not investing themselves in their appearance; in order to 'empower' them through femininity, the show must first get them to care about how they look. As Clinton says to Katie after she's been transformed, 'And now that you know you can look this great, you can pay more attention' (Katie 2006). In other words, in learning to care, Katie can now take responsibility for her appearance. In her final voice-over, Katie concurs with this assessment, saying 'For me this show should be called "How to Care" because I just didn't care before. … It feels crazy to say it but I feel pretty today and I don't truly believe it's only exterior' (ibid.). Katie has learned to invest in her appearance and derive pleasure from it. She also does a kind of work on herself through investing in her appearance – she feels pretty on the inside, which is to say, she feels better about herself. The show has expanded her capacity to appreciate and invest in herself. Taking responsibility for her appearance renders her appearance a site through which she can exercise agency, make choices, and work on herself. She has become the 'actively responsible' neoliberal subject.

Femininity is also tied to enabling the 'right' romantic choices. Shireen, a Latina single mother, was nominated by her friends and family for the title of worst-dressed bachelorette for her tight, skin-baring outfits. The episode begins with a round of speed-dating, after which, unbeknownst to her, Shireen is evaluated by three middle class bachelors. Their evaluation is negative and dismissive, and one commented that she showed too much skin. In the course of the show, Clinton tells Shireen that she is not attracting the kind of man that she wants to be with, implicitly suggesting that Shireen was attracting lower class men rather than middle class men with her display of uncontrolled sexuality. Her overtly sexual version of femininity is portrayed as both lower class and as insuring her lower class status (preventing her from getting a good job and a good man). In order to manage herself and her life, Shireen must reform herself and her dressing to attract the 'right' man. In the end, Shireen sees herself through middle class femininity by choosing to wear a longer, fitted but not tight dress After her makeover, she again meets with the three bachelors who now evaluate her in positive terms: cute, approachable, nice, and fun. Shireen comments that she feels pretty, that she deserves her new look and that she's now attracting a more 'sophisticated guy'. Now that Shireen looks like a middle class feminine woman, she can attract a middle class man; in the show, looking middle class is a route to upward mobility.

Dressing well is also directly tied to upward mobility through the world of work. Most of the participants presented with the rationale of work are young women beginning their careers, though some professional women are also told that they will be taken more seriously if they dress well. Alana, the resistant participant discussed above, was treated to a similar before-and-after frame as Shireen, though this time with an interviewer for a job rather than for a date. A graphic designer, Alana has just graduated from college and is interested in working on window displays at a major department store. In viewing Alana's secret footage, Stacy and Clinton comment that her look is not professional and that she stands out as a 'loose cannon'. They show a 'top window designer' at Macy's her 'secret footage' and he agrees with their assessment. Stacy and Clinton tell Alana that to be taken seriously, she must dress professionally. After her makeover, as Alana looks at herself in the mirror with Stacy and Clinton, she says 'I feel like it makes me feel more assertive like I can go in there and say give me the job' (Alana 2005). Stacy tells Alana that 'now you look the part' (ibid.). Stacy and Clinton surprise Alana by sending her for an interview with the top designer who initially critiqued her. After her interview with him, he gives her a glowing report, saying she looked both professional and creative (the hat, see above). The show teaches that looking the part is necessary to getting the part; by becoming normatively feminine, Alana is able to impress the interviewer and presumably, will land a job soon. Alana learns to become a professional through dressing as one; she learns to value her appearance as a site of agency. In being transformed, Alana becomes a neoliberal feminine subject, pretty, consuming, normatively feminine, and prepared to get the job.

Conclusion

In his essay 'The Fashion Police: Governing the Self in *What Not to Wear*', Martin Roberts uses the frame of governmentality to look at the British version of the show, but comes to very different conclusions. Though I cannot speak to his analysis of the British show, I would like to consider his claims with regard to my analysis of the American show.[8] For Roberts, the British version of the show follows post-feminist logic as it 'empowers' women through making them feel sexy. Roberts argues that while the show treats embracing one's sexiness as a kind of power over patriarchy, he echoes Bartky in arguing that this embrace is really just obedience to patriarchy. On the US show, 'empowerment' is not about power over men through looking good to men, but being 'empowered' to succeed in both the private and the public realms. The product of normative femininity is not pure sexiness (an extreme to be avoided) but rather competency, the demonstration of the 'actively responsible' self. Roberts compares the show to a 'cop show' where the participant is led to make the 'right' choice through 'coaxing and coercion' (Roberts 2007, 234). Indeed, Roberts offers no narrative of *transformation*, arguing that surface and depth are confused in the show as the outside appears to substitute for the inside. In contrast, in my analysis of the American show, the participant's desire is central to the project of transformation. Rather than being punished and pushed, the participant is transformed through her own agency and the shaping of her desire. Middle class tastes are not simply inculcated in the participant; rather she is transformed into a middle class subject through internalizing the split subjectivity of femininity. In both our analyses, consumption is key in the production of femininity, but for Roberts, consumption is what defines femininity and the mode of citizenship promoted on the show. Perhaps the differences between our analyses can be partially accounted for by the differential workings of class in the US and Britain, given the US myth that everyone is middle class and potentially upwardly mobile.[9] In the US version of

---

8   Roberts acknowledges that the American show is 'kinder [and] gentler' than the British show (Roberts 2007, 247).

9   With regard to the British *WNTW*, Angela McRobbie argues that participants could not move up in class to the level of the show's hosts (McRobbie 2004, 99–104). Such a move upward is imaginable on the US show (especially given the fact that Stacy and Clinton are both marginal and privileged as, respectively, a gay man and a Jewish woman).

the show, femininity emerges as a means of self-mastery and upward mobility; the participant does not simply become a consuming citizen, but a neoliberal citizen.

As Laurie Ouellette writes, 'Reality programming is one site where neoliberal approaches to citizenship have in fact materialized on television' (Ouellette 2004, 232). In *WNTW*'s discourse of neoliberalism, femininity is articulated as a mode of self-cultivation that will ensure domestic, economic, and personal security. Participants are taught to see their style, their clothes, and themselves as an investment. As Nikolas Rose writes regarding the logic of 'advanced liberalism', participants are taught to '"enterprise themselves" to maximize their quality of life through acts of choice' (Rose 1996, 57). In other words, as Stacy says, 'Intelligent people use their style well' (Laura 2005). As discussed above, one should 'use style' to enhance one's efficacy and self-esteem. As Stacy and Clinton suggest to Shireen, she could 'use style' by dressing 'well' in order to attract the right kind of man. As they suggest to Alana, she should 'use style' to get a job by 'dressing the part', that is to say, dressing professionally to be seen as a professional. Concern with appearance does not signify a lack of ambition but rather the opposite: the person who really cares about doing well will do everything, including dressing well, to ensure her success. As Rose argues, neoliberalism enables 'govern[ing] at a distance' by producing the consumer-citizen as the 'actively responsible individual' (Rose 1996, 43 and 57). In *WNTW*, the participant takes on the task of disciplining herself and becomes a better neoliberal citizen by learning to monitor herself through the split-subjectivity and the appearance ideal of normative femininity. In the end, *WNTW* offers a fantasy in which upward mobility is guaranteed through femininity; if only everyone would 'take responsibility for themselves' through the tools of normative femininity, they would be successful.

Normative femininity is itself redefined through its articulation with neoliberal citizenship. Joan Riviere (writing in 1929) argues that femininity is always a masquerade put on to cover up masculine ambition (Riviere 1986). Femininity effectively hides ambition because femininity can only mean that one is for others (men) and not for oneself. As discussed above, Bartky and Berger endorse a similar meaning of femininity; it is to shape the self to please the gaze of powerful others. In *WNTW*, the dual structure of femininity is reshaped as a self-discipline that ensures success in both the public and the private sphere. To look good advances one's chances of getting a job, getting a raise, or getting a good mate, because looking good means that one cares and wants to do well. On *WNTW*, as appearance is defined as another field of action, judgment, and competition, the objectification at the heart of femininity is figured as a mode of agency. Femininity is required by *WNTW*, but making use of femininity in such a way essentially alters the meaning of femininity. This iteration of femininity marks it as a tool for the self under a neoliberal regime where every subject must make use of every possible advantage. This model of femininity is not a reaction to dependency, but rather a reaction to persistent anxiety in an uncertain world. In *WNTW*, femininity is to be *for oneself*, ambitious and upwardly mobile; normative femininity demonstrates that one is a competent, 'actively responsible' agent.

Bibliography

Barry, A., Osborne, T. and Rose, N. (1996), 'Introduction', in A. Barry, T. Osborne and N. Rose (eds), *Foucault and Political Reason* (Chicago: University of Chicago Press).

Bartky, S.L. (1990), *Femininity and Domination: Studies in the Phenomenology of Oppression* (New York: Routledge).

Berger, J. (1977), *Ways of Seeing* (London: British Broadcasting Corporation and New York: Penguin Books).

Bordo, S. (1993), *Unbearable Weight* (Berkeley: University of California Press).

Burchell, G. (1996), 'Liberal Government and Techniques of the Self', in A. Barry, T. Osborne and N. Rose (eds), *Foucault and Political Reason* (Chicago: University of Chicago Press).

Dean, M. (1999), *Governmentality: Power and Rule in Modern Society* (London: Sage Publications).

Duggan, L. (2003), *The Twilight of Equality?: Neoliberalism, Cultural Politics, and the Attack on Democracy* (Boston: Beacon Press).

Foucault, M. (1991), 'Governmentality', in G. Burchell, C. Gordon, and P. Miller (eds), *The Foucault Effect: Studies in Governmentality* (Chicago: The University of Chicago Press).

Foucault, M. (1995), *Discipline and Punish: The Birth of the Prison*, translated from French by Alan Sheridan (New York: Vintage Books).

Gordon, C. (1991), 'Governmental Rationality: An Introduction', in G. Burchell, C. Gordon and P. Miller (eds), *The Foucault Effect: Studies in Governmentality* (Chicago: The University of Chicago Press).

McRobbie, A. (2004), 'Notes on "What Not to Wear" and Post-feminist Symbolic Violence', *Sociological Review* 52:2, 99–104.

Miller, T. (2006), 'Metrosexuality: See the Bright Light of Commodification Shine! Watch Yanqui Masculinity Made Over!', in D. Heller (ed.), *The Great American Makeover: Television, History, Nation* (New York: Palgrave Macmillan).

Ouellette, L. (2004), '"Take Responsibility for Yourself": *Judge Judy* and the Neoliberal Citizen', in L. Ouellette and S. Murray (eds), *Reality TV: Remaking Television Culture* (New York: New York University Press).

Ouellette, L. and Murray, S. (eds) (2004), 'Introduction', in L. Ouellette and S. Murray (eds), *Reality TV: Remaking Television Culture* (New York: New York University Press).

Palmer, G. (2004), '"The New You": Class and Transformation in Lifestyle Television', in S. Holmes and D. Jermyn (eds), *Understanding Reality Television* (London: Routledge).

Riviere, J. (1986), 'Womanliness as Masquerade', in V. Burgin, J. Donald and C. Kaplan (eds), *Formations of Fantasy* (New York: Methuen).

Roberts, M. (2007), 'The Fashion Police: Governing the Self in *What Not to Wear*', in Y. Tasker and D. Negra (eds), *Interrogating Post-Feminism* (Durham: Duke University Press).

Rose, N. (1996), 'Governing "Advanced" Liberal Democracies', in A. Barry, T. Osborne and N. Rose (eds), *Foucault and Political Reason* (Chicago: University of Chicago Press).

Cited shows

Alana, *WNTW* (2005), TV, TLC, 8 April.
Aysha, *WNTW* (2004), TV, TLC, 3 September.
Camilla, *WNTW* (2006), TV, TLC, 12 May.
Elizabeth, *WNTW* (2003), TV, TLC, 19 December.
Katie, *WNTW* (2006), TV, TLC, 23 June.
Laura, *WNTW* (2005), TV, TLC, 4 February.
Michelle, *WNTW* (2006), TV, TLC, 14 July.
Misti, *WNTW* (2003), TV, TLC, 12 December.
Sohni, *WNTW* (2005), TV, TLC, 21 January.
Tish, *WNTW* (2004), TV, TLC, 3 December.

Chapter 6

Foodie Makeovers: Public Service Television and Lifestyle Guidance

Isabelle de Solier

In 1997 Australia's multicultural public television broadcaster, the Special Broadcasting Service (SBS), launched a new show called *The Food Lovers' Guide to Australia*. Unlike most Australian food programmes, this was not a cooking show. Its hosts, Joanna Savill and Maeve O'Meara, were not TV 'chefs'. They were food consumers, not food producers. They were food lovers, or 'foodies', and as such they represented the perspective of the viewer, who was also assumed to be, or interpolated to become, a food lover.

The Food Lovers' Guide was a huge success for SBS; its first season was the highest rating production in the network's 18-year history, and four more series were made over the following decade (Savill 2007). Significantly, it was the first programme to explicitly target an audience of 'foodies' or amateur food connoisseurs, and initiated a shift in the direction of the food programming of Australia's public broadcasters. Over the decade that's followed, SBS, and even more so the national public broadcaster, the Australian Broadcasting Corporation (ABC), have given their food programming a makeover to target it towards foodie viewers, to the point where they now produce the most stylish and foodie-oriented programmes on terrestrial television.

While the crucial issue of the role played by lifestyle television in the changing nature of public service television has been the focus of some discussion in the UK (see Brunsdon 2003; Dover and Hill 2007; Moseley 2000; 2001), it has not been investigated in Australia. This is because, in contrast to the UK, the contemporary boom in lifestyle TV in Australia has primarily occurred on commercial television – with the exception of food television, which has conversely taken over public service broadcasting. This chapter, then, examines the unique role played by food television in the makeover of public television in Australia, in the political and economic context of reductions in government funding and increasing commercial pressures. It analyses the history of lifestyle programming on the public broadcasters which, in the 1990s, was given a makeover to focus almost exclusively on food programming; and demonstrates how this food programming itself was made over to target the middle class lifestyle of foodies.

While one of the main claims of academic literature on lifestyle television is that it teaches viewers 'how to live', there has been little research into audience perceptions and uses of lifestyle television to date (see for example Dover and Hill 2007; Skeggs et al. 2008). This chapter draws on audience research conducted with

50 foodies to determine whether these makeovers of public television have been successful in their appeal to foodie viewers, and whether these viewers use the public broadcasters for lifestyle guidance. It argues that the public service broadcasters now operate as influential lifestyle guides which both target existing foodies, and seek to make over other middle class viewers into foodies, thus popularizing this lifestyle. It considers this project in the context of the economics of the 'foodie boom' and other governmental strategies at state and local levels which seek to make over their citizens into foodies through publicly sponsored commercial lifestyle television. The chapter argues, then, that the state – alongside capitalism – is a powerful player in the contemporary foodie boom, which uses lifestyle television to produce a population of foodie-citizens.

Money, money, money: The economic makeover of public service television

Contemporary Australian broadcast television is made up of five channels: two publicly funded (ABC and SBS) and three commercial (Seven, Nine and Ten). Unlike the UK, where the BBC has traditionally played a dominant role, Australia's public channels are minor players in a broadcasting sector characterized by commercial dominance and stability: the commercial channels share almost 80 per cent of audience ratings (fairly evenly), compared to the ABC's 16.5 per cent, and SBS's much smaller 5.5 per cent (Dale 2007).

Public service broadcasting in Australia was based on the Reithian model for the BBC, with its goal to 'inform, educate and entertain' citizens. The national broadcaster, the ABC, began in 1956 alongside Seven and Nine (see Cunningham 2000). As well as producing local content, it has traditionally imported a lot of programmes from the BBC, leading many to see it as fostering an Anglo-centric version of national identity. Thus SBS was established in 1980, 'with a brief to appeal to all Australians and to provide for them a multicultural perspective that was not available on the more solidly Anglo-Celtic services of the ABC' (Jacka 2000, 57). With 75 per cent of programmes originating overseas, in more than 60 languages, it aims to produce a sense of multicultural or cosmopolitan citizenship.

Australia's public broadcasting has never been funded as well as the British. In 2004, for example, public broadcasting in Britain received three times as much as Australia as a percentage of GNP (Starr 2004). Where the BBC is funded through licence fees (as was the ABC until 1974), both the ABC and SBS are funded through taxpayer's money (Jacka 2000, 55). SBS's marginal status in comparison to the ABC means that it has only ever received a fraction of the latter's funding. In 2006–07 it received $177 million, around a fifth of the $823 million allocated to the ABC (ABC 2007, 63; SBS 2007, 101).

In the 1990s, both channels suffered reductions in funding, as public broadcasters around the world faced increasing pressure to operate with a commercial logic as a result of neoliberal economic policies. In 1996, Howard's Liberal-National Coalition government announced the largest funding cuts in the ABC's history of $66 million (12 per cent) over the following two years, forcing it to seek commercial revenue (Inglis 2006, 383, 596–7). Over the 1990s 'ABC Enterprises' (responsible for consumer products and services) increased its annual revenue from $688,000 to $11.3 million. The number of new products released each year – such as books, DVDs and CDs – increased from 230 to 648 (ABC 2006). By 2006–2007, the ABC received $185.2 million (18 per cent of total revenue) from sources other than government funding (ABC 2007, 63).

The 1990s saw significantly more commercial pressures placed on the marginalized SBS. In 1991, Hawke's Labour government transformed it into an independent corporation which introduced advertising before and after programmes, and in 2006 it introduced advertising within programmes. In 2006–2007, SBS supplemented its government funding with $50 million from the sale of goods and services (22 per cent of total revenue), of which $41 million came from advertising and sponsorship (SBS 2007, 101). While its main source of income remains taxpayers' money, such advertising revenue clearly throws into question the channel's status as a 'public' broadcaster; it is now more comparable to the 'commercial public service broadcasters' ITV, Channel 4, and Channel 5 in the UK (see Livingstone et al. 2007, 615).

This neoliberal approach to public service broadcasting – characterized by reductions in public expenditure and increasing commercial pressures – has been criticized for threatening the existence, integrity, and public service ethics of such broadcasters. One fear is that it will diminish the quality of programming, by reducing costly television formats such as drama, documentaries, news, and current affairs, as occurred with the BBC and ABC in the 1990s (Born 2004; Brunsdon et al. 2001; Inglis 2006). This is not always the case, as SBS's introduction of in-programme advertising led to a doubling of drama production and prime time news (Neill 2007). In the UK, lifestyle and reality TV have been at the centre of debates about the decline of public service broadcasting, as they are seen as emblematic of the shift from 'hard' to 'soft' programming, with its privileging of the individual over society, the private sphere over the public, and the personal over the political (see Moseley 2000; 2001). These programming changes are seen to have changed the mode of address of public broadcasters from 'citizens' to 'consumers', traditionally the mode of commercial channels. Interestingly, while the broader debates about the decline of public broadcasting have also been waged in Australia, lifestyle television has not been at the heart of such debates. The reason for this is the different history of lifestyle programming on Australian television.

Food, glorious food: The makeover of public lifestyle television

What we now know as 'lifestyle television' began its career on Australian TV on the commercial channels. In 1961 Channel Seven screened *My Fair Lady*, in which 'a supposedly "ordinary" housewife is given a make-over and transformed into a ravishing beauty' (Harrison 1994, 258). In contrast to the BBC – which produced shows like *Cookery* and *Television Garden* from 1946 (O'Sullivan 2005, 31) – the ABC came relatively late to lifestyle television (and SBS much later). Yet from the mid-1970s, the ABC carved out the origins of a number of genres of lifestyle television, including the home/DIY show (*Handyman* 1976), the travel show (*Holiday* with *Bill Peach* 1977–1981), and later the garden show (*Home Grown* 1985). The commercial networks soon copied its lead with shows like Nine's *Burke's Backyard* (1987–2004) and Seven's travel show *Escape* (1988).

The ABC continued programming these genres of lifestyle television in the early 1990s, with shows like *Holiday* (1987–1994), *Gardening Australia* (1990 onwards) and *The Home Show* (1990–1993). This last programme caused controversy as it was sponsored by various companies, a strategy developed in response to earlier funding cuts, and blurred the line between disinterested programming and advertorial (Jacka 2000, 60). The early 1990s also saw the commercial networks increase their programming of such lifestyle genres, with Nine's copy of *The Home Show* called *Our House* (1993–2001), and the travel shows *Getaway* (Nine 1992 onwards) and *The Great Outdoors* (Seven 1993 onwards).

In contrast to expectations, the ABC did not increase its programming of these lifestyle genres after the mid-1990s funding cuts – it decreased them. The boom in home, garden, travel and makeover shows has occurred largely on commercial television in Australia, unlike the UK where 'public service broadcasting has championed lifestyle' (Dover and Hill 2007, 30). While *Changing Rooms* and *Ground Force* were lifestyle hits for the BBC, they were locally formatted by channels Nine and Seven respectively. Indeed, these two largest commercial channels have broadcast all the home-related lifestyle shows that have characterized the recent explosion, including Nine's *Renovation Rescue*, *Backyard Blitz*, *Location Location* and *The Block*, and Seven's *Better Homes and Gardens*, *Room for Improvement*, *Auction Squad*, *Hot Auction* and *Hot Property*. Since the mid-1990s then, the home, garden and travel genres of lifestyle television have migrated from public broadcasting to their new homeland of commercial TV, with the ABC currently having one garden show but no home or travel show in its schedule.

Interestingly, food programming has followed the opposite trajectory. Food was one of the earliest forms of 'lifestyle' programming on Australian television, and had its origins on commercial TV. It began with *Entertaining with Kerr* on Channel Ten in 1965, and continued with *King's Kitchen* in the 1970s and 1980s. The ABC came late to culinary television – it was not until the 1980s that it produced *Come and Get It* with Peter Russell-Clarke. The financial pressures of the 1990s led to a distinct change in the food programming of Australia's public service broadcasters. For SBS, this meant the introduction of food programming to a channel which had generally been lifestyle-free, while the ABC experienced an even bigger explosion of food programming in its own schedule.

In addition to this increase in the number of food programmes, there has been a distinct change in the type of programmes produced and screened by the public broadcasters and the audiences to whom they speak. These public food shows do not target the traditional audience of culinary television – middle class suburban housewives – through women's daytime programming, as commercial cooking shows continue to do (see de Solier 2005, 469). Screened during prime time, they both target and attempt to cultivate an educated and sophisticated audience of 'foodies', or amateur food connoisseurs. The foodie is a middle class lifestyle-based identity, whose cosmopolitan mode of connoisseurship epitomizes 'highbrow' (see Bourdieu 1984; Gans 1999; Levine 1988) culinary taste in contemporary Australia. Public food shows now speak to such members of the educated cosmopolitan classes, with the cultural and economic capital to put stylized food production and consumption to work in the production of the self.

In targeting their address to such amateur food connoisseurs, these new public food shows are more similar to the 'hobby' programmes of early television than to other contemporary lifestyle programmes. As Charlotte Brunsdon writes: 'The hobby genre … addressed the amateur enthusiast. By the end of the programme, the listener would know how to do something. The new makeover programmes are different in that they offer a different balance between instruction and spectacle … and they most commonly address their audience as customer or consumer' (2003, 10). As we will see in the next section, foodie viewers learn new skills and knowledge from watching these programmes.

SBS has primarily targeted this foodie audience through the genre of the food documentary, which seeks to educate viewers not only in pragmatic culinary knowledge but also in theoretical gastronomic knowledge, often of an anthropological nature. This was epitomized by the aforementioned *Food Lovers' Guide to Australia* (1997–2005). The different segments of this show profiled foodies' main interests: restaurants, *haute cuisine* chefs, specialty produce and producers, food art, and 'authentic' ethnic cooking by migrant families. *The Food Lovers' Guide* was clearly targeted to a sophisticated urban cosmopolitan audience, rather than to the migrants who starred in it cooking their traditional dishes. Chris Lawe Davies writes that since introducing advertising, SBS has imagined its audience as 'less the stereotype of the working-class migrant with poor English and more the urban cosmopolitan of varying ethnicities' (cited in Jacka 2000, 63). The need to attract an AB demographic (senior managers and professionals) in order to secure advertising led SBS to construct its advertising around the image of the urban cosmopolitan. The *Food Lovers'* hosts epitomize this image: well-educated, professional, urban, Anglo-Australian women, venturing into country farms and migrant homes in search of culinary (and cultural) difference. Yet this identity of the culinary cosmopolitan host was originally carved out by non-Anglo migrants: it began with Pria Viswalingam, an upper middle class sub-continental, and his *Fork in the Road* series in 1992, which ran for nine seasons over the next 14 years. This was followed by Ghanaian Dorinda Hafner's *Taste Of …* series in the mid-1990s, which was sold to 48 countries (ABC 2008). SBS's more recent shows have continued the trend towards Anglo-Australian hosts, such as Barry Vera's *Feast* series (2005–2006) and Ron Brown's *Chefs of the Great Restaurants of the World* (2007).

Following the success of programmes like *Food Lovers' Guide* on SBS, the ABC too began to target a foodie audience in the late 1990s, but it did so through the more traditional genre of the cooking show. One of its main strategies was to appeal to foodies' highbrow culinary taste by introducing *haute cuisine* chefs as the hosts of cooking shows, with Stefano de Pieri's *A Gondola on the Murray* (1999), Stephanie Alexander's *A Shared Table* (1999), and Jacques Reymond's *Secret Recipes* (2001) (and continued today with *The Cook and the Chef*, 2006 onwards). These programmes all drew on elements from *Food Lovers' Guide*: the first two were produce-based and showed extra-culinary scenes of the hosts visiting regional producers (similar to Rick Stein's programmes, like *Food Heroes*, which the ABC imports); while the last was more anthropological, profiling the 'authentic' ethnic cooking of migrants in their homes. Like *Food Lovers' Guide*, which achieved merchandizing through videos, DVDs, and annual *SBS Eating Guides* to Sydney and Melbourne, these programmes offered videos, cookbooks (*Shared Table* and *Gondola* – which also spawned a CD), and were all sold on to Australia's pay-TV food channel, LifeStyle FOOD.

The twenty-first century has seen the ABC pursue a more middlebrow audience, in addition to a highbrow foodie audience, which is where it differs from SBS. It has done so through the new mode of 'middlebrow' (Rubin 1992) or 'high-pop' (Collins 2002) 'lifestyle' cooking shows, which it originally imported from British public broadcasters, such as *The Naked Chef*, *Nigella Bites*, and *Ainsley's Gourmet Express*. These lifestyle cooking shows translate highbrow taste into easy home cooking (as Jamie puts it: restaurant food 'stripped' down to its bare essentials) and place a popular emphasis on entertainment and celebrity through extra-culinary scenes of the lifestyle or private life of the host (see Hollows 2003a; 2003b; Moseley 2001; de Solier 2005). They not only teach viewers how to cook, but how to acquire sophisticated foodie lifestyles through commodity consumption and culinary production. Whilst still speaking (in part) to a highbrow foodie audience, these programmes seek to popularize the foodie lifestyle by targeting 'the masses', which is evidenced by their eventual adoption and repetition by the commercial networks.

Yet it is not Australia's commercial channels that have taken up this entertainment and celebrity oriented format in their own productions, but the ABC. Its two main lifestyle cooking shows, *Kylie Kwong* (2003; 2006) and *Surfing the Menu* (2004–2006), have been highly successful both locally and internationally (see Newman and Gibson 2005; de Solier 2005). In addition to merchandizing through cookbooks and DVDs, and local sales to LifeStyle FOOD, series 1 of *Surfing the Menu* sold to around 20 countries, while series 1 of *Kylie Kwong* sold to over 50 countries and was a 'ratings winner' for LifeStyle FOOD, which co-produced the second series (ABC 2004; 2005).

In contrast, the current commercial cooking shows – Nine's magazine-based *Fresh: Cooking with the Australian Women's Weekly* and Ten's *Huey's Cooking Adventures* (see de Solier 2005) – are the least celebritized and entertainment-driven programmes on Australian TV. Both are didactic, with no extra-culinary scenes of food production or the host's (un)sophisticated lifestyle. Screened during the day, they still target middle class suburban housewives, rather than public broadcasting's professional sophisticates. Neither programme has sold overseas, nor do they have DVDs, and only *Huey*'s programme has cookbooks as *Fresh* operates as a promotional platform for *Australian Women's Weekly* cookbooks and magazines. So whilst the commercial networks created the cooking show as an entertainment and celebrity focused genre, they have drifted away from this approach as the ABC has taken it up, in an interesting reversal of public and commercial television.

The ABC, through its quantity and diversity of cooking shows, has become the main player in the televisual production, promotion and popularization of the foodie lifestyle. Yet the national broadcaster's power as an influential lifestyle guide does not end with TV. In 2001, ABC Enterprises launched its own monthly glossy food magazine: *delicious*. The magazine claims to target foodies, as its media kit states:

'delicious readers are discerning, passionate foodies who love to cook' (*delicious* 2007, 3). Its point of difference from competitors is its emphasis on celebrity TV chefs, who contribute most of the recipes and grace the cover. The magazine functions both as a source of additional revenue, and a means of cross-promotion for ABC's celebrity chefs and food programming. *delicious* became the market leader within two years. In February 2007, it had a readership of 428,000, compared to 338,000 for *Donna Hay*, 305,000 for *Gourmet Traveller*, and 144,000 for *Vogue Entertaining and Travel* (*delicious* 2007, 6). It is now a global brand, with editions in the UK and Netherlands, and plans underway for the USA and Asia. In print media, as in television, the ABC has become a powerful player in the stylized foodie cultures of the twenty-first century.

Since the 1990s, then, Australia's public broadcasters have increased their food programming, and explicitly targeted and cultivated an audience of foodie viewers for whom their programmes offer lifestyle guidance. While SBS's programming has maintained its focus on a highbrow foodie audience through gastronomic documentaries, the ABC's importation and local production of 'lifestyle' cooking shows and *delicious* magazine – which are increasingly entertainment and celebrity focused – demonstrate its attempt to appeal to a middlebrow audience, as it seeks out higher ratings and sales in competitive media markets. Thus while the more commercial (and marginal) SBS started this trend in 'foodie' programming, the more taxpayer-funded (and much larger) ABC has cornered the market by capturing both a highbrow foodie audience and a middlebrow culinary audience through its combination of programmes and products. Indeed, the ABC appears to be branding itself as *the* foodie channel: at a recent conference on the future of the food media, an ABC radio presenter said the new head of ABC television wants the channel to 'own food' (Razer 2007). Thus the taxpayer-funded national broadcaster has become the biggest player in contemporary foodism, as it seeks to popularize the traditionally highbrow foodie lifestyle amongst citizen-viewers.

Why, then, have both the ABC and SBS turned to food programming – and not other forms of lifestyle programming – in response to commercial pressures since the 1990s? One explanation concerns economic value. In terms of the cost of production, food shows are less expensive than makeover shows like home renovation programmes, as they have fewer hosts and require less expensive materials, and most don't require the recruitment of 'ordinary' people as participants. As we have seen, food programmes offer significant opportunities for merchandizing through DVDs, cookbooks, and magazines. And finally, because they are not reality- or makeover-based, they offer greater potential for repeat screenings, sales to local pay-TV channels, and particularly outright exports to international markets (see Bonner 2005). Another explanation concerns cultural value. As Rachel Moseley writes, 'there is programming in this [prime time] slot which offers more "acceptable" forms of knowledge within the lifestyle mode, about antiques, stately homes and tradition, and on the cultural history of DIY and interior design, for instance' (2000, 301–2). Food offers such an 'acceptable', high-cultural form of lifestyle knowledge for Australia's public broadcasters, who, unlike the BBC, have steered away from producing reality- and makeover-based forms of lifestyle television, as a point of distinction from their more 'lowbrow' commercial siblings.

'I've learnt quite a lot from TV shows': Foodie viewers and the makeover of the self

How have foodies responded to the recent wave of food programming by Australia's public broadcasters? Has the broadcasters' strategy of targeting a foodie audience been successful? To answer these questions this section draws on audience research I conducted with 50 foodies in Melbourne in early 2007 as part of a broader research project into the foodie lifestyle. Participants were recruited through the 'Epicure' food supplement of Melbourne's broadsheet *The Age*. Twenty individuals were selected for face-to-face interviews (10 women, 10 men), while another 30 self-selected to respond to email surveys (23 women, 7 men). Their ages ranged from early twenties to late sixties, with the largest group in their thirties. While most were Anglo-Australian, 25 per cent claimed European heritage and 10 per cent Asian heritage, with 20 per cent born overseas. They were predominantly urban, with 80 per cent living in inner city suburbs. All were middle class, many with high levels of cultural and/or economic capital. Most were highly educated, with the majority (70 per cent) having completed a university degree, and 40 per cent were undertaking or had completed some form of postgraduate study (including three PhDs). The majority were employed in upper middle class professional/managerial occupations and new middle class (or 'new *petite bourgeoisie*') occupations – 'new cultural intermediaries' and 'lifestyle and body "experts"' (see Bourdieu 1984, 359; Featherstone 1991, 77). None were working class, but ten were currently unemployed (retirees, students and housewives). Their personal incomes ranged from zero (unemployed) to $150,000. The average for those receiving an income was $67,000, with 40 per cent earning $80,000 or more.

Most of the foodies in the study claimed to watch, and enjoy, food television. There was little variation according to gender or age, as both women and men of all ages watched such programmes. The 'foodie viewer', then, is different to the 'typical lifestyle programme viewer' found by Caroline Dover and Annette Hill (2007) in the UK, who was more likely to be a woman in her twenties or thirties. Where Dover and Hill found that retirees hardly watch lifestyle television, all the retirees in my study watched food television.

The majority of the foodies watched and preferred the food programmes shown on public television, which was a result of the greater number of programmes offered by the public broadcasters, the programme scheduling (unlike public food shows which screen during prime time, local commercial cooking shows are screened during the daytime so many participants were unable to watch them), the genre of food programmes they produced, and the 'quality' or cultural value attributed to such programmes. The main sub-genres preferred by foodie viewers were cooking shows and gastronomic documentaries, which are the mainstay of public food television. Most viewers did not like the reality TV-based sub-genres of culinary game shows such as *Ready Steady Cook* or makeover shows like *Honey, We're Killing the Kids*, both BBC programmes which have been locally formatted by Channel Ten. For example Sally, a 28-year-old fashion publicist who 'loved' most food television said: 'I don't like things like *Ready Steady Cook* – rarely put together interesting dishes – more for the masses than the "foodies".'

At issue here are questions of taste and class, as fans like Sally seek to distinguish yuppie foodies like herself from 'the masses' by highlighting their different taste in food and food television. As her comment suggests, the commercial networks are commonly seen as catering for the 'masses' with their more 'popular' (read: boring) culinary taste, and/or reality TV-based formats. These styles of food programming are seen as 'cheap' and 'entertainment-driven' forms of commercial television, as opposed to the 'high quality' productions of the public broadcasters, with their glossy and stylized visual aesthetics, and highbrow culinary taste formations epitomized in the figure of the *haute cuisine* chef. Indeed, it is most likely the lack of reality TV and makeover shows in Australia's public food programming which makes it appealing across demographics as well as creating the perception of it as a more 'respectable' form of lifestyle television.

All the foodie viewers said they found food television both entertaining and informative, and that they had acquired new knowledge and skills from watching such programmes. Where Dover and Hill's study of lifestyle television found that less than 10 per cent of viewers claimed they learnt practical things from such programmes (Dover and Hill 2007, 35), all the foodie viewers in this study claimed to have learnt practical things from culinary television, such as new recipes and ingredients, culinary skills and techniques, and which equipment to use for particular purposes. They also claimed to have learnt more theoretical gastronomic knowledge about food production and farming, and anthropological knowledge about the food practices of different cultural groups. Indeed, foodie viewers seek out programmes that are informative. As Gareth, a 54-year-old retired teacher said, 'I want more in-depth information', which he found in public television shows like SBS's *Food Lovers' Guide* and the ABC's current cooking show *The Cook and the Chef*. Thus foodie viewers like Gareth look to public television programmes for lifestyle guidance, to gain further training in foodie tastes, practices and knowledge: in short – how to live life as a foodie.

The Food Lovers' Guide was undoubtedly the most popular programme amongst foodie viewers, as it offered information on a range of topics of interest to them – restaurants, chefs, ingredients, producers, and migrant families' culinary practices. One of the reasons it is so popular is precisely because it's *not* a cooking show – because it provides a range of theoretical information and guidance beyond the *applied* knowledge of culinary skills. This was especially important for Emily, a 42-year-old foodie who is physically unable to cook due to a disability, who wrote that her favourite food show was '*Food Lovers' Guide* because it shows more than just cooking e.g., produce, restaurants, food stores, etc.'.

The ABC's current prime time cooking show, *The Cook and the Chef* – which continues in the highbrow tradition of *haute cuisine* produce-based programmes – was the most popular *cooking* show amongst foodie viewers. Again, they liked it for the high level and detail of information. Jennifer, a 65-year-old vegetarian foodie, writes that because the hosts

> have a good theoretical knowledge of ingredients and methodology, I find some of their tips (even the simple ones) useful. For example, always cut eggplants with a serrated knife. This sounds trivial but is a really useful tip for me, as we use them at least twice a week.

The persona of the hosts – Maggie Beer, a food writer and restaurateur, and Simon Bryant, Executive Chef at the Hilton Hotel in Adelaide – was also appealing. Jennifer went on to say, 'I find Maggie and Simon entertaining and informative, also lacking in pretension.' Alan, a 61-year-old real estate agent, contrasted them with the younger celebrity chefs hosting 'lifestyle' cooking shows: 'Jamie doesn't appeal to me (probably because of my age), nor does Nigella. I'm more a Rick Stein or Maggie Beer type. They are more interested in the food than themselves.'

It was in relation to the more middlebrow 'lifestyle' cooking shows that the gender and age differences characterizing Dover and Hill's (2007) 'typical lifestyle programme viewer' came into play for culinary television – the foodie viewers who liked such programmes tended to be younger, mostly in their thirties and forties, and also tended to be women. Yet while all viewers enjoyed extra-culinary scenes of producers and ingredients in food programmes, even the foodie viewers who liked these lifestyle cooking shows did not like their emphasis on the celebrity chef and extra-culinary scenes of their lifestyle or private life. As 34-year-old Linda said: 'I am interested in what and how they cook, not their private lives.' Amongst all foodie viewers, the ABC's lifestyle cooking shows *Surfing the Menu* and *Kylie Kwong* were viewed as less 'popular' and of a higher quality than their British counterparts *The Naked Chef* and *Nigella Bites*, due in part to their *haute cuisine* chef hosts' more serious attitude towards food and cooking.

The phenomenon of celebrity TV chefs in general divided foodie viewers, but not along clear age or gender lines. Some foodies liked the fact that celebrity chefs have drawn more attention to food in contemporary society. Rowena, a 47-year-old human resources manager, said she thought the rise of celebrity chefs was 'Great – it's a good thing to be talking and thinking about food than say just focusing on sport. Some of the chefs do great things for the community, e.g. Jamie Oliver, Stefano de Pieri.' Others, however, were strongly opposed to 'celebrity chefs', such as Rachel, a 36-year-old accountant, who said that

> They should get off the tv and we should be showing real food on tv – show the people who have been cooking for 30 years because their parent(s) cooked, and their parents before them and it's the family business. We need to show the history of food and where it's come from. Not some fly-by-nighter person who wants to show off their kids on tv and sell their favourite songs on CDs because it's called diversifying and extracting an extra few dollars from people's pockets. And he'll be replaced by the next trendy whoever with a new and improved marketing ploy.

Interestingly, Rachel (and others) only characterized 'lifestyle' TV chefs such as Jamie Oliver and Nigella Lawson as 'celebrity chefs', and not other TV chefs such as Rick Stein or Gordon Ramsay, who are both global television celebrities with numerous restaurants and product lines to their names. This is presumably because of the relative lack of focus on their private lives in their respective programmes, but also because of the higher cultural value attributed to their personas and programmes (which are perceived as 'authentic') as opposed to the 'popular' (and 'plastic') status of 'lifestyle' TV chefs.

Presumably due to the high emphasis placed on celebrity TV chefs within its pages, the ABC's *delicious* magazine was not popular with the foodies in the study, even amongst those who watched and liked 'lifestyle' cooking shows. Whilst *delicious* claims its readers are 'discerning, passionate foodies', none of the foodies in this study bought the magazine on a regular basis: the most popular magazine amongst these foodies was the more highbrow *Gourmet Traveller*, which has a greater focus on *haute cuisine* restaurant chefs (not TV stars), culture and travel, and appeals to their anthropological and cosmopolitan sensibilities. In comparison to the foodie demographics outlined earlier, the majority of *delicious* readers are women and are not in full-time employment, which suggests a greater proportion of middle class housewives (with an average household income of \$94,430) (*delicious* 2007, 3). It appears then that the ABC's *delicious* magazine is speaking to a more mainstream middlebrow audience – even more so than its 'lifestyle' cooking shows – to whom it popularizes the traditionally highbrow foodie lifestyle.

This audience research has shown that the strategy employed by Australia's public service broadcasters since the 1990s of targeting their food programming towards a foodie audience has been mostly successful. The majority of foodie viewers watched public food programmes, and preferred them over commercial shows. The public broadcasters produced the most popular food programmes amongst foodie viewers: SBS's documentary series *The Food Lovers' Guide*, and the ABC's highbrow cooking show *The Cook and the Chef*. In terms of merchandizing, some foodies owned cookbooks from ABC shows, and a few had seen their TV chefs perform live. This demonstrates that foodies are certainly using the public broadcasters as significant and influential guides in their pursuit of a foodie lifestyle.

Yet the ABC's *delicious* magazine, while claiming to target a foodie audience, has not been successful amongst this sample of foodies, primarily due to its high emphasis on celebrity. ABC's middlebrow 'lifestyle' cooking shows – *Kylie Kwong* and *Surfing the Menu* – with their focus on entertainment and celebrity, have not been as successful at appealing to all foodie viewers, only appealing to a younger female segment of this audience. These offerings are seen as too 'popular' for some foodies, in contrast to the more highbrow programmes which appeal to all foodie viewers. Thus while SBS has remained focused on a highbrow foodie audience, the ABC is also speaking to a broader mass middle class audience through its middlebrow 'lifestyle' cooking shows and *delicious* magazine. In doing so, the national broadcaster is actively popularizing highbrow foodie tastes and practices amongst a more mainstream culinary population, which it seeks to transform – or makeover – into foodies.

State makeovers: Cultivating foodie-citizens

The targeting, promotion and production of foodie viewers by Australia's public television broadcasters must be considered in the economic and cultural context of the 'foodie boom' of which it is both a cause and effect. Over the past decade, food has increasingly come to the fore in consumption, leisure and lifestyle practices, and more people are identifying as 'foodies' than ever before. In Australia, as elsewhere, food is big business. The restaurant industry is booming: 10,000 new businesses have entered the industry over the past five years, making a total of 37,700 in 2007

(Restaurant & Catering Australia 2007). Food festivals are another area of rapid growth. Australia's largest festival, the Melbourne Food and Wine Festival, began in 1993 with 12 events – in 2007 it had 140 events, including 'The International Flour Festival' and 'Wicked Sunday' which drew 120,000 people over one weekend. This 'foodie boom' has of course included an explosion of food media. We have witnessed an exponential rise in the number and range of food magazines, cookbooks, food blogs, and of course, TV shows, which are our focus here. These media function as lifestyle guides, instructional manuals which teach their audiences competency in the cultural codes of foodism, or how to acquire culinary and gastronomic cultural capital (see Bourdieu 1984; de Solier 2005).

This chapter has suggested that Australia's public service broadcasters function as such lifestyle guides, by targeting, training and producing a population of foodies. Yet this strategy should not be seen in isolation, but in the context of other governmental strategies aimed at promoting and popularizing this lifestyle. The Melbourne Food and Wine Festival, for example, is sponsored by both the local (Melbourne) and state (Victorian) governments, which both encourage foodism amongst their citizens and offer lifestyle guidance through TV – not public TV, however, but commercial TV.

The Melbourne City Council promoted the foodie lifestyle in its TV show *That's Melbourne* (2004), which formed part of its broader campaign of promoting the inner city as a space of commodity consumption and leisure to suburban citizens. The programme resembled a travel show but focused on Melbourne alone, and was targeted towards its own citizens rather than tourists. It was screened in Victoria on Channel Nine, and was co-hosted by game-show host Livinia Nixon, comedian Dave O'Neil and ex- Australian Rules footballer Garry Lyon. The show encouraged viewers to engage in foodie practices of visiting the city's cafes, bars and restaurants, explicitly teaching them how and where to consume food and drink in a sophisticated manner. It showed Melbournians how they could (or should) construct urban identities through stylized culinary consumption, suggesting that such consumption is a form of cultural city-zenship, and that good city-zens are foodie city-zens.

The Victorian state government also used commercial television to promote the foodie lifestyle to its citizens, through its sponsorship of Channel Seven's food tourism series *The Food Trail* (2006). In contrast to *That's Melbourne*, where the foodie lifestyle was played out in the space of the city, *The Food Trail* sought to teach suburban Melbournians how to perform this lifestyle in the spaces of regional Victoria. Modelled on *The Food Lovers' Guide*, *The Food Trail* replaced the urban female hosts with a suburban male host, actor Paul Mercurio, who visited a range of regional food producers, wineries and restaurants, for whom the programme functioned as an advertisement.

It is interesting that neither of these government sponsored TV shows were screened on the public broadcasters, especially considering their niche in food TV. Yet this is because neither of these programmes were targeted at existing foodies, at the urban professional audiences of public food television. Indeed, none of the foodies in my study watched *That's Melbourne*, and only two watched *The Food Trail*. Rather, these government sponsored programmes targeted the 'unsophisticated' suburban 'masses', the aspirational lower middle class, through mainstream commercial media and pop-culture hosts. The hosts reflected their audience as they too had no culinary or gastronomic cultural capital, but were undertaking projects of the self in order to acquire such cultural capital and sophisticated foodie identities. These programmes, then, sought to makeover unsophisticated suburbanites into stylish foodies by teaching them how to spend their leisure time and money pursuing foodie tastes and practices, thus popularizing this lifestyle amongst the 'masses'.

The ideological work of promoting and popularizing foodism that is occurring at a national level through the food programming of Australia's public television broadcasters should be seen in the context of similar governmental strategies at state and local levels operating through commercial television, as part of a broader move to produce a citizenry with sophisticated culinary tastes and skills, who use stylish food in a stylization of the self. The state then, alongside capitalism, must be understood as a powerful player in the contemporary foodie boom. All these state initiatives are clearly speaking to citizens as citizen-consumers, telling them how and where to spend their money on food. Yet it is not about consuming indiscriminately, or being a glutton – and definitely not about becoming obese (indeed, the obesity crisis appears beyond the reach of style-oriented public television, a signifier of 'bad taste' and the province of the lower classes and commercial television, such as *The Biggest Loser* and *Honey, We're Killing the Kids*). Rather, it is about reflexively consuming 'high quality' culinary goods and services in particular stylized ways, and putting this consumption to work in the production of a self-identity as a foodie.

These state agencies, then, are actually guiding culinary consumption to a close degree, providing highly detailed and prescriptive lifestyle guidance through television for 'proper' citizens to follow. As Bev Skeggs and Helen Wood have pointed out in relation to the lifestyle guidance offered by Channel 4's programmes like *Wife Swap*, which 'teaches mothers how to mother', this is not a neoliberal approach but a Scottish moral liberal approach: that is, that people need instructing (Skeggs 2007). It's not the autonomous neoliberal subject free to construct themselves through their own culinary choices in the market, but a liberal subject who needs to be trained in their culinary consumption choices and lifestyle by the state. Ironically for public broadcasting, this moral liberal approach to culinary consumption is a product of neoliberal economic policies.

The foodie-citizen is one of the new forms of 'legitimate', 'respectable', consumer-citizenship being promoted by the state in late capitalist liberal democracies. This signifies a new relationship between the state, citizens, and food. It is no longer merely an obligation of citizenship to eat healthily according to the food pyramid and nutritional guidelines promoted by governments in the 1980s, or for women to know how to cook such healthy meals as part of the labour involved in their gendered cultural citizenship. In the twenty-first century, the state's culinary address to citizens is divided down class lines. As obesity has become a new marker of working and lower class bodies – lower class Australian children are twice as likely to be obese (Stark 2007) – health issues still dominate the state's address to these classed citizens, as they are encouraged to fulfill the new obligation to not be obese. In contrast, in the state's address to middle class citizens the emphasis has shifted from health to style, as all members – regardless of gender – are expected to possess 'good taste', consume sophisticated gourmet meals, and acquire the culinary skills required to 'create' them (not just cook them). This is a mode of consumer-citizenship that is only available to certain citizens, members of the middle class who have the economic and cultural capital necessary to participate in it.

The question begs, then, whether this foodie-citizen is a citizen at all, or merely a consumer pursuing their self-interests of lifestylization to the exclusion of other social and political concerns (see also Miller 2007). While for many foodies, their interest in food is primarily a project of self-production through gastronomic knowledge and practices, there is a growing awareness of and concern for food politics amongst this lifestyle group. The multicultural politics of food are those most heavily advocated in the state's promotion of foodism in Australia, particularly in the case of public television, and are those about which most foodies have an interest and awareness. Yet for some foodies, the international, environmental and economic politics of food are integral to their foodism, despite their relative absence from the state-funded foodie media. For example Sam, a social worker, describes how his interest in food has made him aware of the power relations that structure the world he lives in:

> Through an awareness of food I see connections with all else, the social as in class and power, the economic as in "development" and international trade relations, the political, the environmental, and the cultural. Food is universal, in that we all need it, but within that there are a plethora of layers which bring connection and understanding of people and places in the world I live in.

Sam's foodism is increasingly tied to a cultural politics of food, and has played an integral role in making him a socially aware local and global citizen. Thus while public television promotes culinary consumption as a means of stylization of the self, the foodies who watch such programmes are not uninformed consumers but highly educated citizen-consumers who also see it as a site for the enactment of a politics of consumption. While most of the state promotions of foodism, including public television, do not address such politics at present, there is clearly potential for them to do so in the future, as foodies look to them not only for lifestyle guidance, but for political awareness. As Toby Miller writes: 'If properly engaged, the cultural politics of food could be central to everyday citizenship' (2007, 143).

This chapter exposed the role played by the state as a lifestyle guide in the current foodie boom, by examining how it has used lifestyle television to promote this cultural identity. It focused on the public service broadcasters, the ABC and SBS, who adopted this role as gastronomic lifestyle guide during the commercial pressures of the 1990s to financial success. It showed that while the more commercialized SBS was the first to target foodie audiences through the genre of the food documentary, it is the larger, more publicly-funded ABC which has become the most powerful player in contemporary foodism, through its combination of highbrow *haute cuisine* cooking shows and middlebrow 'lifestyle' cooking shows and *delicious* magazine. As we saw from the audience research, these public broadcasters function as influential lifestyle guides for contemporary foodies. The chapter argued that these strategies of public television must be seen in the broader context of local and state governmental strategies which promote foodism through commercial lifestyle television, and seek to popularize it amongst the aspirational suburban 'masses'. Thus in the twenty-first century, the state is using both public and commercial lifestyle television to attempt to produce a population of sophisticated foodie-citizens.

Bibliography

ABC (2004), 'Global Popularity for Series 1 and 2 of Surfing the Menu', <http:// www.abc.net.au/abccontentsales/s1267866.htm>, accessed 16 November 2007.

ABC (2005), 'Announcing Kylie Kwong: Simply Magic', <http://www.abc.net.au/ abccontentsales/s1483884.htm>, accessed 16 November 2007.

ABC (2006), 'About the ABC – History of the ABC: The 90s', <http://www. abc.net. au/corp/history/hist7.htm>, accessed 11 March 2007.

ABC (2007), *Annual Report 2006–07* [online] <http://www.abc.net.au/corp/annual_ reports/ar07/>, accessed 7 November 2007.

ABC (2008), 'Talking Heads: Transcripts: Dorinda Hafner', <http://www.abc.net. au/talkingheads/txt/s1570610.htm>, accessed 3 January 2008.

Bell, D. and Hollows, J. (eds) (2005), *Ordinary Lifestyles: Popular Media, Consumption and Taste* (Maidenhead: Open University Press).

Bonner, F. (2005), 'Whose Lifestyle is it Anyway?', in D. Bell and J. Hollows (eds) (2005), *Ordinary Lifestyles: Popular Media, Consumption and Taste* (Maidenhead: Open University Press).

Born, G. (2004), *Uncertain Vision: Birt, Dyke and the Reinvention of the BBC* (London: Secker & Warburg).

Bourdieu, P. (1984), *Distinction: A Social Critique of the Judgement of Taste* (London: Routledge).

Brunsdon, C. (2003), 'Lifestyling Britain: The 8–9 Slot on British Television', *International Journal of Cultural Studies* 6:1, 5–23.

Brunsdon, C. et al. (2001), 'Factual Entertainment on British Television: The Midlands TV Research Group's "8–9 Project"', *European Journal of Cultural Studies* 4:1, 29–62.

Collins, J. (ed.) (2002), *High-Pop: Making Culture into Popular Entertainment* (Malden, MA: Blackwell Publishers).

Cunningham, S. (2000), 'History, Contexts, Politics, Policy', in G. Turner and S. Cunningham (eds) (2000), *The Australian TV Book* (St Leonards: Allen & Unwin).

Dale, D. (2007), 'Imported Shows … Who Needs Them?', *The Age*, 1 December, p. 3.

delicious (2007), 'Delicious Media Kit August 07', <http://www.fpc.com.au/sites/ del/del_2007_08-Delicious_Media_Kit_August07.pdf.>, accessed 4 September 2007.

Dover, C. and Hill, A. (2007), 'Mapping Genres: Broadcaster and Audience Perceptions of Makeover Television', in D. Heller (ed.) (2007), *Makeover Television: Realities Remodelled* (London and New York: I.B. Tauris).

Featherstone, M. (1991), *Consumer Culture and Postmodernism* (London: Sage).

Gans, H. (1999), *Popular Culture and High Culture: An Analysis and Evaluation of Taste* (New York: Basic Books).

Harrison, T. (1994), *The Australian Film and Television Companion* (East Roseville, NSW: Simon & Schuster).

Heller, D. (ed.) (2007), *Makeover Television: Realities Remodelled* (London and New York: I.B. Tauris).

Hollows, J. (2003a), 'Feeling Like a Domestic Goddess: Postfeminism and Cooking', *European Journal of Cultural Studies* 6:2, 179–202.

Hollows, J. (2003b), 'Oliver's Twist: Leisure, Labour and Domestic Masculinity in *The Naked Chef*', *International Journal of Cultural Studies* 6:2, 229–248.

Inglis, K.S. (2006), *Whose ABC? The Australian Broadcasting Corporation 1983–2006* (Melbourne: Black Inc).

Jacka, E. (2000), 'Public Service TV: An Endangered Species?', in G. Turner and S. Cunningham (eds) (2000), *The Australian TV Book* (St Leonards: Allen & Unwin).

Levine, L. (1988), *Highbrow/Lowbrow: The Emergence of Cultural Hierarchy in America* (Cambridge, MA: Harvard University Press).

Livingstone, S. et al. (2007), 'Citizens and Consumers: Discursive Debates During and After the Communications Act 2003', *Media, Culture & Society* 29:4, 613–38.

Miller, T. (2007), *Cultural Citizenship: Cosmopolitanism, Consumerism, and Television in a Neoliberal Age* (Philadelphia, PA: Temple University Press).

Moseley, R. (2000), 'Makeover Takeover on British Television', *Screen* 41:3, 299–314.

Moseley, R. (2001), '"Real Lads Do Cook ... But Some Things are Still Hard to Talk About": The Gendering of 8–9', in Brunsdon et al. 'Factual Entertainment on British Television: The Midlands TV Research Group's "8–9 Project"', *European Journal of Cultural Studies* 4:1, 32–9.

Neill, R. (2007), 'Identity Crisis', *The Australian* [website] (3 November), <http://www.theaustralian.news.com.au/story/0,25197,22673746-16947,00.html>, accessed 7 November 2007.

Newman, F. and Gibson, M. (2005), 'Monoculture versus Multiculinarism: Trouble in the Aussie Kitchen', in (eds), D. Bell and J. Hollows (eds) (2005), *Ordinary Lifestyles: Popular Media, Consumption and Taste* (Maidenhead: Open University Press).

O'Sullivan, T. (2005), 'From Television Lifestyle to Lifestyle Television', in D. Bell and J. Hollows (eds) (2005), *Ordinary Lifestyles: Popular Media, Consumption and Taste* (Maidenhead: Open University Press).

Razer, H. (2007), 'Getting on TV – How to Do it and is it Worth it?', panel discussion at 'Out of the Frying Pan: Future of the Food Media' Conference, Melbourne Food and Wine Festival, 26 March.

Restaurant & Catering Australia (2007), 'Industry Snapshot: Issue 1, 2007', <http://www.restaurantcater.asn.au/rc/content.aspx?id=11>, accessed 1 October 2007.

Rubin, J. (1992), *The Making of Middle/Brow Culture* (Chapel Hill: University of North Carolina Press).

Savill, J. (2007), 'Getting on TV – How to Do it and is it Worth it?', panel discussion at 'Out of the Frying Pan: Future of the Food Media' Conference, Melbourne Food and Wine Festival, 26 March.

SBS (2007), Annual Report 2006–2007 [online], <http://www20.sbs.com.au/sbscorporate/index.php?id=392>, accessed 7 November 2007.

Skeggs, B. (2007), 'The Moral Labours of Transformation on Lifestyle Television', paper presented at the Media Moralities Workshop, The State Library of Victoria, 23 November.

Skeggs, B., Thumim, N. and Wood, H. (2008), '"Oh Goodness, I *am* Watching Reality TV": How Methods Make Class in Audience Research', *European Journal of Cultural Studies* 11:1, 5–24.

Solier, I. de (2005), 'TV Dinners: Culinary Television, Education and Distinction', *Continuum: Journal of Media & Cultural Studies* 19:4, 465–81.

Stark, J. (2007), 'Children's Obesity Rates Keep Rising', *The Age* [website] (20 July), <http://www.theage.com.au/news/national/childrens-obesity-rates-keep-rising/2007/07/19/1184559956554.html#>, accessed 15 February 2008.

Starr, J. (2004), 'An Alternative View of the Future of Public Television', <http://www.cipbonline.org/JerrysAlternateView.htm>, accessed 7 November 2007.

Turner, G. and Cunningham, S. (eds) (2000), *The Australian TV Book* (St Leonards: Allen & Unwin).

Chapter 7

Shame on You:
Cosmetic Surgery and Class
Transformation in *10 Years Younger*

Julie Doyle and Irmi Karl

Introduction

"It looks like she shouldn't be on the beach."

"It looks disgusting to be honest."

(Comments made by the British public on Nerys, a participant on *10 Years Younger*, pre-cosmetic surgery, *10 Years Younger* 2006d)

"It has been worth all the pain, heartache and humiliation. I feel good about myself now. I look good and feel good."

(Comment made by Laura Hammond after facial cosmetic surgery, *10 Years Younger* 2006c)

The year 2004 saw the emergence of yet another makeover show on British terrestrial television, *10 Years Younger in 10 Days*. Adding a new twist to the already established diet of makeover programmes, it combined the fashion and nutrition advice presented in programmes such as *What Not to Wear* (BBC1, UK) and *You Are What You Eat* (Channel 4, UK), with the cosmetic surgery so far witnessed on cable/ satellite TV shows such as *The Swan* (FOX, US) and *Extreme Makeover* (ABC, US; Living, UK).[1] Its success spawned the second series *10 Years Younger* (2005).[2] Both series featured facial cosmetic surgery, and style and fitness advice, to knock ten years off the perceived age of the predominantly female contestants, following public polls in city centres across Britain, and in holiday resorts. The second series shifted the success of the makeover towards the essential role of facial cosmetic

---

1   *Extreme Makeover UK*, is modelled on its US counterpart. The series entered its third season in 2008.

2   Whilst the first series was entitled *10 Years Younger in 10 Days*, featuring a '10 day' makeover cycle, the implementation of increasingly extensive cosmetic surgery in subsequent series demanded a much longer production time frame to allow participants to recover from various surgical interventions before their final style makeover. This necessitated the title change to *10 Years Younger*.

surgery. However, the quest for youth and beauty did not stop at the face: series 3 and 4 (2006–7), called for an 'all-over cosmetic transformation' (*10 Years Younger* 2006a) for women, featuring face and body modifications on a so far unprecedented scale on British terrestrial television.

The ability of television programming to cross national and cultural borders is already widely acknowledged. As British and US versions of Reality TV programming continue to influence each other, 'The focus on personal confession, modification, testing and the perfectability of the self in Reality TV has become transnational' (Bignell 2005, 40). Nevertheless, it would be an omission to neglect analytic perspectives that address particular styles of audience address and 'local' differences within global television culture. This chapter provides a critical examination of the British makeover programme *10 Years Younger* in the context of wider ranging discussions of cosmetic surgery and body modification, (post)feminism and consumerism, gender and class transformation. We consider UK Channel 4's decision to air *10 Years Younger* to be a milestone not only in terms of introducing (extensive) cosmetic surgery onto British terrestrial television, but more specifically into the public service broadcasting arena.[3] This, it will be argued, signifies and further intensifies the media's contribution towards the class re-education project implicit in Third Way politics and neoliberalism more generally, and New Labour politics in particular (Karl 2007).

As US makeover shows and fictional programmes featuring cosmetic surgery have proliferated in recent years, academic interest, especially in feminist quarters, has also been growing. By far the most attention has been given to US programmes such as *Extreme Makeover* and *The Swan* (Banet-Weiser and Portwood-Stacer 2006; Heinricy 2006; Heyes 2007; Tait 2007). However, although the literature points out that these cosmetic makeover programmes predominantly feature working class and lower middle class women, comparatively little analytical emphasis is put on the class factor in this reality TV (sub)genre. As Skeggs has argued, 'class is so insinuated in the intimate making of self and culture that it is even more ubiquitous than previously articulated, if more difficult to pin down' (Skeggs 2005, 969). This chapter aims to contribute towards work on cosmetic surgery programmes by more specifically making connections between body and class transformations.

We argue that cosmetic surgery is being legitimized as a form of female empowerment within contemporary media discourse through narratives of individual choice and self-liberation. The concept of choice needs to be critically examined within the context of popular post-feminist and neoliberal ideologies of the self which focus upon individual responsibility and consumer agency, thereby rendering invisible structural and social inequalities. In consumer society, the authentic self expresses itself through practices of consumption, where the body becomes a privileged signifier of the inner self. However, these discourses are gendered in that they work predominantly upon womens' bodies, but more crucially, assigning value and (moral) worth through a particular classed ideal of the self achieved by bodily transformation. In the context of *10 Years Younger*, processes of public shaming

---

3   Channel 4, although entirely commercially self-funded, holds a remit of public service obligations.

are employed to render working and lower middle class female bodies worthless and wanting. Whilst the subsequent transformations are figured as attainable to all women, they serve to reinforce class differences by identifying certain kinds of bodies as worthless in the first place, leaving unquestioned the cultural and economic resources required for access to and maintenance of the transformed body.

Cosmetic surgery, feminist interventions and questions of class

Within feminist theory, cosmetic surgery has been condemned and more recently rehabilitated (Negrin 2002). Criticisms of cosmetic surgery are that it colonizes women's bodies in conforming to ideals of female beauty through technological intervention (Bordo 1993; Jeffreys 2005). Central to feminist discussions of cosmetic surgery is the relationship, or conflict, between individual choice and social oppression. For Jeffreys, cosmetic surgery, like other beauty practices, is 'not about women's individual choice or a "discursive space" for women's creative expression, but … a most important aspect of women's oppression' (Jeffreys 2005, 2). Susan Bordo argues that a discourse of individual choice has become naturalized so that it is difficult to politically question such practices. Barbara Brook states that 'while "choice" appears to be egalitarian, there are dominant preferred patterns of "beauty" and "normality" that are, on examination, Caucasian and which impose their own parameters on those choices' (Brook 1999, 79).

Kathy Davis, however, has argued for a recognition of the positive aspects of such technologies for women seeking an embodied sense of self, leading to a degree of self-empowerment (Davis 1995). Nevertheless, Tait argues that Davis' focus on surgical consumers has 'enabled the domestication of cosmetic surgery within feminist scholarship' (Tait 2007, 121). The gains of second wave feminism are clearly at risk in the light of popular post-feminist renderings of female empowerment through individual (surgical) transformation *vis-à-vis* efforts to transform social and ideological structures as a means of women's liberation (Tait 2007). As media sites featuring, promoting and normalizing surgical culture multiply, it is becoming more difficult to criticize surgical culture and to have those criticisms valued as credible.

Cressida J. Heyes investigates the paradox of the homogenizing and 'normalizing' effects of surgical makeovers and the feelings of 'uniqueness' and individuality women express. In her reading of the televisual cosmetic surgery makeover, she argues that such programmes, presenting cosmetic surgery as 'taking charge of one's destiny, becoming the person one always wanted to be, or gaining a body that better represents the moral virtues one has developed, are all forms of working on the self within a regime of normalization' (Heyes 2007, 28). Problematically, 'normalization' (as a historical ontological process) is concealed by essentializing identity talk in these shows ('Let the *real* you shine through'). The decision to undergo cosmetic surgery is, according to Heyes, portrayed as a courageous choice for the active and self-determined individual. There is little or no room left for the woman who tries to live with her less than perfect body; 'this choice is often subtly construed as passive or resigned' (Heyes 2007, 28). For her, the key to understand and, importantly, resist the allure of cosmetic surgery resides exactly in 'grasping the paradox that we sometimes act as if our uniqueness is best expressed through conformity' (Heyes 2007, 29). We ought to remember that by rejecting cosmetic surgery we are *not* rejecting individuality, but certain disciplinary technologies and the unequal systemic power relations they produce and support.

As Heyes has pointed out, the target market for cosmetic surgery is predominantly white women between the ages of 25 and 45 (Heyes 2007). Makeover programmes such as *The Swan*, *Extreme Makeover* and *10 Years Younger* specifically identify working class and lower middle class participants as in need of transformation of the self through all-over 'beauty' treatments. With reference to the history of the US and the American dream, Heinricy points out that prior to the Depression only wealthy women could be found on the pages of *Vogue*: 'The magazine served to show the masses how wealthy people should look and act, thus reinforcing class difference. Beauty appeared to be a by-product of wealth ... Being beautiful was not seen as possible for poor women, thus naturalizing class difference in terms of beauty' (Heinricy 2006, 152). Nevertheless, soon after, processes of commodification required women of all classes to purchase products for the upkeep of their bodies, as 'consumption was the duty of American citizens; it would fuel the economy and save the nation ... Of course, this consumption was gendered and classed' (Heinricy 2006, 153).

As Gimlin has pointed out (see Heinricy 2006, 160), the body has long become the signifier of the self and moral character, partly due to mind/body dualism: 'It is a sign of the failure of the mind if the mind cannot properly control the body ... Exercise, makeup, and plastic surgery are actually ways of correcting a wayward moral character, one that excessively consumes or lacks discipline'. Banet-Weiser and Portwood-Stacer consider the selection of working class women as part of the American dream, 'where those of a lower socio-economic class can succeed at becoming middle-class subjects ... Although the subjects of reality television may actually represent a more diverse range of identities than previously seen in the medium, the outcome of these subjects' transformations is usually a mainstreaming, a construction of a new, improved self who conforms even more readily to dominant norms' (Banet-Weiser and Portwood-Stacer 2006, 266–7). The success of reality television and more specifically (cosmetic surgery) makeover programmes in this sense very much depends on the continuous re-rendering of class differences and re-education of the wayward working classes. Nevertheless, in order to sustain the idea of social mobility, also very closely linked to the politics of New Labour in Britain, class signifiers may become more and more implicit, meaning that class differences are not fading, but are becoming more ubiquitous.

Post-feminism, consumer culture and the disavowal of class

Feminist theorists have critiqued the concept of post-feminism for its promotion of a neoliberal discourse of individual responsibility and consumer choice. As Banet-Weiser and Portwood-Stacer comment, 'consumer post-feminism is often individualised and constructed as personal choice or individual equality' (Banet-Weiser and Portwood-Stacer 2006, 257). Here, female empowerment is conceived as a project of self-liberation, which, as Stephanie Genz argues, figures 'private lives and consumer capacities as the sites for self-expression and agency' (Genz 2006, 338). The individualization of women within post-feminism is thus markedly different 'from an historical feminist emphasis on social change and liberation' (Banet-Weiser and Portwood-Stacer 2006, 257).

In a British context, the politics of neoliberalism, with its promotion of individualism, are engendered in New Labour's commitment to the ideology of *The Third Way* (Giddens 1998 in McRobbie 2000, 97) which 'seeks to reconcile the irreconcilable' by 'combining elements of left social democracy with right neo-liberalism' (McRobbie 2000, 100). An expressed commitment to tackling social inequalities is accompanied by an endorsement of the free market economy and capitalism. The focus upon individual responsibility is a key characteristic of The Third Way, helping to create the conditions for social acceptance of a reduction in state welfare and an increase in the rights and responsibilities of the individual consumer. McRobbie argues that whilst The Third Way may borrow language from feminism and seek to encourage girls and women into education and employment, the kinds of women imagined in the discourse and politics of The Third Way are white and middle class, 'deeply consumerist and embracing an individualism within the family unit' (McRobbie 2000, 100).

Consumer culture promotes commodities as central to the construction of self and identity, where the 'ideals of an authentic inner self' are 'expressed through consumption practices as technologies of the self' (Cronin 2000, 275). The individual self within consumer culture, responsible for its own maintenance, represents a classed self in a number of ways. Firstly, as a cultural practice, consumption inscribes and produces the individual, assigning value to the self. The value assigned to the self through participation in consumer culture operates as a form of exchange-value (Skeggs 2004). However, not all selves are equally valued within these processes of exchange. Historically, the working classes have been assigned less value than the middle classes, an inscription which continues in contemporary society. As Skeggs contends, the discourse of individuality serves to render invisible the class based nature of the conception of the individual self and personhood by naturalizing it and disavowing the structural and symbolic mechanisms involved in its formation and perpetuation. Only by examining what kinds of persons are given value and by whom, or 'how different forms of culture and labour are given value and how these can be exchanged or not' (Skeggs 2004, 71) can class be made visible in the conception of the self.

Secondly, the very concept of the individual self is the historical product of an Enlightenment middle class (bourgeois) and masculine notion of personhood (Skeggs 2004). This manifests itself in the figuration of both an inner and outer self, or mind and body, as constitutive of the individual. The idea that the inner self can be expressed through the outer self – often through its appearance – is a middle class concept which privileges certain forms of symbolic expressions (of the self) above others. Bourdieu identifies taste as one of the symbolic expressions of the self, where the acquisition and display of cultural knowledge and competency defines the middle class self. The acquisition and demonstration of taste is linked to habitus, which involves 'an interrelationship between the development of the body and people's social location' (Shilling 2003, 111). The body becomes a primary signifier of class, where 'individual classes come to develop and occupy a similar habitus' and therefore display similar tastes (Crompton 1998, 148). However, as Bourdieu argues, only certain forms of taste are deemed worthy. If habitus 'is the member's internalisation, as natural, of the tastes of his or her class', then this marks 'only some for distinction' (Frank 1991, 67).

This privileging of certain expressions of self (in the form of taste) leads to the third manner in which the self is classed, that is, through the assigning of moral value. Skeggs argues, 'How people are valued (by different symbolic systems of inscription; by those who study them; by systems of exchange) is always a moral categorisation, an assertion of worth' (Skeggs 2004, 14). Historically the (white) working class have been devalued, represented variously as excessive, disgusting, shameless and lacking in taste (Skeggs 2004). Thus, judgements of worth and value are (middle) classed, where particular bodies get inscribed as worthy/worthless.

Rather than class becoming less important, it has become more ubiquitous. Class inequalities are made less visible through the concept of the individual, where interest in the self 'as a way of generating exchange-value' (Skeggs 2005, 965) has come to define contemporary class relations. This makes it difficult to analyse and critique class relations, as the self appears removed from any social structures. It is through culture that class is now being reworked and should thus be analysed (Skeggs 2004). As our analysis of *10 Years Younger* will show, class is central to the workings of makeover culture and the specific promotion of cosmetic surgery as a means of accruing exchange-value. However, before moving onto the analysis of the programme, we will now explore how shame is involved in the constitution and (re)workings of the (classed) self.

Shame, the self and the workings of class

Most makeover shows identify an aspect of the participant's self or environment as in need of improvement. Generally, participants agree to changes by concurring with the negative evaluation of their selves offered by the makeover 'experts'. Participants either feel already inadequate or are made to feel inadequate through the makeover process. Recent affect theorists have explored how the feelings of inadequacy or failure – upon which makeover shows are premised – are associated with feelings of shame that are intimately linked to the self (Ahmed 2004; Probyn 2005). As Ahmed has argued, 'to acknowledge wrongdoing means to enter into shame' (Ahmed 2004, 101). Shame relates to 'how the self feels about itself' (Ahmed 2004, 103). Although shame may feel like the revealing of an essential inner aspect of the self, Ahmed points out that feelings of shame are reliant upon the relation of self to other. This relationship is what defines and authorizes the feelings of shame, rather than being 'in' the subject. Thus, 'shame becomes felt as a matter of being – of the relation of self to itself – insofar as shame is about appearance, about how the subject appears before and to others' (Ahmed 2004, 104–5). The reliance of shame upon the subject/object relation is important to acknowledge, particularly as shame is often experienced as an inner bodily emotion.

Shame functions to construct and maintain the boundaries of the self (and body) within the cultural values of a given society, helping to define what kinds of bodies are valued, and those that aren't. As Skeggs (2004) reminds us, the notion of an individual self – of inner and outer – is a specifically bourgeois and masculine concept. Shame, experienced as an inner emotion but dependent upon the subject's outer appearance to others, is therefore also classed. The perceived inadequacies of self through which shame works are premised upon moral values that are inherently (middle) classed. The denigration of the white working class (woman), in popular culture and political rhetoric, as shameless, excessive, disgusting and immoral (Skeggs 2004) thus illustrates how what is considered to be shameful (and its corollary, disgust) is constituted through a gendered and classed value system.

Like Ahmed, Elspeth Probyn explores how shame is premised upon a relation of self to others within a system of cultural value. However, Probyn views shame as a productive emotion because 'admitting shame is much more likely to spur consideration of why one feels ashamed' (Probyn 2005, xiii). Thus 'It is productive in how it makes us think again about bodies, societies and human interaction' (Probyn 2005, xviii). Whilst this may be the case for those selves who are in a position to be self-reflective, i.e. the middle class individual self, it fails to acknowledge the classed position which enables self-reflection (or even makes it desirable), or the cultural resources needed to be able to do so. Arguably, the notion of shame as productive potentially reproduces a class based set of values and relations, from which the most injurious discourses of shame have emerged.[4] In the following analysis, we explore the limitations of the surgically transformed self of reality TV through an exploration of the ways in which *10 Years Younger* reaffirms a neoliberal, post-feminist conception of the self, through its deployment of class signifiers to shame the women into achieving middle class femininity. The moral responsibility placed upon the individual renders invisible the class differences and inequalities upon which the very notion of the self is premised.

10 Years Younger: Normalizing cosmetic surgery

Once a week, *10 Years Younger* presents its audiences with the story of a personal transformation. Judged and shamed by 'the great British public' on their age-appearance and their general looks, the female participants submit to a makeover regime prescribed by a panel of experts, including cosmetic surgery, dental treatment, fashion re-styling, make-up and hair. This is followed by a second public age poll after the participants' transformation, with more positive results concerning the estimated age.

Following a tradition established by women's magazines, the programme format offers a range of authoritative voices with regards to matters of femininity, beauty, health and well-being (Blood 2005). Like the magazines, the programme positions

---

4   See Julie Torrant (2007) for a critique of Probyn's theories of shame, based upon her presentation of 'affect' as post-class. For a discussion of the productive and multi-directional power of shame, as it is 'put to work' across a variety of reality television programmes, see Gareth Palmer (2006).

the female body as the locus of her self-identity, but one that must be 'regarded as permanently flawed and always in need of remedial work' (Blood 2005, 64). *10 Years Younger* zooms in on the bodies of the female participants to highlight their designated problem zones such as face, breasts, bum and thighs. Their failure to live up to the norms of Western, white, heterosexual, middle class femininity is exposed.

> We live in a world where youth is prized above all else. A world where we are constantly reminded of the need to look good or feel good. But apparently the message still hasn't got through to some people. (Male voice-over, *10 Years Younger* 2006a)

The apparent irony in programme introductions such as this creates a distance between the viewers and the participants to be judged. They nevertheless invite women viewers to accept the 'truth' about the importance of youth and looks, to question our own potential deviations from the desirable standards and to 'learn' how to correct them. Personal change and self-improvement are at the centre of *10 Years Younger*. These discourses reflect neoliberal politics and post-feminist ideology. By linking health, emotional well-being and age appearance to beauty, cosmetic surgery is being introduced into and validated as crucial to the transformation.

> Male voice-over: She hasn't had a decent haircut in 15 years and is a stranger to the skin care counter (visuals: Jeni pours a glass of white wine). She fuels her stressful job with fizzy drinks and then there is the cigarettes (Jeni coughing).
>
> Jeni: I feel so hopeless, really, it's just a horrible mess.
>
> Male voice-over: A horrible mess that's making her look older than her years. (*10 Years Younger* 2006b)

As Nettleton and Watson argue, 'To appear inappropriately "old" or to be "mutton dressed as lamb" in our contemporary society appears to be a source of tension' and may result in 'loss of status' as members of society and as women (Nettleton and Watson 1998, 18). The programme presents the female participants as having lost their social lives, for example, turning into a 'virtual recluse', as well as their femininity: 'when I first looked at [the family photo] I was like, where's Nerys? 'cause it just looks like, where's the woman' (Nicky Hambleton-Jones, *10 Years Younger* 2006d). The solution offered to the women is presented as a neat package, with cosmetic surgery placed alongside the other makeover aspects and subsequently normalized:

> Male voice-over: Surgery to remove the fleshy eyelids and bags, chemical peel to reveal younger skin, botox to smooth her troubled brow, haircut, colour and, yes, you heard right, a perm. And finally Nicky will try to bring her wardrobe back from the edge. (*10 Years Younger* 2006b)

This normalization is enhanced by the set-up of experts, where male cosmetic surgeon Jan Stanek commands this title alongside the dentist, hairdresser, make-up artist and stylist. Visually, this is supported by seating them next to each other, to be summoned by programme presenter and fashion stylist, Nicky Hambleton-Jones, to present their diagnosis and solution. Each of the episodes repeatedly shows the experts at work side by side, as a split screen effect features them in the operating theatre, dentist treatment room, hair and beauty salons, creating a seemingly level playing field. The programme goes through great pains to highlight that cosmetic surgery is not to be taken lightly, constituting the hardest part of the transformation. Nevertheless, its consolidation into the traditional beauty regimes is quickly re-established as the viewer learns that each of the makeover steps is the most difficult one. The achievement and maintenance of a beautiful youthful appearance requires hard work.

As Glassner has pointed out, 'For many people, cosmetic surgery is enticing precisely because they think of it as an active endeavour – as one more piece in a comprehensive health-and-fitness programme' (Glassner 1995, 170). This view of cosmetic surgery is bound to gain increasing acceptance, 'given our tendency to confuse beauty with health' (Glassner 1995, 170). *10 Years Younger* certainly contributes towards this trend and confusion of health, age and beauty markers. Here, cosmetic surgery is presented as the logical accompaniment to a diet and fitness regime:

Male voice-over: She managed to lose an astonishing five stone through diet and exercise (visuals: Heather lifts weights and bounces on a trampoline). But she wasn't left with the body she dreamt of.

Heather: Quite a few people have said have I been ill, cos there is a lot of weight lost from my face.

Heather's friend: I thought oh my god, you poor thing, after having done all this hard work.

Male voice-over: This is the battle plan: the eyebags will have to go, the cheeks will be plumped up with fat from her stomach, she'll get modest breast implants, the excess skin sliced away [and] she'll be given a Hollywood smile.

Nicky: You're such an inspiration to so many women out there. Why do you think you were so driven to being slimmer and having better boobs and a flat stomach?

Heather: Well, I think that image is quite important.

Nicky: You've lost the weight, you've had the surgery. The worst is now over. (*10 Years Younger* 2006a)

The surgical transformation is presented as an objective and subjective process. The physical transformation is presented as something that the experts do to the women's bodies, articulated as a challenge, a battle, work and a rescue package that begins with surgery and ends with clothes restyling. The women subjectively embrace the body modifications on offer as the promise of a new or improved self. Heather Williams declares, 'This is my second chance and I'm gonna go for it' (*10 Years Younger* 2006a) and Laura Hammond exclaims, '[Surgery] is just everything to me and it means the world to me' (*10 Years Younger* 2006c). Finally, Nicky Hambleton-Jones tells Jeni:

> Nicky: Jeni. I can see that deep down inside that there is still a gorgeous sexy woman. Our challenge – myself and all the experts I've got lined up – is to really rediscover that and give you back that confidence.
>
> Jeni: Yes please. (*10 Years Younger* 2006b)

The transformations offered in *10 Years Younger* are experienced by the women as a positive form of self-empowerment. Heather says, 'I can't thank you enough for doing this for me' (*10 Years Younger* 2006a). Jeni declares, 'I just feel so much lighter about life I can go out there and enjoy' (*10 Years Younger* 2006b), whilst Nerys exclaims, 'For the first time I actually feel pretty and feminine' (*10 Years Younger* 2006d).

The programme is keen to assign agency to the individuals in choosing cosmetic surgery. The male voice-over states, 'Cosmetic surgery is a big step and it may not be the answer for everyone. Heather thought long and hard and reached a decision to go ahead' (*10 Years Younger* 2006a). However, we argue that the concept of individual choice understood as self-empowerment remains firmly rooted within the limitations of a neoliberal, consumerist discourse of the self. Here, access to the cultural and economic resources to maintain such a sense of self-empowerment are left unquestioned. The class based nature of this conception of the self is rendered invisible through the overriding discourse of self-empowerment presented by the programme. However, the very brutal process of social judgement and public shaming of the women, staged by the programme, undermines the very notion of individual choice, revealing the class relations upon which it is premised.

Shame, blame and the classed female body

Shame can express itself through feelings of inadequacy. Skeggs explains that shame 'requires if not an actual audience before whom my deficiencies are paraded, then an internalised audience with the capacity to judge me' (Skeggs 1997, 123). *10 Years Younger* makes this internal audience actual, through public parading and shaming. Taken onto the streets of British cities, each week the individual women are displayed to the public, and 100 members are asked to comment upon and judge their age and looks. The moment when the results of the first age poll are revealed to the women through video footage is introduced by Nicky Hambleton-Jones as 'the worst part where people really think of the way that you look' (*10 Years Younger* 2006a). Watching the video clips, the women are variously shocked and horrified: 'I didn't think I looked as old as what they said' (Heather, *10 Years Younger* 2006a); 'It's shocked me because I see myself all the time and I didn't know I looked that bad' (Nerys, *10 Years Younger* 2006d). The women readily agree with the judgements made – 'I do look like a granny though, I do' (Nerys, *10 Years Younger* 2006d); 'Yes I look like a wreck really, I mean most of the time' (Jeni, *10 Years Younger* 2006b) – internalizing the 'truth' of external judgement and blaming themselves: 'I don't know what to do to undo the damage that I've done to myself' (Laura, *10 Years Younger* 2006c); 'I just let it all go really' (Jeni, *10 Years Younger* 2006b). The process whereby the women agree to the judgements made demonstrates the workings of shame. Skeggs argues, 'shame requires the recognition that I am, in some important sense, as I am seen to be' (Skeggs 1997, 123).

Whilst shame functions in the programme as a means of authorizing cosmetic surgery in the attainment of heterosexual, youthful femininity, the shaming is also premised upon the achievement (and failure) of class status and distinction. From a variety of backgrounds and places, including Manchester, Bradford, Stow-on-the-Wold and Essex, the women are categorized as the Essex girl, the country bumpkin, the single mother and the middle class professional. Heather Williams is described as an Essex girl who loves sunbathing and smoking. Heather's inappropriateness is based upon a femininity that is classed. Her clothes are criticized for being too 'tarty', 'too young', or 'mutton dressed as lamb', and her hair for being too blonde (*10 Years Younger* 2006a). Her clothes are described as in bad sexual taste, excessive, obvious and thus common. The goal of the transformation is to make Heather's femininity more appropriate through understatement. She will have 'modest boobs', that are not 'oversized melons … just a decent handful', new teeth that 'are the right shade of white to make her dazzling but not phosphorescent', clothes that are less 'bling' and more 'shabby chic', make-up that is 'natural and subtle' and hair that is 'expensive blonde', not 'cheap and trashy' (*10 Years Younger* 2006a).

Respectability becomes one of the key ways in which some groups are othered, take for example the stereotype of the Essex girl. As Skeggs confirms, 'respectability is one of the most ubiquitous signifiers of class' (Skeggs 1997, 1). Historically, the working classes have been othered, where respectability as 'a property of middle-class individuals' becomes 'a standard to which to aspire' (Skeggs 1997, 3). The subject's internalization of notions of respectability, and the fear that accompanies women's failure to achieve respectable heterosexual femininity, is apparent in the programme. Although positioned as an Essex girl by the male voice-over and experts, Heather herself identifies as an Essex girl. Asked to justify why she has gone to extreme measures to transform herself (the emphasis is placed upon the female participants to justify their radical transformation) she states:

> I think that image is quite important. I'm quite an image person, I suppose. I mean I come from Essex of course (laughter from Nicky and Heather) and use a sun bed. To look nice as I possibly can. (*10 Years Younger* 2006a)

Heather defends herself by stating that image is important, identifying with a gendered discourse of beauty, whilst also identifying herself consciously as an Essex girl and its associated stereotypes that represent inappropriate/excessive working class femininity. Heather's final assertion that she wants to look as nice as possible demonstrates the negotiation of gender and class in the attainment of a morally respectable femininity. The programme perpetuates the stereotype of the dumb blonde, framing her predominantly as a mother and wife by choosing not to tell us her occupation. The photographs that Heather shows to Nicky as evidence of her weight loss (prior to the makeover) include pictures of her two graduation ceremonies. Yet in the programme these photographs signify as the 'truth' of Heather's changing body rather than as evidence of her academic achievements.

Cosmetic surgery becomes integral to the achievement of femininity, but in ways that are dependent upon the class markers of the participant. For Heather, an entire 'reshaping' is needed, where she 'has essentially been taken apart and put back together again' to create something new (*10 Years Younger* 2006a). From Stow–on-the-Wold, Jeni Ingram's transformation to respectable femininity is not to create something new, but to 'rediscover' 'that gorgeous sexy woman' that has been hidden 'deep down inside' (*10 Years Younger* 2006b). Whilst Jeni is still shamed and blamed for her appearance, the transformation is presented as a rediscovery of something she already had but had temporarily lost. Cosmetic surgery will enable Jeni to 'to turn back the clock'. As Nicky Hambleton-Jones comments, 'With all that surgery, I'm wondering whether you're getting to look like you used to?' (*10 Years Younger* 2006b). Rediscovery of the lost self is articulated following Jeni's clothes restyling.

Nicky: This to me is the Jeni of 10, 20 years ago I saw in the pictures. Remember that girl?

Jeni: It's starting to come back. I feel kind of feminine in it.

Nicky: It's the you we've brought back. (*10 Years Younger* 2006b)

Thus, Jeni had only temporarily lost her status (and exchange-value) as a middle class woman. The surgery has enabled her to express her inner self, and to restore her class distinctions.

The contrasting transformations of Heather and Jeni illustrate how cosmetic surgery is being promoted as part of the process of the achievement of respectable femininity for all women, yet achievement that encompasses different journeys based upon habitus, and thus limited by these. The subtle distinctions between discovering a lost self and attaining a new self illustrate how class is involved in the 'intimate making of self and culture' (Skeggs 2005, 969), where some women are positioned as having the cultural competency and knowledge – the taste – already, whilst others need to acquire this through consumer practices. Whilst the programme appears to offer cosmetic surgery as a means of erasing class differences through conformity to a middle class female body ideal, it actually reinforces these differences through its denigratory use of class signifiers to shame women into the transformation. Furthermore, by commodifying the body, the economic inequalities which affect access to cosmetic surgery practices are erased (Negrin 2002), as well as the cultural resources necessary for the upkeep of this new self.

The public shaming of the women also draws upon wider social discourses of health, informed in turn by the discourses and representations of class. The majority of the women are criticized by the male voice-over for unhealthy diet and lifestyle: 'Sun, smoking and an absence of anything approaching skin care have left her [Laura Hammond] with a lamentable complexion' (*10 Years Younger* 2006c); 'Nerys' addiction to food was becoming a health hazard' (*10 Years Younger* 2006d). The experts support this view: 'She has aged prematurely as a result of [smoking]' (*10 Years Younger* 2006a): 'As a smoker you do actually get bad gums with it, gum disease' (*10 Years Younger* 2006b). The health of the British nation has been a recent and growing concern for the New Labour government and the British media.[5] *10 Years Younger*, reflecting other media voices, discursively links bad eating habits, obesity and working class culture, thereby invoking a morally inflected and classed value system.

The surgery must go on

Series 3 and 4 of *10 Years Younger* included a number of 'Bikini Specials', featuring the most extensive surgical interventions in the programme's history, notably a '360 degree body-lift' (*10 Years Younger* 2006e). The commonalities shared by the female participants here are radical weight loss as a result of gastric bypass surgery and excess skin to show for it. By introducing one of the participants as coming from Bradford (in the north of England), 'the fattest city in Britain', and integrating commentary from obesity surgeons, the programme establishes obesity as a public/national health issue (*10 Years Younger* 2006e). However, this is contrasted by the subsequent presentation of weight loss surgery and cosmetic surgery as the choice and responsibility of the individual woman in the light of her personal failure:

> Married to a city business man, Lorraine was a lady who lunched too much. Munching her way up to a size 22, she subsequently tried and failed at many diets, and eventually opted for weight loss surgery to drop down to her current petite size. (Channel 4 2006)

The health risks associated with (morbid) obesity are established through the programme's narrator and subsequently internalized by the women themselves:

> Male voice-over: Nerys' addiction to food was becoming a health hazard.

> Nerys: At my heaviest, when I was 20 and a half stone, my BMI was 41, which is morbidly obese. It really worried me because my grandfather had dropped dead with a heart attack … I suddenly realized that here I was a mother with four children which depended on me and my weight had got to such a stage that I was putting my life at risk. (*10 Years Younger* 2006d)

All the women represented have turned to weight loss surgery 'in a last desperate attempt to slim down' (Channel 4 2006) after a long string of failed diets. Weight loss surgery becomes established as the new (healthy) way to lose weight, signifying a diet that seemingly does not fail and generating a new woman in the process. By readily accepting weight loss surgery as the only option, and by selecting these participants in the first place, the programme contributes towards the normalization of this surgical procedure, promoting it as part of already established discourses and repertoires of dieting and health. Weight loss surgery is presented as a 'common

---

5   2006 saw two Department of Health reports, one forecasting the development of obesity to 2010, the other presenting a more general 'Health Profile of England'.

sense' option in the public 'war on obesity', making it difficult to argue against such surgical practices, that would have been considered extraordinary only a few years ago.[6]

Weight loss surgery and the loss of weight are only the initial steps for these women on their journey of self-transformation. Cosmetic surgery is now being called for to address the consequences of rapid weight loss – to restore all-over youthful good looks, without which the project is not only incomplete, but considered worthless:

> Kate (Nerys' friend): I think it must be really crippling when you've gone through such an ordeal and gone through such a big operation … to then look down on your body and think "Why did I bother?"

> Nerys: It's not just ugly and unsightly, it's actually a disfigurement. Very wrinkly, very ugly and quite hideous to look at. I'm more self-conscious now without clothes than when I was hugely obese. (*10 Years Younger* 2006d)

The message is that a woman cannot feel good unless she looks good, youthful and healthy. Weight loss surgery may well become an increasingly attractive option for more and more women as part of their quest to obtain the body beautiful, especially since *10 Years Younger* re-assures us that cosmetic surgery can take care of the potentially ugly side of rapid weight loss. In this sense, weight loss and cosmetic surgery are beginning to reinforce and legitimize each other in classed public discourse.

Conclusion

> Not only is elective cosmetic surgery moving out of the domain of the sleazy, the suspicious, the secretively deviant, or the pathologically narcissistic, it is *becoming the norm*. This shift is leading to a predictable inversion of the domains of the deviant and the pathological, so that women who contemplate *not using* cosmetic surgery will increasingly be stigmatised and seen as deviant. (Morgan 2003, 175)

As Morgan has pointed out, cosmetic surgery is increasingly being normalized. *10 Years Younger* contributes to this normalization by reproducing dominant discourses of the self, virulent in (British) neoliberal politics and post-feminist ideology, with their emphasis on individual responsibility and consumer choice. Whilst a lot of critical attention has been devoted to the examination of US originated programming, we have argued that the analysis of class difference and class relations has been largely neglected,[7] specifically in the context of British cosmetic makeover shows.

---

6   See Karen Throsby (2008) for a discussion of how weight loss surgery patients position themselves in the 'war on obesity' as participants, rather than as objects of denigration, through the discourse of 're-birth'. Throsby shows the difficulty in claiming the identity of the post-surgical 'new me' as it requires both familiar and novel techniques of normalization of the post-weight loss surgery body.

7   See Angela McRobbie (2004) for a discussion of the promotion of class antagonism in reality TV makeover shows with reference to British New Labour politics.

Conceptions of the self promoted by such programmes need to be understood as inscribed by a middle class exchange system which assigns value and worth to certain kinds of bodies/selves (Skeggs 2004; 2005), thereby perpetuating a system of inequality under the guise of the possibility of re-education and social mobility.

Through an examination of the British makeover show *10 Years Younger*, we have illustrated how class signifiers are used to shame the female participants into the surgical transformation. These significations can be linked to the historical denigration of white working class women as excessive, tasteless and wayward. The transformations offered by the programme reproduce class stereotypes, presenting middle class versions of the (transformed) self as attainable by all women. In doing so, the programme appears to erase class differences whilst simultaneously creating and reinforcing them.

Bibliography

Adkins, L. and Skeggs, B. (eds) (2004), *Feminism After Bourdieu* (Oxford: Blackwell).

Ahmed, S. (2004), *The Cultural Politics of Emotion* (Edinburgh: Edinburgh University Press).

Ahmed, S., Kilby, J., Lury, C., McNeil, M. and Skeggs, B. (eds) (2000), *Transformations: Thinking Through Feminism* (London: Routledge).

Banet-Weiser, S. and Portwood-Stacer, L. (2006), '"I Just Want to Be Me Again": Beauty Pageants, Reality Television and Post-feminism', *Feminist Theory* 7:2, 255–72.

Bignell, J. (2005) *Big Brother: Reality TV in the Twenty-first Century* (Basingstoke: Palgrave Macmillan).

Blood, S.K. (2005), *Body Work: The Social Construction of Women's Body Image* (London: Routledge).

Bordo, S. (1993), *Unbearable Weight: Feminism, Western Culture and the Body* (London and Berkeley: University of California Press).

Brook, B. (1999), *Feminist Perspectives on the Body* (London: Longman).

Bunton, R., Nettleton, S. and Burrows, R. (eds) (1995), *The Sociology of Health Promotion: Critical Analyses of Consumption, Lifestyle and Risk* (London: Routledge).

Channel 4 (2006) '10 Years Younger', <http://www.channel4.com/life/microsites/0-9/10yy/index.html>, accessed 14 June 2006.

Crompton, R. (1998), *Class and Stratification: An Introduction to Current Debate* (Cambridge: Polity).

Cronin, A.M. (2000), 'Consumerism and "Compulsory Individuality": Women, Will and Potential', in S. Ahmed, J. Kilby, C. Lury, M. McNeil and B. Skeggs (eds), *Transformations: Thinking Through Feminism* (London: Routledge).

Davis, K. (1995), *Reshaping the Body: The Dilemma of Cosmetic Surgery* (London: Routledge).

Department of Health 2006, 'Forecasting Obesity 2010', <http://www.dh.gov.uk/
en/Publicationsandstatistics/Publications/PublicationsStatistics/DH_4138630>,
accessed 30 May 2007.

Department of Health 2006, 'Health Profile of England', <http://www.dh.gov.uk/
en/Publicationsandstatistics/Publications/PublicationsPolicyAndGuidance/DH_
4139556>, accessed 30 May 2007.

Escoffery, D.S. (ed.) (2006), *How Real is Reality TV? Essays on Representation and
Truth* (Jefferson, NC: McFarland and Company Inc. Publishers).

Featherstone, M. (1991), 'The Body in Consumer Culture', in M. Featherstone, M.
Hepworth and B. Turner (eds) (1991), *The Body: Social Process and Cultural
Theory* (London: Sage).

Featherstone, M., Hepworth, M. and Turner, B. (eds) (1991), *The Body: Social
Process and Cultural Theory* (London: Sage).

Frank, A.W. (1991), 'For a Sociology of the Body: An Analytical Review', in M.
Featherstone, M. Hepworth and B. Turner (eds) (1991), *The Body: Social Process
and Cultural Theory* (London: Sage).

Genz, S. (2006), 'Third Way/ve: The Politics of Post-feminism', *Feminist Theory*
7:3, 333–53.

Glassner, B. (1995), 'In the Name of Health', in R. Bunton, S. Nettleton and R.
Burrows (eds) (1995), *The Sociology of Health Promotion: Critical Analyses of
Consumption, Lifestyle and Risk* (London: Routledge).

Heinricy, S. (2006), 'The Cutting Room: Gendered American Dreams on Plastic
Surgery TV', in D.S. Escoffery (ed.) (2006), *How Real is Reality TV? Essays
on Representation and Truth* (Jefferson, NC: McFarland and Company Inc.
Publishers).

Heyes, C.J. (2007), 'Cosmetic Surgery and the Televisual Makeover: A Foucauldian
Feminist Reading', *Feminist Media Studies* 7:1, 17–32.

Jeffreys, S. (2005), *Beauty and Misogyny: Harmful Cultural Practices in the West*
(London: Routledge).

Karl, I. (2007), 'Class Observations: "Intimate" Technologies and the Poetics of
Reality TV', *Fast Capitalism 2.2.* <http://www.fastcapitalism.com>.

McRobbie, A. (2000), 'Feminism and the Third Way', *Feminist Review* 64, Spring
2000, 97–112.

McRobbie, A. (2004), 'Notes on "What Not to Wear" and Post-feminist Symbolic
Violence', in L. Adkins and B. Skeggs (eds) (2004), *Feminism After Bourdieu*
(Oxford: Blackwell).

Morgan, K.P. (2003), 'Women and the Knife: Cosmetic Surgery and the Colonization
of Women's Bodies', in R. Weitz (ed.), *The Politics of Women's Bodies: Sexuality,
Appearance and Behaviour* (Oxford: Oxford University Press).

Negrin, L. (2002), 'Cosmetic Surgery and the Eclipse of Identity', *Body and Society*
8:4, 21–42.

Nettleton, S. and Watson, J. (eds) (1998), *The Body in Everyday Life* (London:
Routledge).

Palmer, G. (2006), '*Video Vigilantes* and the Work of Shame', *Jump Cut: A Review of
Contemporary Media* 48, Winter 2006 (published online), <http://www.ejumpcut.
org/archive/jc48.2006/shameTV/text.html>, accessed 18 September 2007.

Probyn, E. (2005), *Blush: Faces of Shame* (Minneapolis, MN: University of Minnesota Press).

Shilling, C. (2003), *The Body and Social Theory* (London: Sage).

Skeggs, B. (1997), *Formations of Class and Gender* (London: Sage).

Skeggs, B. (2004), *Class, Self, Culture* (London: Routledge).

Skeggs, B. (2005), 'The Making of Class and Gender through Visualizing Moral Subject Formation', *Sociology* 39:5, 965–82.

Tait, S. (2007), 'Television and the Domestication of Cosmetic Surgery', *Feminist Media Studies* 7:2, 119–136.

Throsby, K. (2008), 'Happy Re-birthday: Weight Loss Surgery and the "New Me"', *Body and Society* 14:1, 117–33.

Torrant, J. (2007), 'The "New" Shame-faced Partisans of Capital: A Critique of Elspeth Probyn's Blush', *The Red Critique* Winter/Spring 2007, <http://www.redcritique.org/WinterSpring2007/thenewshamefacedpartisansofcapital.htm>, accessed 20 June 2007.

Weitz R. (ed.) (2003), *The Politics of Women's Bodies: Sexuality, Appearance and Behaviour* (Oxford: Oxford University Press).

TV programmes

10 Years Younger (video recording) (2006a) Channel 4, January 12.
10 Years Younger (video recording) (2006b) Channel 4, January 19.
10 Years Younger (video recording) (2006c) Channel 4, February 2.
10 Years Younger (video recording) (2006d) Channel 4, May 3.
10 Years Younger (video recording) (2006e) Channel 4, May 10.

Chapter 8

Revealing the Inner Housewife: Housework and History in Domestic Lifestyle Television

Laurel Forster

A: I don't understand why everyone talks as though all housewives have a miserable time. Lots of women like being housewives.

B: It's ridiculous to pretend that anyone actually *likes* cleaning floors and washing dishes – how can they? Housework is awful work. It's lonely and boring. There's nothing to show for it – it's all got to be done the next day. You don't get paid for it either.

Speaker A and speaker B could be two contestants on the domestic lifestyle television programme *Wife Swap* battling out their opposing viewpoints at the end of the show. Or script A could be delivered by the presenters on *How Clean is Your House?*, imploring a reluctant housewife to get more involved in her domestic duties or perhaps by Anthea Turner on *The Perfect Housewife* explaining why housework is such fun, whilst script B could easily be the contestant's retort. However A and B are none of these, they are two sides of a debate about housework used as an illustrative prototype conversation in Ann Oakley's sociological study of housework, published in 1974, over three decades ago (Oakley 1974, 186). As Oakley points out, there are two different approaches here: A is talking about the role of the housewife, whilst B is discussing the actual domestic chores. Oakley in her conclusion draws attention to the distinction between feelings about housework and the orientation to the housewife role: 'While the former is a question of job satisfaction in the home, the latter refers to the whole construction of psychological femininity and its "fit" in a social world predicated on gender differences' (Oakley 1974, 184–5). It is precisely this difference between the pleasurable status of being a housewife and the drudgery of unpaid physical domestic chores which has presented a dichotomy for feminism for decades. It highlights both the joy and the unhappiness associated with attending to the domestic. Furthermore it is precisely this split in definition between role and chores which differentiates the domestic lifestyle programmes viewed on recent British television. By considering these programmes in the context of previous moments when housework became a matter of prominence, this chapter explores the different aspects of and approaches to housewifery presented on lifestyle programmes and, more broadly, questions why housework has become so prominent on our television screens at the start of the new century.

Recently, a number of reality lifestyle television programmes have focused on the domestic and housework: *How Clean is your House* (Channel 4 2003); *The Perfect Housewife* (BBC3 2006); and *Wife Swap* (Channel 4 2003) are of particular interest here. To differing degrees, these programmes concentrate on how we live in and manage our homes, they delve into our psychological relationships with the space we inhabit and seek to make links between the physical task of housework and our mental health. Highlighted in these programmes are issues of cleanliness (dirt is frequently regarded as the enemy), tidiness, household management, childcare and domestic responsibilities. Often strongly linked to this is a question about whether women work within or without the home. And whereas feminism, particularly 1970s feminism, has always had a troubled relationship with the housewife, domestic lifestyle television of the new century both embraces and relies upon promoting the value of the stay-at-home wife and mother as a point of reference. In assuming the significance of the housewife, difficult and broader ideological issues are avoided. As such these programmes echo the 'opt out revolution' of 2003–4, where a flurry of newspaper and magazine articles supported, as Vavrus has argued, a neoliberal regime of old-fashioned family arrangements (Vavrus 2007, 47–63). This continuing investment in the domestic sphere on our television screens helps to sideline political engagement with feminist concerns of the present and of previous decades.

Nonetheless, the resurgence of interest in lifestyle and domesticity has its roots in the feminism of the 1970s when housework and domestic issues became sites of political contestation, and the work of the home and the role of housewife were differentiated, one being linked to the labour market and the other to historical notions of femininity. Feminist activism in the 1970s brought previously-hidden aspects of women's lives to the fore. Women's marches and demonstrations demanded that attention should be paid to issues which directly affected women's lives such as contraception and equal pay, or at least access to the workplace. As part of this consciousness raising, domesticity and work at home became politicized too. The idea of the 'housewife' became highly problematic for feminism. Betty Friedan, Germaine Greer and Ann Oakley in early second wave feminism all attacked the image of the housewife, urging women to reject a role of servitude; women were encouraged to create value in their lives outside the home. There were prominent articles in feminist magazines such as *Spare Rib* which engaged with Marxist debates about wages for housework, as well as in other engagements with the feminist debate in more mainstream women's magazines like *Cosmopolitan* and women's pages of the daily press (see Coates 1974, 28–9; Freeman 1973).

In both the feminist and the regular press, irony and political earnestness existed side by side concerning the age-old issue of women's unpaid and largely unacknowledged work in the home. Some mainstream press engaged in popular ridicule of strident feminism, and even some parts of the feminist press indulged in banter, name calling and the caricature of anti-feminists. The role of the 'feminist', whatever she was, had multiple manifestations: she might be the political activist, perhaps rejecting the domestic trap of the nuclear family to support wider campaigns; or she might adopt the role of 'earth mother' left over from the countercultural 1960s, pursuing feminine authenticity of identity by baking wholemeal bread and wearing home-made clothes. The 'feminist lifestyle' then was never one-dimensional. Even in the strident 1970s there was a lifestyle choice for women regarding the way they were encouraged to interact with their home and domestic life.

There were a number of fundamental issues not really addressed by feminism at this time, such as the disparities in class, race, wealth, education and aspirations. Whilst the feminist press might have elided such differences in order to bring collectively more important issues to the public scene, other media explorations of women's domestic lives in the 1970s were more persistent in reflecting these differences between women. This can be exemplified by two generically different televisual examples from the decade. Mike Leigh's 1973 *Hard Labour* of the Play for Today strand (BBC1, 12 March 1973), depicts class differences between women most starkly when Mrs Thornley, a hard-working and unassuming working class woman arrives after a long bus journey to clean another woman's house only to find her middle class employer still languishing in bed reading the paper, and is dismissively asked to 'do the usual'. A very different view of women was visible through the highly popular Southern Television programme *Houseparty* (1972–1981) which performed on the TV screen the ritual of the coffee morning and became a mode of articulating female lifestyles, with conversation round the studio-set kitchen table ranging around domestic skills and paid work. Women's changing roles between home, work and family were a normalized expectation in this environment and homemaking and paid working skills were both seen as valid parts of the cohesion and variety of women's lives. Both the fictitious play and the drop-in coffee morning simulation provoked much interest and both reflected differently upon women of the time.[1]

The second wave feminists of the early 1970s have since been criticized for devaluing family work and even, as Johnson and Lloyd argue, for inventing the 'happy housewife myth' of the 1950s in order to avoid looking at the contradictory nature of women's relationship to the domestic and the outside world. 'The "happy housewife myth" was not simply a product of popular culture conjured up in advertising but also – a myth of a myth – conjured up by feminism in the attempt to construct a narrative that would make sense of and dispel the sense of contradiction and tension women felt between public achievement and femininity' (Johnson and Lloyd 2004, 11). Feminists of the 1990s and 2000s, in what has been identified as 'third wave feminism', have further problematized feminism and housework (Heywood and Drake 1997). They have debated whether women ever could be 'happy housewives' and whether in fact women of these later decades have been failed by the claims of their feminist mothers of the 1970s who argued that women could succeed simultaneously in worlds of work and home (see Hakim 1995). For instance, Hakim has argued that 'The unpalatable truth is that a substantial proportion of women still accept the sexual division of labour which sees homemaking as women's *principal* activity and income-earning as men's *principal* activity in life' (Hakim 1996, 179). Nonetheless, the 1970s was a moment when the subject of housework was forcefully made public, there was serious debate and women's roles were questioned. The debate about gendered space of the home has continued and broadened with ideas

---

1   *Houseparty* was so popular it was taken up by Thames Television.

which define differing zones, media and technology in the home and of course consumption for the home, itself a gendered activity.

Portraying the domestic on British television

The home as a major site of gender struggle has long supplied numerous scenarios both comic and serious for popular media. British television for decades now has used the home as a basis for many of its highly successful sitcoms, comedy series and even historical dramas such as *Bless this House* and *Upstairs Downstairs*. *Upstairs Downstairs* (London Weekend Television, 1971–75), an instantly popular and award-winning series, followed the fortunes of a prominent Edwardian household. It was set in a grand London town house and the storylines which emphasized the butler, cook and maidservants were at least as interesting, if not more so, than those of the upper class family members. Of particular interest was the superbly nuanced dominance and mastery over the household enjoyed by the butler and the cook. Class conflicts abounded and in this reversal of class dominance the authority of the servant classes was obtained not through ownership, of course, but through the hard labour necessary to maintain a large Edwardian household. *Upstairs Downstairs* was one of many period dramas of the 1970s as this was a time when the Edwardian era was held particularly high in nostalgic esteem. Such was the lasting impact of this drama series that a reality TV programme *The Edwardian Country House* (Channel 4 2002) did its best to emulate the atmosphere of class tensions so dramatically and nostalgically portrayed in *Upstairs Downstairs*.

The home has recently been re-idealized as a haven of harmonious order and tranquillity, and David Chaney's discussion of the 'enchantment of sentimentality' helps us in part to understand why (Chaney 2002, 155). In evoking an idealized household of an imagined bygone era, domestic lifestyle programmes are able to produce a nostalgic yearning for a perfect home and family. Here, imagined order and calm replace chaos and frenetic, perhaps technologized, activity. This sentimental ideal lies behind these programmes as a latent force informing the direction and content of this genre of reality television. In the collective imagination of the audience, uncertain of its values and objectives, there must be an ideal way to manage your home. This halcyon home is known by no one but can be imagined by all: home was a tranquil place, clutter hadn't been invented, and a sense of calm pervaded from surfaces and cupboards to smooth the metaphorical crumpled sheets of the inner psyche. Domestic lifestyle programmes offer differing modes of containing the domestic space: *How Clean?* combines old-fashioned cleaning, even evoking the image of a Victorian housekeeper, with scientific gloss; *Wife Swap* intervenes in questions of class and homemaking and *Perfect Housewife* idealizes the attainment of a middle class domestic space where creativity, efficiency and productivity abound and where true feminine contentment is to be found. Regardless of mode, current domestic lifestyle programmes aim to elevate the supremacy of the domestic realm for women in particular: the exterior world may be chaotic, complex and virtual, but the interior world can be made ordered, straightforward, and responsive to the 'real' functions of everyday living. Moreover these programmes encourage the viewer to rediscover for herself the happiness to be found through homemaking.

Domestic didacticism in *How Clean is Your House?*

In the series *How Clean is Your House?* (Channel 4 2003) two indisputable experts, Kim Woodburn and Aggie MacKenzie, redoubtable women both, with levels of authority that knowingly invite comedic and parodic viewer responses, enter and inspect an 'ordinary' person's home, proclaim it unspeakably, even dangerously filthy, and then proceed to demonstrate processes of 'proper' cleaning. White coats and fur-trimmed rubber gloves are donned, a team of cleaners employed and a systematic scouring ensues. These women combine two quite different approaches to professional dirt control. Aggie draws on her experience in working for the Good Housekeeping Institute (the part of *Good Housekeeping* magazine which tests products and recipes) as a journalist to lend scientific authority to her approach to dirt. Kim has an altogether more complex appearance: seemingly very 'dressed up' with evening jewellery and her hair piled up high, she suggests a 1960s working class sense of glamour.[2] This TV demeanour is at odds with the graft of cleaning, possibly posing an intentional incongruity with her own background as a cleaner since the age of 15. Certainly Kim's is a no-nonsense approach to domestic chores as she is portrayed being practical, enthusiastic and energetic. The unusual combination of scientific and practical authority may well be responsible for two out of the couple's three books reaching the home and property best seller lists (*Bookseller* 2007, 40). The programme has been popular at home and abroad, with five series in the UK, some of which have been aired internationally in the US on BBC America, in Canada on W Network, and in Australia on UK TV. There have been foreign versions in a range of countries including France, The Netherlands, Iceland and the Philippines, in addition to a US version aired on Lifetime Network (2004). A Canadian version called *Kim's Rude Awakenings* is currently calling for Canadian families to apply.

This show is didactic reality television. The contestants are used as the means by which the viewing public may be informed and educated about the dangerous implications of keeping a dirty house, the potential consequences to family health, and most importantly the methods by which dirt and grime may be overcome. *How Clean?* illustrates a tangible sense of coming to terms with and dominating the domestic space. Dirt and grime are seen as the enemy, to be exposed, beaten back and banished. As a regular feature of this programme, hidden dirt is revealed by Aggie, not just by peeking behind the kitchen appliances, but also microscopically via a scientificized, laboratory-based analysis of any suspicious-looking bacteria lurking in the contestants' homes. This usually results in the dramatic revelation of near-fatal bacteria. The harmful dirt and grime harboured in the exposed households is given a horror-film style treatment by borrowing dramatic zooms, close ups and

---

2   Kim's appearance is acknowledged in the promotional on-line video where Aggie is said to call Kim 'Hagrid in drag' and Kim refers to her own press coverage in describing herself as a cross between Mother Theresa and Madam Whiplash! Retrieved from: <http://www.channel4.com/4homes/ontv/how_clean_is_your_house/index.html>, March 2008.

scary audio effects from the genre to emphasize the terror lurking in such a filthy household. A useful side effect of this technique is to augment the ignominy heaped upon the slovenly contestant.

In episode two of the first series, 'Climb a Mountain of Laundry', Kim and Aggie are to be found expressing disgust and disdain as they inspect untidy food cupboards and scrape muck with painted fingernails from behind the cooker of a disordered household of seven children and a completely overworked Mum. During the family interview the husband states that he simply will not participate in the housework explaining that: 'Catherine doesn't have to go out to work, so Catherine should be able to find some time during the day to do a bit of cleaning and tidying.' This evokes only very mild responses from the presenters and Catherine herself. Other issues, which might interest contemporary viewers, and which were certainly of interest to feminists in the 1970s, remain unexplored here, such as reasons for the unusually large family; the unaccommodating response of the husband regarding housework; and the sheer exhaustion of the mother (who can barely participate in the programme let alone look truly shamed). These issues are all sidelined by the format and structure of the programme and as a result feminism remains only latent. McRobbie has noted that in the present climate of post-feminism, 'feminism is invoked in order that it is relegated to the past' (McRobbie 2004, 262). But in television lifestyle programmes such as *How Clean?* feminism is not even given the prominence of a failed imperative; it is silently marginalized as though it were an inappropriate conceptual framework. What has taken its place is performed domestic responsibility, where, for the benefit of the cameras, as in the above example, the whole family including the baby and the reluctant husband are themselves instructed, and then demonstrate, newly learnt traditional cleaning skills. More complex issues of sustainable and equitable divisions of labour and reward are ignored as cleaning is reduced to a mere family game, apoliticized and 'naturalized' as part of home life for all family members. The overriding narrative remains one of the battle against the enemy – dirt – and only secondarily the lifestyle that has lead to it.. The story is made no more complex than many a simple advert for a cleaning product. Other broader, more significant points remain unexamined, perhaps only existing as provocative discussion points for the viewers at home. Aggie does make a later jibe at the husband when he does not offer to help move the microwave oven, but actual root causes and the domestic circumstances of the dirty home, as well as his part-responsibility for it, remain unexplored and unresolved.

The format demands that the contestants participate in the cleaning of their home and Kim manages to motivate all the children to join in the mass clear out and clean up. As the children are filmed cleaning and tidying, the narrator frames his commentary in terms analogous to school homework. However, conversation with one child reveals the extent to which supremacy must be given to domestic chores: when the girl says she prefers to read a book than clean the house, it is clear that housework must be seen as equally important as reading. In this regime housework is to be privileged, and less culture may have to be consumed in the home in order to allow time for domestic chores. Housework here is not a lifestyle choice, but a basic necessity to ensure the well-being of the family. The combined authority of the domestic doyenne in the housekeeper-tutor, and scientific laboratory 'proof' of threat of disease, are seen to have a greater authority than the claims of feminism.

A sense of old-fashioned thoroughness prevails as our experts advocate the value of using white vinegar and bicarbonate of soda to return the bathroom to a pristine state, eschewing the modern expensive proprietary products in favour of their traditional household cleaning hints and tips. As they reveal their long-forgotten methods for removing limescale using only white vinegar, there is a sense of reinventing the Victorian housekeeper, or at the very least her trusty virtues, in the guise of the modern housewife, passing on hitherto forgotten domestic lore to the modern hapless participant. Aggie is even quoted in the *Guardian* as saying 'In supermarkets, the shelves are full of products but we actually need very few things [to keep a home pristine].'[3] Nonetheless, this devotion to old-fashioned methods and techniques of a pre-consumerist variety has not prevented the programme's producers from accepting sponsorship deals from Lever Faberge's Cif (a modern cleaning cream) and product placements from Clorox and in the US, Proctor and Gamble, nor from considering launching a range of their own branded spin-off products from Consuma.[4] Besides incongruities between the overall message of the presenters, based on skill and experience and a devotion to the home, and the commercial lure of product partnerships, representing speed, economy and the home-as-unit, there are other slippages too. For instance, there is a slippage in class position between working class capability and middle class helplessness, and this is furthered by the presenters who, with Kim's comic-glamorous appearance and Aggie's schoolmarm approach are clearly 'outsiders'. History too is toyed with as the commanding housekeeper of the nineteenth century is evoked whereas the feminist activist of the 1970s is nowhere to be found. The modern feminist is eclipsed by this image of the past – the representation which 'works'. In this housework-as-horror genre of domestic lifestyle TV, dirt is seen as a tangible opponent to a well-ordered household, and other wider issues are ignored or at best skirted around. *How Clean?* is not about female choices regarding housework – there can be no choice in whether or not to keep a clean house – the tone is dictatorial: the imperative is towards making better choices and re-educating inefficient housewives.

Comparing housewifery in *Wife Swap*

In the same year as *How Clean is Your House?* Channel 4 also launched another new domestic lifestyle programme: *Wife Swap* (Channel 4 2003). Two female participants, whose differences are announced by extra-diegetic narration so that potential conflict is set up from the outset, undertake to swap roles and lives for two weeks. The first week they live in the other household according to the other woman's house rules (set down in a manual), while in the second week they are allowed to instigate changes according to their own preferences. Although the title

---

3   'If your mum could see this … ' *Guardian*, 4 June 2003.

4   See *Advertising Age*, 7 February 2005, Vol. 76, Issue 6, Special Section, p. 2; *Marketing*, 1 April 2004, p. 4; *Marketing Week*, 28 October 2004, Vol. 27, Issue 44, p. 12; *Brandweek*, 6 September 2004, Vol. 45, Issue 31, p. 6.

'Wife Swap' has overtones of sexual licence between couples, or 'swingers' of the 1970s, the focus is entirely on the household and not on exchanging sexual partners! There are some similarities of subject matter with *How Clean?* concerning issues of domestic order but *Wife Swap*, as an 'unscripted' reality show, probes much deeper in exposing other, more sensitive, areas of modern domestic life. It has been hugely popular, attracting 5.7 million viewers within three weeks of airing,[5] and having six UK series by 2007 and a US version. The programme offers the ultimate in reality TV voyeuristic pleasures: an intimate look into the daily functioning of other people's homes and families. The two wives are very often of different class backgrounds, and revealed in titillating opposition for the viewer's entertainment are the mundane details of their everyday lives. At the very least, to enable the show to function, it is likely that the women will have certainly made different lifestyle choices regarding the world of work, partners, approach to bringing up children and managing their homes. The differences between wives are often ferociously defended which lends a *frisson* to the incomprehension of one woman's life by another.

Bourdieu has discussed minor differences as 'diversity within homogeneity' where 'the singular habits of the different members of the same class are united' and major differences as those occurring between a different class or group (Bourdieu 1977, 86). A good example of class difference is made manifest in episode four of the first series which focuses on 'Lizzie' and 'Emma'. Emma, who works outside the home, describes herself as 'aspirational', and the programme emphasizes her detached house, two cars and two children from the outset. Her dream lifestyle would be to own a mansion, with a swimming pool and a butler. Lizzie on the other hand has eight children and lives on benefits with her partner in a council house.

Opportunities abound in this episode for judgement and disapproval. Ken Loach has described the programme thus: '*Wife Swap* ridicules people, making them look stupid and trying to put them in a position where they will row. It's puerile and disgusting.' (*Broadcast* 2007, 25). The show invites, even demands, comparison both between the contestants and between the viewer's own household and those of the televised families. There are stages of enquiry throughout: firstly there is the exposé of other 'ordinary' people's lifestyles; secondly the delving into the unseen family systems and dynamics; and thirdly the process of rationalizing differences. At each of these stages there is the potential for antagonism between viewer and participants, between families and the 'swapped' women, and ultimately between the women themselves. Conflict remains important throughout each episode of *Wife Swap*. Sites of contestation are domestic work; cleanliness; food choices and eating habits; income; husbands; social life; and other lifestyle choices. All of these factors are displayed to test the wives' devotion to home and family. What could be seen as tediously repetitive 'fly on the wall' reality TV is reframed into a suspense-filled narrative of tension and conflict because of the staged confrontation at the end of the show. This ending, where both sets of re-united couples come together is where all four adults, but frequently mostly the wives, can justify their lifestyle choices and practices. In the case of Lizzie and Emma, Emma maintains a middle class

---

5   Retrieved from BBC news website <http://news.bbc.co.uk/2/hi/entertainment>, 22 January 2003.

detachment whilst Lizzie is overrun by her emotional disapproval of Emma's hands-off attitude to motherhood and keeping house. Lizzie's earlier emotional outburst when she perceived Emma to be a 'home-wrecker' was in fact so uncontrolled that the usual course of the two week exchange was curtailed in this particular episode.

The display of raw emotions such as anger, jealousy or despair is provoked and encouraged at the end meeting of the two couples for the entertainment of millions of viewers. What previously would have remained private has been violated and this in turn exposes the violence that women do to themselves and each other. Women's private lives have been slyly exposed by a disapproving intruder who prefers her own different systems, and now is the moment of condemnation and justification. In this climax disagreement is expected, argument is anticipated and even physical violence has been displayed. So much has already been exposed about the way the women run their homes by this point that the big reveal is not only in the raw emotion of the women often struggling to articulate their whole raison d'être, although this is often shocking and heart-wrenching enough, but also in the secondary comments made by husbands and children. The surprise is not that a more ordered household or home-cooked meals may improve general well-being, but that in an act of supreme disloyalty, the opinions of their nearest and dearest may just be voiced. These remarks, sometimes supportive but also often undermining, act as the final and supreme judgement on the woman's chosen mode of running her family. As Palmer has suggested, the access to reality is often through the unpredictable responses (Palmer 2004, 180), and in *Wife Swap* this is to be found in the final outpouring of opinion and resentment, long withheld under the constraints of nuclear family domestic life by the contestant's kith and kin. In the 'Lizzie and Emma' episode, much is revealed on the margins of the programme: there are suggestions of immoral codes, kept just beyond the viewer's reach; lies, love and jealousy all bubble to the surface. Whatever the revelations, narrative bias ensures that judgement is passed, so that although the programme is ostensibly about lifestyle choices of the homemaker, really it is about class disapproval. The privacy of the domestic is exploded by *Wife Swap*, and whilst exposing the public behaviour of others has long been media fodder, now this TV programme enables judgement to be passed on what used to be the most private of domains: the family at home. The focus is not directly on the labour of domestic chores as in *How Clean?*: it is an assessment of the participant's compliance with the unspoken rules of general housewifery, an assault on her femininity, her approach and attitude to the role of housewife. Woman is set against woman in *Wife Swap*. Comparison and judgement are central, there is no feminist unity amongst women here. Each woman is judged to stand or fall in relation to that unknowable and unattainable gold standard of feminine perfection.

Performing middle class propriety in *The Perfect Housewife*

The Perfect Housewife (BBC3 2006) offers to provide help on the domestic front with a wide range of housewifery skills. The stress here is on performance. The unspoken premise of the programme suggests that through a certain style of homemaking, and certain domestic patterns, a middle class veneer of taste and behaviour may be acquired. This performance, the programme seems to imply, will not only improve the self-respect of the contestant (and viewers of course) but will also act as a statement of class membership. The host of the programme is Anthea Turner. Turner's performance is itself a reinvention of her old celebrity self. As the *Perfect Housewife* she implores us all to be better housekeepers and as such she suggests a younger British version of Martha Stewart. But it should be noted that Turner's credentials in the area of homemaking are especially dubious given that she had been described as the 'perfect home wrecker' in the press after her part in a divorce case (Hanks 2006). Her personal integrity seemed further threatened when she sold her wedding photos to *OK!* magazine and also appeared to be advertising Cadbury's chocolate at the same time. Portrayed as breaking up one family, and making a commodity of her wedding, more than a little irony was attached to her new TV role as a model homemaker. Nonetheless, as the 'perfect housewife' Anthea offers endless advice about running a home and demonstrates her domestic prowess to two hapless contestants in this show. The contestants compete (the prize is a mop) for Anthea's approval each week, which will be granted to the person (usually a woman) who most closely follows Anthea's advice and methods around the home.

Unlike the rather fixed subject position of *How Clean is Your House?*, there are a number of ways in which the viewer is encouraged to consume *Perfect Housewife*, adopting various subject positions. We can link the unreality of Anthea's life as a housewife with the animated Anthea augmented by the music from the sitcom *Bewitched* (ABC Network, 1964–72);[6] we can tune in to the narrator's sardonic mockery of Anthea's over-the-top display of housewifery, making her seem like a parody of herself; we can mentally store the interspersed set pieces of advice given by a previously-recorded Anthea; or we can empathize with the contestants, who are given ample time to feel inferior to Anthea's domestic supremacy.

There is more than a touch of fantasy about this programme in the improbable persona of housewife Anthea, both in her expectations of the contestants and in her manner of running a middle class home. In the very first episode Anthea demonstrates the correct way to fold a towel, edges in first and so on. In making sure all the raw edges are hidden, the towel folding stands as a metaphor for the control and seamlessness needed in the successful middle class home. What Anthea is demonstrating in all she does is 'the "right" kind of femininity' where individuals may compensate for their own inadequacies by following the guidance of television's experts.[7] When Anthea shows us her ordered linen cupboard she offers viewers a shrine to unreality in the modern domestic world. But this is the height of domestic performance to which the contestants must aspire. Whereas in the Victorian era the middle classes 'aspired to a performance of housework invisible to those of highest status within the house' (Bryden and Floyd 1999, 7), in the twenty-first century, ironically, it is the lady of the house who must undertake these chores in order to achieve a similar class status. Imagined class migration through correct towel folding may seem ludicrous,

---

6   There was also a more recent film: *Bewitched* (Nora Ephron 2005).

7   For a related discussion see Helen Wood and Beverley Skeggs 'Notes on Ethical Scenarios of Self on British Reality TV' in S. Moorti and K. Ross (2004) 'Reality television', *Feminist Media Studies* 4:2, 203–31, p. 206.

even the contestants snigger, but the invisibility of the labour involved in creating a beautifully presented linen cupboard and the order it represents is the epitome of the desired controlled environment of the middle class household. If the quest is to become a perfect housewife, make no mistake, the holy grail is class acceptance.

The fairy tale of Anthea's own housewifery skills, sprinkling her fairy dust (the animated Anthea twinkles stars) on lesser mortals, helps us to understand the attraction of this lifestyle programme. Her wealth and gorgeous home are enviable, but the principle of order, even regimentation, in the home is where the real focus lies. Whilst she could clearly afford not to have to do her own housework, the point is she makes a virtue of what other women would see as chores bordering on drudgery. However, the contestants in this first episode provide a challenge to Anthea not wholly typical of the total series. Both Ann Marie and Kate also have lovely homes; their problem is that they are not performing their class status through their homes, or at least not Turner's version of class-bound domestic display. Ann Marie is in fact very witty, unable to control her scepticism at the faux seriousness of the towel demonstration, and suggesting that Kate is 'going over to the dark side' by appearing to accept Anthea's instruction. As the programme continues Anne Marie proves herself to be much more articulate than Anthea by expressing a more deeply thought-through rationale. Anne Marie argues a point about wanting to preserve her current lifestyle and role as full time Mum, identifying strongly with the presence of the children in her home, evidenced through her son's pictures on the wall. However, the format of the competition ensures that the much-treasured children's drawings must now be regarded as clutter and hidden away from general view. Anthea is allowed to look a little heated as she insists on this trivial compliance with her rules. What must dominate in the home is an impenetrable gloss which conceals all: mess; children; and, of course, the effort involved in achieving the gloss. Time, Anthea repeatedly assures us, will be saved by her methods. Needless to say, the time needed for this standard of housewifery, and the sacrifice of other more pleasurable activities is of course, in a middle class way, completely hidden. What Anthea offers are not just tips on being an expert housewife but access to a wholly class-determined way of living. Viewers are invited to behave in a certain way by reflecting on given modes of taste and choice, with the promise that, if they follow all the rules of the Anthea Turner school of middle classness, their claims to inclusion in that group will be irrefutable.

Consumerism, of the middle class variety, is inextricably linked with lifestyle in this programme, from the opening shots of Anthea's own home, a Lutyens-style country mansion, to the relentless call by Anthea for appropriate storage containers for all corners of the home, to the types of food appropriate for a stylish party. Class is determined by the performance of certain codes of behaviour in housekeeping. Appearances, orderliness and the correct mode of purchase are very good places to start: white towels and bed linen are less vulgar than other more practical colours; party food does not include sausages on sticks and must be presented on beautiful tableware; for drinks it is best to stick to champagne! Lip service is paid to the notion of recycling, not because it saves the planet but because it offers a system for ordering the rubbish. In this TV model, the role of housewife is a 'performative one' in which as, Giddens argues, there is an expected division between appearance and self-identity (Giddens 1991, 58–9). In this case, the performance of the housewifery role is at a distance from the inner, originating sense of self. If then, the contestants can perform the role of a perfect housewife they can subsume any sense of inner identity and create firm middle class allegiances. Do all this, Anthea implores, and you will be happy. The link between an orderly home and a contented mind is made with alarming frequency. But even the regular press despaired at Anthea's performance: 'Watching Turner's control-freakery is moderately entertaining for a few minutes, but it's not enough to compensate for the neurotic air hanging over proceedings. And the format is setting back the cause of feminism by decades, if not centuries. Somebody put this back on the shelf.' (Hanks 2006). For, in a total reversal of early second wave feminism, in Anthea's fantasy world a woman need look no further than the confines of her domestic domain with its clear surfaces and tidy cupboards for self-fulfilment.

* * *

Housework is reinvented in domestic lifestyle programmes as something more than the drudgery of domestic chores exposed by feminists. In twenty-first century parlance, being a housewife has become a lifestyle choice. The choice is not whether to accept or reject the role of housewife, but which type of housewife to be, following highly standardized female identities. The removal of any larger dissent or debate about conforming to the housewifely role has allowed lifestyle television to present a complacent and unchallenging gender politics. Women need, it seems, to be retrained in the art of housekeeping not only because their skill levels have declined but because they have forgotten the 'joy' of keeping house. Lifestyle television in these programmes adopts a Reithian zeal to offer women a valuable opportunity to become refocused on the home. In a world where a postmodern sense of a disconnected self may leave a woman feeing disempowered, apolitical and unable to relate to the outside world, inside the home, so these television programmes would have us believe, is the possibility of a return to the security of a meaningful, well-defined role. Housekeeping has once more acquired a worthy status, and becomes a route by which a woman may newly feel in command of her life and confident in her redefined position in the family and in society.

   These programmes suggest that the cure for a fractured identity is mastery over the domestic environment. The actual systems and management of home living are seen as having an impact on psychological health as they represent the link between the interiority of the individual and the functioning of that individual in society. By regaining control over the domestic the housewife gains well-being and a feeling of command over the self and thus her life. In this way a direct link is made between the chores of housework and potential happiness. Arguing against any feminist antipathy to the restrictions domesticity has placed on women's lives, domestic order is promoted as a strong, rooted and wholesome lifestyle choice for women. It is perhaps indicative of their gender politics that most domestic lifestyle programmes are primarily aimed at women.[8] They aim to restore the worthiness of housekeeping as a profession, with power, control and accomplishment as rewards with deeper meaning than mere wages for a job well done. In keeping an ordered household the housewife regains her sense of purpose which in turn provides a route to psychological health for herself and the whole family too who may now be better able to face the chaos of the world outside.

If women have lifted their gaze from their domestic interiors over the past few decades and become distracted by things like careers and political interventions, then this recent flurry of domestic lifestyle television programmes offers to refocus women's attention back on the home. Female viewers must *relearn* how to keep house, otherwise they might develop problems for themselves like the poor souls whose lavatories and fridges are shamefully revealed in such public viewing. In order to deliver their messages, domestic lifestyle television programmes are simple in structure. The viewer can anticipate the reveal at the end – everyone knows what a tidy house looks like – but the true reveal is in the participants' emotional outpouring at the end that can range from angry indignation to tearful gratitude. What is revealed here is the emotional landscape of the home. In this way housework, a seemingly unlikely subject for mass viewing, is packaged for consumption by millions in the guise of ever-popular cathartic self-therapy.

The image of the real, ordinary housewife then, as currently transmitted on British television, is not a site of feminist discourse but an opportunity to adopt a particular persona learnt through the world of lifestyle TV. Unlike the 1970s when enquiry into women's lives (either through personal or political avenues) resulted in multiple interpretations of female and feminist identity, domestic lifestyle programmes of the early twenty-first century offer little variety in the relationship of women to the home. A consistent image becomes a powerful one though, and the identification of the viewer with the domestic matriarch such as that suggested by Charlotte Brunsdon concerning British soap operas may be related here. Brunsdon's 'fantasy of ordinariness, of femininity achieved' helps us to understand the power of domestic reality programmes too (Brunsdon 2000, 66–71). The housewife on television, be she a member of the public or a celebrity posing as a housewife, operates as a figure which epitomizes the fantasy of ordinary femininity and as such, can be used to reach the underbelly of sensibilities in unconfident female viewers, to educate and inform them through the guise of entertainment. This fantasy of femininity in lifestyle television can display delightful class nuances, satisfy our cravings for voyeurism, chastise us, or make us feel self-satisfied in our own domestic practices, and perhaps most importantly of all, make us cringe with embarrassment when we see our own behaviour reflected on the screen. But thankfully for those worried about 'making it', domestic femininity is both significant and achievable.

---

8   For example, although *Wife Swap* often includes the roles of husbands (who often take much of the responsibility for housework and cooking), the makers of the programme, RDF, make it clear on their website that it is the women who change households, and that they remain the main focus of the show, 'The two women of each family trade places for ten days to see what it is like to live in another family's home.' Retrieved from <www.rdftelevision. com/categories.aspx?cid=2&pid=144>, May 2008.

Perhaps most disconcertingly of all, we can see that these programmes, by disengaging the role of housewife from feminist politics, make the figure of the housewife open to interpretation and manipulation from other, less woman-centred political arenas. Housework repackaged as therapy and as a means of reclaiming femininity serves a number of purposes: it offers entertaining instruction; it encourages conformity of an otherwise disparate group to a single idealized image of womanhood; it provides the perfect medium within the home from which to view other domestic spaces and reflect on our own; and it serves an increasing need for a narrative of the self. Furthermore, it registers housework as an apolitical potential career for women. Even if women of the twenty-first century have little stability and many distractions, even if feminism is a disputed term and there is no actual agreed definition of femininity, there can be little doubt that the modern politics of lifestyle and consumerism require women to be houseproud. So little surprise then that television and the popular genre of lifestyle TV are used as a medium through which to enlighten and retrain women in the historic art of housekeeping.

The research for this article was carried out under the aegis of the project on the 1970s at the University of Portsmouth which is supported by the Arts and Humanities Research Council

Bibliography

Bell, D. and Hollows, J. (eds) (2005), *Ordinary Lifestyles: Popular Media, Consumption and Taste* (Maidenhead: Open University Press).

Bookseller (2007), Issue 5278:40, 27 April.

Bourdieu, P. (1977), *Outline of a Theory of Practice* (trans. Richard Nice) (Cambridge: Cambridge University Press).

Broadcast (2007), 21 September: 25.

Brunsdon, C. (2000), *The Feminist, The Housewife and the Soap Opera* (Oxford: Oxford University Press).

Bryden, I. and Floyd, J. (1999), *Domestic Space: Reading the Nineteenth-century Interior* (Manchester: Manchester University Press).

Chaney, D. (2002), *Cultural Change and Everyday Life* (Basingstoke: Palgrave).

Coates, J. (1974),'Shared Housework', *Spare Rib* 25:28–9.

Freeman, C. (1973), 'When is a Wage not a Wage?', *Red Rag*, August.

Giddens, A. (1991), *Modernity and Self-identity* (Cambridge: Polity Press).

Hakim, C. (1995), 'Five Feminist Myths about Women's Employment', *The British Journal of Sociology* 46:3, 429–55.

—— (1996), 'The Sexual Division of Labour and Women's Heterogeneity', *The British Journal of Sociology* 47:1, 178–88.

Hanks, R. (2006), 'Welcome to My Lovely Home', *The Independent*, 17 February.

Heywood, L. and Drake, J. (eds) (1997), *Third Wave Agenda: Being Feminist Doing Feminism* (Minneapolis: University of Minnesota Press).

Holmes, S. and Jermyn, D. (eds) (2004), *Understanding Reality Television* (London: Routledge).

Johnson, M.L. (ed.) (2007), *Third Wave Feminism and Television: Jane Puts it in a Box* (London: I.B. Tauris).

Johnson, L. and Lloyd, J. (2004), *Sentenced to Everyday Life: Feminism and the Housewife* (Oxford: Berg).

McRobbie, A. (2004), 'Post-feminism and Popular Culture', *Feminist Media Studies* 4:3, 255–64.

Oakley, A. (1974), *The Sociology of Housework* (Oxford: Martin Robertson).

Palmer, G. (2004), '"The New You": Class and Transformation in Lifestyle Television', in S. Holmes and D. Jermyn (eds), *Understanding Reality Television* (London: Routledge).

Vavrus, M.D. (2007), 'Opting Out Moms in the News', *Feminist Media Studies* 7:1, 47–63.

Chapter 9

What Not to Buy: Consumption and Anxiety in the Television Makeover

Deborah Philips

In his 1836 parody of academic endeavours, *Sartor Resartus*, Thomas Carlyle invents a Germanic Clothes-Philosopher, Herr Teufelsdröckh, whose principle is:

> in this one pregnant subject of CLOTHES, rightly understood, is included all that men have thought, done, and been: the whole external Universe and what it holds is but Clothing and the essence of all Science lies in the PHILOSOPHY OF CLOTHES ... (Carlyle 2002, 84)

If Carlyle was using Herr Teufelsdröckh ironically, *What Not to Wear* is a programme dedicated to fashion and to the principle that the essence of self-improvement lies in the Philosophy of Clothes. As Herr Teufelsdröckh advises, 'For neither in tailoring nor in legislating does man proceed by mere Accident'; 'professional' guidance is required to guide the uninitiated through the Philosophy of Clothes.

Trinny Woodall and Susannah Constantine were the first presenters of the show (and remain the biggest names in British fashion makeover; with their departure from the BBC and move to ITV in 2006, Trinny and Susannah had to leave the format and the title of *What Not to Wear* behind and to reinvent new variations of their partnership and styling). In all their programme formats, self-worth is mapped onto the ability to choose and to wear clothes with 'style', and they present themselves as 'helpers' in the transformation of the self. In the conclusion to one episode in their 2006 incarnation on the ITV series *Trinny and Susannah Undress*, Trinny and Susannah congratulate each other on their achievement:

> It's been a complete transformation in two short weeks ... It's like their whole life situation comes through their clothes ... so it's an emotional change as well as a physical one ... (*Trinny and Susannah Undress*, ITV, 10 October 2006)

The language of personal transformation has increasingly become part of the fabric of everyday life; a slogan for a chain of fitness centres proclaimed in 2007, 'Be Yourself, Only Better!' (Fitness First). This discourse of physical and moral improvement is a standard feature of the television makeover, in which discipline and proper training are shown to effect a personal transformation. The training and discipline promoted by *What Not to Wear* is that of appropriate forms of consumption; the presenters give a subject the means of purchasing and advise them in their acquisition of clothing and accessories.

In her study of fashion as a sign system, Alison Lurie suggests that there are those who are simply inept at mastering the language of clothes:

> Unfortunately ... there are ... many persons who do not dress very well, not because of lack of money but because of innate lack of taste. In some cases their clothes are merely monotonous, suggesting an uninteresting but consistent personality. Others seem to have a knack for combining colors, patterns and styles in a way that ... suggests personal awkwardness and disharmony. (Lurie 1982, 21)

Like Lurie, the presenters of *What Not to Wear* believe that there is such a thing as 'innate taste' and that there are those who simply lack it. Paradoxically, these presenters also insist that this taste can be taught and that their set of rules can overcome 'personal awkwardness'. Trinny and Susannah are among the many current guides found in fashion journalism whose mission is to redress this 'innate lack of taste' and who claim to convert the sophisticated language of fashion into high street accessibility. The title of Trinny and Susannah's 2004 book is *What You Wear Can Change Your Life*; like Lurie, they assume that a failure to 'dress well' is indicative of a failed and unproductive life. An inability to read the runes of the fashion system is seen to constitute a personal and moral failure. Barthes has explained this process:

> the *unfashionable* is part of the system, it is to incur a moral condemnation ... the institution of the Fashion sign is a tyrannical act: there are *mistakes* in language and *faults in Fashion*. Moreover it is in direct proportion to its very arbitrariness that Fashion develops an entire rhetoric of Law and Fact, all the more imperative because the arbitrariness it must rationalize or naturalize is unchecked. (Barthes 1985, 216)

Trinny and Susannah literally enact this rhetoric of Law and Fact – morally censuring their subjects for being 'unfashionable' and asserting the unquestionable imperatives of the 'fashionable'. Their 'rules' (outlined in the accompanying books to the series) are a central element in the narrative of the programme; these are carefully explained to the programme's makeover subject, and tyrannically imposed over her own taste and choices.

There is a regular trope in the programmes of the conflation of the subject's life and their clothes in which the judgement of the clothes becomes a judgement on the self; as in this concerned address by the presenters to one subject: 'Your wardrobe has been where your life has been, tired, fusty and old-fashioned' (*What Not to Wear*, 28 November 2004). In rescuing their subjects from fashion disaster, the fashion tastemakers are restoring harmony and redeeming their subjects from personal neglect. The fashion television makeover can be understood an embodiment of what Barthes has termed the 'Fashion' sign:

> ... the Fashion sign, like all signs produced within what is called mass culture, is situated, one might say, at the point where a singular (or oligarchical) conception and a collective image meet, it is simultaneously imposed and demanded. (Barthes 1985, 215)

The fashion television makeover is precisely the imposition by an oligarchy of stylists of a singular conception of 'taste' onto the subject of the makeover, who has, by applying and agreeing to appear on television demanded that imposition. Since Barthes undertook his survey of the fashion press in 1963, magazines devoted entirely to shopping have emerged. The fashion system of the magazine is increasingly determined by the garments available in high street stores and fashion advice has unapologetically transmuted into the promotion of branded names. In *What Not to Wear*, transformation is achieved through the consumption of brands: the subject is sent out shopping, and the shops are clearly identifiable. Just as in the television makeovers of houses and rooms, (in which the paints and furnishings and fabrics are clearly priced and sourced), the brands of clothing used in the transformation are clearly marked with their labels and price in the final display. As Bourdieu explains, the role of the 'tastemaker' is to impose consumer needs:

> in order to be able to sell the symbolic products they had to offer, they had to produce the need for them in potential consumers by a symbolic action ... tending to impose norms and needs, particularly in the areas of lifestyle and material or cultural consumption. (Bourdieu 1979, 345)

Trinny and Susannah are themselves a brand, and have been so since their first column and website, a brand that is confirmed and endorsed by their television visibility. Besides their successful line of books, they are involved in a range of marketing and product promotions and have directly lent their name to commercial endorsements, most visibly in their advertising campaign for a brand of instant coffee. A line of hosiery is promoted under their name as the 'Trinny and Susannah Original Magic Knickers™', and they have supported a line of hosiery for 'Tights Please'. Littlewoods, the sponsors of the current ITV show, have a two year deal in which Trinny and Susannah endorse their catalogues and online sales. The Trinny and Susannah brand has now moved to America, after their appearances on BBC America led to underwear endorsements, interviews on *Oprah* and a book entitled *Trinny and Susannah Take on America*.

Their current website 'Trinny and Susannah.com' is styled as 'The Big Survey', which purports to be 'a crusade for real style for real women' but is also a sharp instance of lifestyle marketing and a clever device for market research. The site is full of product promotions and surveys; a privacy policy statement makes it clear that the questionnaires ostensibly designed to 'help you find your own style' will be shared with market research companies.

Trinny and Susannah can be understood as only two among a current media phalanx of 'tastemakers' (in Bourdieu's term), television 'experts' whose expertise is to style your house, your car or your body. Bourdieu has little to say directly about fashion and clothes in his study of taste in *Distinction*, perhaps because the field of clothing consumption is dominated by women, although fashion represents (as he acknowledges) one of the best examples of the imposition of distinction. Fashion offers, he suggests, an 'almost perfect meeting point' (Bourdieu 1979, 259) between the fields of production and of consumption. Bourdieu is writing of a time when the couturier held sway in Paris, and he identified the 'tastemaker' as necessary to the late eighteenth century patron anxious at the moment of industrialization and consumer choice. The transition from the twentieth into the twenty-first century

may not be an equivalent moment of historical change but the status anxiety that
Bourdieu describes among the bourgeois art buyers has echoes in the confusions of
contemporary consumers.

In the twenty-first century the fashion system now brings the collections of elite
designers to high street stores across the globe; international celebrities and designer
names have 'created' collections for chain stores: Stella McCartney for H&M
and Giles Deacon for New Look are recent examples. The contemporary woman
consumer is presented with an apparent infinite variety of fashion garments and with
a fashion press that is full of bewildering dictums on how to select and combine
items. Trinny and Susannah assume a natural 'right' over the world of fashion; they
present 'style' as an eternal truth that transcends history and the economic. They
position themselves as a conduit between the arcane 'rules' of haute couture and the
bewildering accessibility of high street fashion, prepared to convert their cultural
capital into shopping advice.

The fashionable consumer is required both to conform to the regulations of the
season while simultaneously maintaining the eternal rules of style, in an impossible
resolution of the 'classic' and the 'fashionable'. But it is worth remembering the
rhetoric that Barthes ascribes to his personification of fashion:

> that absolute, dogmatic, vengeful present tense in which Fashion speaks ... the murder
> it commits of its own past, as if it vaguely heard that possessive voice of the slain year,
> saying to it: *Yesterday I was what you are, tomorrow you will be what I am* (Barthes 1979,
> 273)

This dogmatic voice of fashion is constantly reiterated in style and celebrity
magazines, where what is construed as 'in' and what is 'out' is fiercely charted in
weekly and monthly columns, and is personified in the presentational style of Trinny
and Susannah.

The participants in the fashion makeover show are seen confronted with an array
of fashion outlets and the expert becomes their guide in steering them through the
potential hazards of the wrong consumer choice. As Trinny and Susannah recognize,
the choice of goods in a global market is fraught with potential pitfalls; the selection
and combination of 'fashion' elements is a clear source of tension for many women
and their promise is that they are experts who can negotiate their subjects through
the complexities of fashion choices to achieve harmony and taste.

A range of postmodern theorists (many citing de Certeau) have suggested that
shopping is a celebratory practice and that the pleasures of consumption offer a
multiplicity of modes of being. This is only one among many critics to have
celebrated the postmodern self in the shopping mall:

> the self now is a virtual object to such a degree of intensity and accumulation that the
> fascination of the shopping mall is in the way of homecoming to a self that has been lost,
> but now happily discovered. The postmodern self as one more object in the simulacra of
> objects. (Kroker and Cook 1989, quoted in Langman 1992, 65)

The shopping mall in *What Not to Wear* is regularly shown to be less of a 'homecoming'
than a source of anxiety and confusion for the female subject. Consumption is, in

the world of Trinny and Susannah and of other makeover shows, not an unalloyed pleasure; as Barthes recognized, it is easy to get fashion wrong. Trinny and Susannah may be professional consumers and make their living by encouraging other women to shop, but they freely acknowledge that shopping is a source of unease: 'we fully appreciate the anxiety it can cause' (Constantine and Woodhall 2002, 140)'. The first *What Not to Wear* book is introduced with a shopping guide divided into three sections – all of which involve guilt: 'no guilt/slight guilt/guilt for days' (Woodhall and Constantine 2002, 74).

This understanding of the anxiety of shopping is however undercut by the superior cultural capital of the 'tastemakers'; their advice is precisely designed to overcome the guilt and anxiety of the consumer and consumption itself becomes a form of therapy. Armed with the 'rules' and professionalized advice of the tastemakers the subject of the makeover is provided with the consumer skills to make sense of the complex lexicon of the shopping mall (and of what Barthes has termed the 'fashion system') and is reassured.

The makeover show has increasingly taken on an ostensibly therapeutic discourse; as *What Not to Wear* developed as a series, these psychotherapeutic claims became more and more explicit. What had begun as the language of empowerment in the dressing room ended with the subject of the makeover literally on the couch, with Trinny or Susannah placed behind her taking notes on her (lack of) taste. In the final series in which these presenters fronted *What Not to Wear*, women were grouped by virtue of a shared 'problem' and set against one another to compete for the privilege of a makeover. In Trinny and Susannah's compassionate phrase (a convention repeated in each programme): the chosen subject 'is the one who could most do with our help', a format that continues with the new presenters. This selection of subjects on the basis of need had uncomfortable resonances of the hugely popular American television show *Queen for a Day*, a radio show which was first televised on NBC from 1955 and which ran for almost two decades. In *Queen for a Day*, women were required to demonstrate which one of them had the most miserable lot in life to win game show prizes and the crown of most pitiable existence. In the later series of *What Not to Wear*, women lined up before the presenters, grouped by virtue of their shared 'problem'. The presenters then discussed behind a screen which of these putative subjects were most in need of their help; the chosen women are then congratulated as 'winners' of a makeover. The transformative powers of fashion and the therapeutic potential of consumption have been extended into Trinny and Susannah's series for ITV, *Trinny and Susannah Undress*, beginning in 2006. Here, the format has moved beyond the single subject into the transformation of a couple, and the presenters' expertise beyond fashion advice into marriage counselling. The series now focuses on communities of women, grouped by geography, age or lifestyle 'problem'.

Each programme in the final series of *What Not to Wear* presented by Trinny and Susannah concentrated on 'problem categories' (in the words of the programmes' website). These problems are exclusively women's problems ('mothers with small children', 'teenage mums', 'women with younger men') and they exist outside any social or economic dimension, manifest only in the women's failure to dress well. The 'problem' is then magically resolved through the purchasing of a new wardrobe, fashionable consumption being shown as capable of overcoming the trials of stressed parenting, a sexist differential between the genders, or the combining of work and motherhood. Trinny and Susannah are stylists of the self who in promoting products and enabling consumers to 'find their own style' claim that they can also restore self-worth. In one interview, Trinny Woodhall recounts the tale of a woman whose lack of self-esteem is evident from the failures of her wardrobe: 'What we found showed such a lack of love for herself. I found it very upsetting' (Woodhall, quoted in Cooke 2004, 27). While there may well have been some basis for this concern for the woman subject, the solution offered by the programme and presenters is entirely one of consumption. The factors that may have made a subject's life miserable – common factors (visible only in the margins of the programme) include lack of childcare, unacknowledged labour, low status work – are magicked away with the promise of a new wardrobe.

Consumption is shown as capable of assuaging class and gender inequalities. Trinny and Susannah's advice in their first book explicitly denies any financial, family or social pressures that might intervene in the process of being well dressed. Any such problems are airily dismissed as:

> comforting excuses – there's the kids, the overdraft, no time nor inclination. Clothes are immaterial, because you can rely on your fabulous personality and your partner is blind to you looking like a tramp, because he loves you just the way you are. At the end of the day this is bollocks. (Woodhall and Constantine 2002, 6)

While much is made in their programmes of Trinny and Susannah's expertise and of their credentials as agents of cultural capital, there is no reference at all to any kind of professional training. Both Trinny Woodall and Susannah Constantine have professional backgrounds in marketing and public relations, and their expertise is entirely derived from fashion journalism. While the programme unequivocally presents them as arbiters of taste and style, this is presented as a natural phenomenon, rather than a set of acquired skills. Their incarnation as 'Trinny and Susannah' began as lifestyle columnists, first with a weekly column in *The Daily Telegraph*, and later, *The Sun*. They first appeared on daytime television on a satellite channel; this then led them to set up an early internet lifestyle site, 'Ready2Shop.com', which collapsed financially in 2000. In 2001, their first dedicated television programme, *What Not to Wear*, appeared on BBC2. Once they had crossed channels and lost this title, they had to reinvent the formula as *Trinny and Susannah Undress*, in which the presenters first worked their skills on married couples. The BBC recruited model Lisa Butcher and singer Mica Paris to take over *What Not to Wear* as presenters; like their forerunners, the programme claims them to be best friends. The new presenters have taken over the combination of cajoling and bullying of their subjects, in the presenting style developed by Trinny and Susannah, and continue to promote an 'absolute, dogmatic' voice of fashion.

Whatever the format, and whoever the presenters might be, their superior cultural capital and social status is confirmed by the editing and presentation of the television narrative. While Trinny and Susannah may claim themselves as the subject's 'friends', there is a constant assertion of class distinction between the presenters and their subjects. The current *What Not to Wear* 'office', where subjects arrive and are assessed, is located in a grand house in an unspecified central London location. Designed with all the trappings of an interiors magazine, the house appears to be the 'natural' habitat of the tastemakers. As the presenters travel to their subject's domain, their class superiority is underlined through editing. On a trip to Hull, Trinny and Susannah's status as first class travellers was established by a shot of first class seats, even before they came into shot. On disembarking they could be overheard remarking (with some surprise) 'This is rather nice', as if to confirm that they had never before been to Hull. This claim to ignorance of any location outside central London is a recurrent trope in the ITV series *Trinny and Susannah Undress* – in which the metropolitan sophistication of the presenters is firmly distanced from the everyday lives of their 'out of town' subjects.

The makeover programme offers a particular conjunction of audience and programme makers – in that the subjects of the makeover are 'ordinary viewers' who willingly submit to what, as Angela McRobbie and Nick Couldry have noted, has become an increasingly ritualized form of humiliation (Couldry 2006; McRobbie 2004). The presenters work as a double act – in which one can be deliberately rude, while the other soothes and empathizes with the subject. The rudeness can be aggressive and abusive – in which not only the woman's fashion sense but her sense of her self (the large majority of subjects are women) and her world are derided. In one programme, Trinny addressed the woman undergoing the experience (a woman with triplets): 'Get a fucking life. … We're … about getting you out of that small boxy world you've got yourself into' (BBC1, 28 September 2004). Susannah later responds: 'You were tough on her, but I know it came from a good place.' The abuse and derision are thus rendered acceptable because they are ostensibly in the best interests of the subject.

A language of personal transformation and a childlike girlishness marks the tone of Trinny and Susannah's address to their audience (and is also there in their names; they can be recognized without surnames). The recurrent tone is one of girlish hectoring, as the subject is subjected to the scrutiny of the presenters; a use of slang implies an intimacy with the reader's body and appears to be that of a good friend observing the subject in the mirror of a communal changing room. This claim to friendship is also there in the string of books that have emerged from the television series:

> think of us as your *best friends* … The information ahead is essential to those of you who want to *feel better about yourselves*. We know how much looking good can change a woman's whole outlook on life. If you look chic, not corporate, you'll perform better … *So, girls, look fab* and get the man, the job, the promotion. (Woodhall and Constantine 2003, 11)

Trinny and Susannah are often cited as examples of good women friends by their fans and they may indeed be good friends with one another (as their chat show appearances suggest), but they are not and cannot be the friend of the subject within the format of the programme. Their role is as professional presenters who appear at a point in the subject's life, only to disappear again. The transformation tastemaker has no knowledge of the subjects' personal history or habitus beyond the fact finding of television researchers.

The subject of the 'makeover' becomes a 'docile body' (in Foucault's term), a 'subject, used, transformed and improved', and willingly complicit in the erasure of their own tastes. *What Not to Wear* enacts an expunging of the subject's personal wardrobe; their personal choice of clothing is subjected to scorn and discarded in a ritual of stripping the subject (both literally and metaphorically). *What Not to Wear* literally enacts a process in which the presenters assume what Foucault has described as a 'machinery of power that explores (the human body), breaks it down and rearranges it' (Foucault 1982, 138). The subject's own self-presentation is broken down by being confronted by their reflection in a 360 degree mirror, their underwear and body shape assessed by the presenters. Their clothing preferences are then rearranged according to the 'rules', the stern term that is used to suggest that there are absolute regulations for dressing. Once initiated into the style advocated by the stylists, the subject is sent shopping and observed by the presenters over a panoptic webcam. If the 'rules' have been breached, the presenters arrive in person to set the subject on the right path through the clothes rails. Subjects are also the object of surveillance beyond the single programme; *What Not to Wear Revisited* may be cheap television, in that it can recycle footage from past programmes, but it is also a means of checking up on the subject's continued commitment to the programme's regime. In one episode, the authoritarianism of the 'revisiting' practice was evident when the subject was surprised at work and told 'We've come to check up on you to see if you've kept to our rules' (*What Not to Wear Revisited*, 13 December 2005).

Trinny and Susannah are enablers in the process of self-transformation, providing not only their expertise but also, crucially, the economic means to provide a new wardrobe, in the form of a cheque. They are *dei ex machina*, or fairy godmothers, who exist outside the world of the subject but are transported into it only for the process of transformation. The transformation and Trinny and Susannah's participation in it apparently exist outside any social or economic context. What is evacuated, along with the subject's wardrobe, is any sense of their own habitus. Family, friends and work colleagues exist only to support the presenters' derisive comments on the subject's appearance and to finally applaud the programme's achievement. In what is the most distressing element of the programme's narrative arc, partners and children are confronted with questions such as 'How do you feel about your Mum's taste?' The subject is then confronted with a tape of disparaging remarks from their close friends and family about their appearance, a process which more often than not reduces her to tears. This is an element in which *What Not to Wear* is demonstrably personally extremely cruel; Nick Couldry has written of the theatre of 'systems of cruelty' in reality television, and this ritual can be read as one such system. The structure of the programme entirely conforms to Couldry's understanding of reality television as a 'secret theatre of neoliberalism' which requires 'continuous loyalty, submission to surveillance and external direction even within the deepest recesses of private life' (Couldry 2006, 1).

Trinny and Susannah have articulated their mission as the empowerment of women, and claim an empathy with their subjects, as Trinny Woodhall put it in one interview: 'Love us or loath us, we've always had empathy with women. We're not there to degrade them. We're there to champion them. We are on their side.' (Trinny Woodhall quoted in Cooke 2004, 27). There is a consistent claim throughout the programme series and books that the (correct) consumption of fashion and beauty products is enabling for women and will in itself create new life opportunities for them. The introduction to the second volume of *What Not to Wear* borrows from the language of feminism; the terms 'stereotypes', 'decisions', 'break free' and 'transformation' are all picked out in bold type. The authors claim:

> we aim to guide the misguided into looking the part for all manner of life-changing moments. The book demonstrates how dressing well can help you get what you want. It will train those bound by what the neighbours say to break *free from stereotypes.* It will urge those who are lacking in confidence to go the extra mile in order to gain that much needed self-belief to win the job, get the bloke or fit in with the sleek sophisticates oiled up on the beach in southern Spain. It will enable girls to make *dressing decisions on their own*, without the help of competitive peers ... (Woodhall and Constantine 2003, 6–7)

Here, the language of female empowerment is defined by 'dressing well'. Female success is framed entirely within the bounds of traditional femininity. The women readers are addressed here as 'girls' and assumed to be rival with one another. The 'life-changing' moment can only be achieved at an individualized level and with the aid of expert helpers; those who demur are dismissed as 'misguided'.

Trinny and Susannah have become a byword for triviality in the broadsheet press, their very names suggestive of insubstantiality. They are considered harmless even by feminists; Elaine Showalter claimed them as her 'guilty pleasure' in a *Guardian* article (*The Guardian*, 3 February 2007). However, as Barthes has pointed out, the language of fashion is incapable of irony:

> Fashion is both *too* serious and *too* frivolous at the same time, and it is in this intentionally complementary interplay of excess that it finds a solution to a fundamental contradiction which constantly threatens to destroy its fragile prestige: in point of fact, Fashion cannot be literally serious, for that would be to oppose common sense (of which it is respectful on principle) ... conversely Fashion cannot be ironic and put its own being in question. (Barthes 1985, 242)

The paradoxical rhetoric that Barthes identifies in the fashion system is readily available in the language of the programmes and books of the fashion makeover. Clothes are described as simultaneously 'funky' and 'classic', as both up-to-date and traditionally 'feminine'. *What Not to Wear* is pitched exactly at the tension Barthes describes – between the serious and the trivial. While consistently acknowledging that what to wear is 'only common sense' and that it should be fun, it is also claimed that it can change your life, as the title of Trinny and Susannah's 2003 book asserts.

Trinny and Susannah belong to a discourse of self-improvement that goes beyond the fashion system as they represent a mechanism by which the regulations and regimen of consumerism have become 'normalized' in everyday life. Unlike those programmes that promote plastic surgery, such as *Extreme Makeover*, Trinny and Susannah (as Elaine Showalter points out in their defence) do not require their subjects to submit to literal surgical operations, but they do undeniably objectivize the self into a normalized regime of taste and style. If *What Not to Wear* falls short of recommending plastic surgery, the female subject is nonetheless prompted to view her body in terms of improvement. The first *What Not to Wear* book (2002) is organized around female bodily parts – with the assumption that body parts will betray the ideal female body; 'big tits', 'no tits', ' big arms', 'big bum', 'no waist', 'short legs/flabby tummy'. The advice given in both books and television programmes does not at any point challenge an impossible ideal of femininity, but instead recommends strategies of dealing with the problems it presents for the less than perfect female body.

The fashion makeover show works as a powerful Cinderella narrative; the 'big reveal' puts the subject at the centre of a transformation scene achieved through the magical powers of television. This fairy tale scenario also works, however, as an assertion of the cultural capital of the tastemaker in the field of fashion; Trinny and Susannah, like fairy godmothers, brook no argument. *What Not to Wear* can be understood as an example of 'the technologies of power' which Foucault has termed 'Governmentality'. Foucault has theorized the 'cultivation of the self' as 'the form of an attitude, a mode of behaviour; it became instilled in ways of living; it evolved into procedures, practices and formulas' (Foucault 1988, 45). Trinny and Susannah can be read as practitioners of such procedures; they are proponents of a certain mode of knowledge, and they can be understood as technologists of the 'self'. There is in *What Not to Wear* the belief, as expressed by Herr Teufelsdröckh, that 'the essence of all Science lies in the PHILOSOPHY OF CLOTHES'; the ethical and moral state of the subject is entirely read from their clothing. A failure to 'look good' (in another recurrent phrase of the presenters) is taken as a failure of self-discipline.

What Not to Wear exercises domination over its subjects, in the guise of help and support. The presenters operate the technologies of power and of the self that Foucault has described as:

> technologies of the self , which permit individuals to effect by their own means or with the help of others a certain number of operations on their own bodies and souls, thoughts, conduct, and way of being, so as to transform themselves in order to attain a certain state of happiness, purity, wisdom, perfection or immortality. (Martin et al. 1988, 18)

The 'big reveal' at the end of each successful transformation shows the subject of the makeover as having achieved that 'state of happiness' (and the immortality of a television appearance) with the help of the television tastemakers. The 'makeover' has, however, now moved beyond television and the pages of fashion magazines, to become a model to support women in and into the workplace. It is a model, however, which remains entirely within the frame of patriarchy, which does not challenge inequalities of gender or class, but which relies entirely on subsidizing clothing and beauty products for aspiring working women.

The success of programmes such as *What Not to Wear* has allowed the values and mode of address of lifestyle coaching and fashion advice to bleed into social policy. The claim of these programmes, that they are there to support women, is now taken as a paradigm for the apparent promotion of women in the workplace. The *What Not to Wear* format of bullying and cajoling women into new modes of fashion fits neatly with a government policy that enjoins women to transform themselves into entrepreneurs. Like Trinny and Susannah, current government initiatives expect women to enter the workforce but fail to supply the economic and domestic support that is needed to sustain them. A 'Dress for Success' scheme was launched nationally in Britain in 2000, which donated appropriate clothing to putative women executives, an initiative organized by Business in the Community and supported by Cherie Blair, then the Prime Minister's wife. In 2007, Gateshead Council celebrated International Women's Day with free beauty and fashion advice from an image consultant for unemployed women (www.gateshead.gov.uk). Children too are now subject to a lifestyle makeover designed by stylists and life coaches. The 2007 Channel 4 programme, *Make Me a Grown Up* uses the format of *10 Years Younger* to instil confidence in insecure young people, with a fashion makeover and (brief) advice from a psychologist. The programme is broadcast under the 'learning' aegis of Channel 4's remit. Herr Teufelsdröckh would happily endorse this emphatic insistence on clothing as the means of accomplishing personal worth and social status: 'The beginning of all Wisdom is to look fixedly on Clothes' (Carlyle 2002).

As Foucault has pointed out, the exercise of discipline and the assertion of domination work as:

> a multiplicity of often minor processes, of different origin and scattered location, which overlap, repeat, or imitate one another, support one another, distinguish themselves from one another according to their domain of application, converge, and gradually produce the blue-print of a general method. (Foucault 1982, 138)

What Not to Wear can be seen as one such 'minor process'; it overlaps and repeats the discourses of fashion magazines, but it also exists in the context of a range of television lifestyle programmes.

The 'reality' show has intruded further and further into private lives – the domestic space is transformed in makeovers of rooms and houses, relationships are transformed with the transferring of partners in *Wife Swap*. It has become literally invasive in body makeover shows – subjects are required to be filmed in their underwear, and in the more extreme makeovers, subject to invasive plastic surgery. These programmes operate in different domains of application, promising the self-improvement to every aspect of life through the transformative power of television and its experts: housing (*Grand Designs*, *Location, Location, Location*), health (*You Are What You Eat*), childcare (*Little Angels*), relocation (*Escape to the Country*), and investment (*Property Ladder*). Together they contribute to a blueprint in which social anxieties and economic decisions are rendered as entirely personal problems which can be resolved through individual endeavour and within the framework of a single episode of a television programme, with the 'magical' help of the presenters.

Bibliography

Barthes, R. (1985), *The Fashion System*, trans. M. Ward and R. Howard (London: Cape).

Bourdieu, P. (1979), *La Distinction: critique social du jugement* (Paris: Les Editions de Minuit).

Carlyle, T. (2002) *Sartor Resartus: The Life and Times of Herr Teufelsdröckh* (Edinburgh: Canongate Classic).

Constantine, S. and Woodhall, T. (2002), *Ready 2 Dress: How to Have Style Without Following Fashion* (London: Orion).

Cooke, R. (2004), 'We're Just As FAT As You When We Take Our Shoes Off', *Evening Standard*, 13 September, pp. 27–8.

Couldry, N. (2006), 'Reality TV, or the Secret Theatre of Neoliberalism' (London School of Economics and Political Science), published as 'La téléréauté ou le theâtre secret du néolibéralisme, Paris', *Hermes*, No. 44, 121–7.

Foucault, M. (1982), *Discipline and Punish: The Birth of the Prison* (Harmondsworth: Peregrine Books).

Foucault, M. (1988), *The Care of the Self. The History of Sexuality, Volume 3* (New York: Vintage Books).

Langman, L. (1992). 'Neon Cages: Shopping for Subjectivity', in R. Shields (ed.), *Lifestyle Shopping* (London: Routledge), pp. 40–82.

Lurie, A. (1982), *The Language of Clothes* (Feltham: Hamlyn Paperbacks).

Martin, L.H., Gutman, H. and Hutton, P.H. (1988), *Technologies of the Self: A Seminar with Michel Foucault* (Amherst: The University of Massachusetts Press).

McRobbie, A. (2004), 'Notes on "What Not to Wear" and Post-feminist Symbolic Violence', *The Sociological Review* 52, 97–109.

Woodhall, T. and Constantine, S. (2002), *What Not to Wear* (London: Weidenfeld and Nicholson).

Woodhall, T. and Constantine, S. (2003), *What Not to Wear 2: For Every Occasion* (London: Weidenfeld and Nicholson).

Woodhall, T. and Constantine, S. (2004), *What You Wear Can Change Your Life* (London: Weidenfeld and Nicholson).

Chapter 10

Making Over the Talent Show

Guy Redden

One of the concerns of recent studies of popular television has been to try to develop understandings of cultural democratization (Holmes and Jermyn 2004, 9). Much contemporary lifestyle programming revolves around the illustration of good, beneficial choices in the lives of those who act as participants. Of great importance is the characterization of the people on whom these discourses depend: in the main they are so-called ordinary people who become the focus of scrutiny. This category does not simply arise from the marking of persons in terms of class, race, gender, or sexuality so as to equate citizens with normative social identities. The ordinariness at stake is better thought of as a kind of layperson status. Members of the public are shown going about their everyday lives. Their televisual interest is predicated on their initial *lack* of qualification or complete competence in some aspect of life, and it is this that warrants the intervention of their counterparts: the experts whose advice enables a process of apparent improvement that is the very core of the shows.

As Lisa Taylor puts it with reference to gardening television, 'ordinari-ization' strategies 'construct a discourse of lifestyle achievability and accessibility' (2002, 480). Experts act as counsellors, assisting their clients in fulfilling their stated desires. In the course of this their superior professional knowledge in matters of taste and behaviour is redistributed to the participants, and by extension to the viewing population as a whole. On the face of it, television of this kind constitutes and illustrates an egalitarian mode of cultural transmission in which the keys to living well are made widely available, enhancing the life chances of its addressees.

However, enfranchisement of the populus in this mediated world is more complex and paradoxical than it may seem. The narrative structure of makeovers and other shows based on personal lifestyle modification require that people are changed in the end. This raises questions about what some of the conditions applied to participation in this world might be. The presence of the public is something more than an unadulterated expression of the *vox populi*. People are there for something to happen to them, to be adjusted, not simply to be 'themselves'. Accordingly, we need to question whether the appearance of citizens on our screens is necessarily progressive in light of the fact that the terms upon which they appear are tightly controlled by the TV formats they are admitted to.

A complicating factor is that televisual ordinary people are not confined to lifestyle shows. Reality television is also focused on observing them, and itself may be seen as part of a trend towards personalization across the media: the tabloid leaning towards personal stories that is evident in chat and soft news (Dovey 2000; Macdonald 2003). Ordinary folk are not the exclusive property of a genre, and interest in them is paralleled by an obsession with celebrity in all its forms. Just as lifestyle shows change the person, a great number of reality game shows are premised upon the achievement of celebrity by participants. Although useful rubrics like 'lifestyle' and 'reality' have been used to capture significant changes in non-fiction television, some of the broad conventions – ordinari-ization and celebritization included – are mobile elements that appear throughout popular media.

This chapter draws upon some of the cross-border traffic between non-fiction genres that feature ordinary people. My interest is how the person-improving narrative logic of the makeover can spread across television beyond the strict genre of that name. The programming in question is the new generation of talent shows that appears to have ameliorated the decline of free-to-air Saturday night television, at least in the UK. A genre that previously peaked in the 1970s and 1980s with *New Faces* and *Opportunity Knocks* has itself been made over. The new versions combine elements of lifestyle and reality with the classic talent search. The melange is no weak rag-bag, but an international killer application that, through the more successful variants, such as those belonging to the *X Factor* and *Pop Idol* franchises, constitutes a strain of widely discussed 'water cooler', or 'event' television (Holmes 2004a, 215).

While the entertainment value of the shows is high, I argue that the currency of the reinvented talent searches lies partly in their articulation of aspirational concepts of personhood that are embedded in the broader neoliberal cultural economy. They offer alluring parables of opportunity and mobility through the assured transformation of winning contestants into celebrities. Yet how democratizing is a model of life-improvement that promises passage to elite status for a few, and where does the implied value system leave the meaning of being 'ordinary'?

Rediscovering the talent show

As Bell and Hollows note, a key feature of lifestyle media is its tendency towards proliferation and hybridization (2005, 9). One reason for this is the diversity of phenomena that can be considered germane to it. At the risk of tautology, lifestyle television could be expected to accommodate any discourse that is about how lives may be lived. In practice, however, this is normally broken down to the minutiae of how individuals could elect to act in particular spheres, say fashion, interior design or cooking. Furthermore, commodity consumption is central to many shows, meaning that the focus is not the full range of conceivable ways of living, so much as ways of styling the self that are mediated by the possibilities of contemporary consumer culture. The experts who effect the refashioning of the personal link that world with the exigencies of industry production, inducing a kind of fruitful personal labour in consumption (Redden 2007).

Nonetheless, the proliferation of the makeover has been marked and has taken it beyond the purview of lifestyle *qua* leisure. Anxieties about health (e.g. *You Are What You Eat*), domestic labour (e.g. *How Clean is Your House?*), and personal finance (e.g. *Bank of Mum and Dad*) are addressed. There has also been a discernible 'behavioural' turn in British shows, many of which showcase the use of tough love to turn people around. These are not already well-intentioned consumer-citizens seeking further self-development, but apparently recalcitrant types whose inability/unwillingness to act properly distinguishes them from implied norms of personhood. They are made to stand for general life failure before their possible redemption under the tutelage of mentors. Of particular interest, in the terms presented by the shows, are: unruly children (e.g. *Supernanny*), unfeminine women (e.g. *Ladette to Lady*), unproductive and aggressive young men (e.g. *Bad Lads Army*), and single mothers (e.g. *Help! I'm a Teen Mum*).

The shifting terrain of makeover television has also seen it embrace the sphere of production. In the UK a number of small-business makeovers have run. They tend to focus on leisure-related businesses (e.g. *The Hotel Inspector*). *Ramsay's Kitchen Nightmares*, in which one of Britain's top chefs advises failing restaurateurs, is the most well known. However, it is just part of a trend towards competitive cookery in which demonstrated improvement in skill of amateur or low-level professional cooks is rewarded by a life-changing prize in the form of a top job or business opportunity. This includes three interlinked series from Jamie Oliver in which young people are trained up (*Jamie's Kitchen*; *Cutting the Apron Strings*; *Fifteen)* and also *Raymond Blanc's The Restaurant* (2007). The aspect of lifestyle at stake is not what can be done with disposable income. It is its necessary corollary; the other side of commodity culture: successful processes of selling one's labour or profiting from that of others.

The new talent shows are congruent with this expansion of lifestyle concern to the realm of work and, more broadly, personal behaviour beyond consumption. There are sound media industry grounds for extending successful formulas across topics and into new formats. Television appears to be increasingly cross-generic in pursuit of programmes that can satisfy multiple audience interests (Morris 2007, 43–4). The personal dramas created by the makeover framework guarantee conflict, resolution and the self-learning of characters in addition to the inherent interest of the topics at hand. The before/after contrast around which the narrative is built and suspense is generated guarantees change (Moseley 2000). It is no wonder then that the means/end fascination created by the makeover can breathe life into such potentially dry topics as time management or financial discipline. It is also no surprise that it can be used to resurrect the once magnificent genre of the talent show.

The new era of talent TV was heralded by *Popstars*, a public contest to find members for a pop group, which was first aired in New Zealand in 1999. After high ratings, and the launch of the group, True Bliss, Australian and British versions were quickly released, followed by numerous others around the world. The bands formed enjoyed huge exposure and instant success; though in the UK only Girls Aloud remain popular at the time of writing. Popstars was soon superseded by Pop Idol and then *X Factor* in the UK. By the mid-2000s talent shows were topping the ratings in many countries. American Idol is by far the most popular prime time series on US television (CNN 2008), and in the UK *X Factor* goes head-to-head with BBC dance show *Strictly Come Dancing* (which is the source of the international *Dancing with the Stars*) on Saturday and Sunday nights, capturing up to 80 per cent of the viewing audience between them during finals (Reality TV World 2005).

Perhaps unsurprisingly, the producers of highly similar singing shows have been involved in legal disputes about format rights. The original British season of *Pop Idol*, which ran in 2002, was even more successful than *Popstars*, launching the careers of the solo singers Gareth Gates and Will Young. However, after the first series 'Idol' was required to drop the 'Pop' from all of its titles to protect the integrity of the Popstars brand (BBC 2004). In turn, Simon Cowell, a record producer and the most famous judge on *American Idol* was the target of copyright claims by Simon Fuller (whose 19TV owns the Idol format) after Cowell launched *X Factor* with Fremantle Media. Given the history of highly similar TV talent shows, the importance of Cowell as an Idol judge, and the financial rich pickings all round, the case resulted in an out-of-court settlement (BBC 2007). All three franchises are still active internationally, and have launched numerous pop groups and solo artists.

Taken together, the shows constitute a revival of TV light entertainment, an area that infotainment (seen as all factual programming with an emphasis on entertainment value) has displaced over recent years (Bonner 2003, 20). However, on the whole the new talent shows eschew the more traditional variety form. Instead they tend to focus on a single skill in the performing arts. Contestants undertake numerous tasks to demonstrate their facility with the discipline under the watch of panel judges and mentors who are professional experts in the specified area. As a result, performances can be scrutinized closely and comparatively in line with industry criteria. This focus on single disciplines is combined with clarity in goals. The prizes for winners are real-world, well-remunerated contracts to work in the chosen field, as with *X Factor*'s UK prize of a one-million-pound recording contract. These high-stakes rewards help to focus the narratives. They also indicate that the shows act as direct routes through which successful contestants, including those who do not win but who are still able to launch entertainment careers, become commodities managed by prescribed culture industry agents (Dann 2004). In a neat and manufactured form of cross-media symbiosis, the 'stars in the making' are also manna from heaven for the convergent media of the celebrity-lifestyle complex which create content by scrutinizing week-to-week and outside-show lives of contestants. In so doing they boost the broader exposure of the performers to the point where they have viable (if often short) careers.

Transforming the talent show

The talent show is now going through a period of diversification somewhat similar to that when the makeover moved beyond interior design and personal appearance in the early 2000s. There is a proliferation of weaker versions of the hits and shows applying talent searches to disciplines beyond pop singing. Some get people competing to be a leading man/woman in musical theatre, adding acting skills into the mix. They offer auditions to find the next Maria (*How Do you Solve a Problem like Maria?*, BBC), Joseph (*Any Dream Will Do*, BBC), Sandie and Danny (*Grease is the Word*, ITV). The BBC seems to have a proclivity for dance shows, including *Dance X* and *Strictly Dance Fever*. But if the Beeb can get celebrities dancing (*Strictly Come Dancing*), ITV can get them dancing on ice (*Dancing on Ice*, ITV).

Having enlivened Saturday night entertainment, talent formulas are breaking into weekday prime time. Lifestyle talent is crossing into makeover territory. In *Interior Rivalry*, Channel 5 home makeover guru Ann Maurice stands as judge and jury not on homes themselves, but on the wannabe interior designers who would make them over. As previously mentioned, cooking television increasingly revolves around competition, with *Masterchef Goes Large* (BBC) being a good example of a population-wide talent search, and *Great British Menu* (BBC) of a celebrity-chef variant. Now we even have a canine talent show, *The Underdog Show* (BBC) where we can find Fun Lovin' Criminals' lead singer Huey pitting his pooch against a motley crew of celebrity mutts in matters of agility and obedience. And we have talent shows set in the world of business, most famously, *The Apprentice*.

These generic transformations arise from industry creativity, which itself militates against the settling of talent TV into a stable genre. Indeed, recent shows have largely been considered under the rubric of 'reality TV'. Couldry (2002, 288), for instance, considers *Popstars* to be one of the first major reality shows in the UK. Holmes regards the singing contests to be the incorporation of music television into the realm of reality programming, helping to revive an area where ratings were flagging in the form of conventional pop performance programmes, such as Top of the Pops (2004b, 151). This makes sense on various levels. Although there are celebrity versions which show known personalities struggling to perform outside their normal craft, most of the shows feature real people, and work up their ordinary status systematically. As Biressi and Nunn note with reference to American Idol, the quality of ordinariness is constructed by a bundle of recurring testamentary techniques which portray the backgrounds, friends and families and the self-commentaries of contestants (2003, 49). Combined with this is the sense that something real is happening to them. The prize of a contract means that someone really will become a performing artist and star, rather than simply play the role. There is much in common with the person-watching mode of television associated with *Big Brother* and similar formats where contestants reveal who they are to an audience that judges them through their repeated performances. Such programmes revolve around a series of unfolding events that leads to a final resolution in the moment of winning, a process that has been marked out by rituals (such as eviction) that generate, fulfil, and deny expectations of who the winner will be and how they will get there (Scannell 2002).

Similar temporal structures are even more elaborate on pop talent shows. *Idol* starts with regional auditions in the community, goes through two further audition stages, and ends up with the 'shortlist' of 10 or 12; the small number of the most talented who we get to know intimately, and who are then subjected to weekly elimination rounds (Coutas 2006, 372; Holmes 2004b, 153). Each stage allows for differences of emphasis and production, contributing to the overall narrative arc in which citizens take extraordinary journeys, one of them to the very end, while the majority return to the generalized public from which they emerged (Cowell 2004, 6).

However, the affinities between talent and reality shows do not mean that the former are derived from the latter. The talent show is a long-standing genre, and, with reality game shows, it stands alongside others which articulate the competitive sociality of capitalism. As Holmes (2007) has shown, quiz shows have provided the most enduring site for the participation of ordinary people throughout the history of television. TV has always presented a range of competition – sport, quizzes, game shows – all of which revolve around the ritualization and evaluation of competitive social behaviour (Whannel 1990). Entertainment value is easily derived from a narrative driven by questions of who will win and lose, with what costs and results. In their structuring and narrating of events, programme makers can exploit the familiar poles of risk, opportunity, chance and serendipity and how they come to bear upon a character's fortunes.

It was rather prescient of Whannel to comment nearly 20 years ago: 'it is noteworthy that television seems increasingly prepared to turn almost anything into the stuff of competition' (108). This was said before a slew of reality TV had stripped the focus of competition right back to form a new kind of popularity contest in which participants themselves, their personal qualities and ways of life as social beings, became the criteria for determining their success or failure.

As John Tulloch notes (cited in Whannel 1990, 105), all game shows have a logic of remuneration whereby a performance of knowledge or skill is exchanged for a reward. While the classic quiz show tests knowledge demonstrated in response to questions, one controversy surrounding reality game shows of the *Big Brother* type is that the merit that is being rewarded is not so clear. A great deal of the disapprobation targeted at them centres on the supposition that they valorize talentless people, thereby feeding a celebrity culture where people are famous for being famous, rather than any kind of outstanding contribution to culture (Biltereyst 2004). However, the talent show rewards achievement in artistic performance and leads to 'deserved' fame. And its reckoning, rating and ranking of skill involve more complex evaluation than the objective tests of knowledge in most quiz shows. Yet, while it deals with matters of taste, such that it is impossible to demonstrate universal right and wrong, reference to standards of performance in the area of skill is necessary. Hence, there is a need for a panel of judges to mediate discourses of evaluation in combination with the audience voting that helps to bring them to conclusion. Much of the distinctive entertainment of the genre derives from the interplay of conflicting opinions surrounding these processes.

Transforming lives

To summarize so far, the new talent searches can be viewed as part of a longstanding swathe of game-oriented programming in which ordinary people appear as participants in some form of competition and are rewarded (or not) relative to how well they do something. What those 'somethings' are, the nature of the rewards, and other elements are subject to variation. The pop talent shows also signal a kind of return to light entertainment – but in different forms from conventional variety and musical performance. The way they are structured as texts is shared with competitive variants of reality TV. In short, the potent mix of suspenseful competition (game show), person-watching (reality TV) and stories of personal transformation (lifestyle) are all added to light entertainment. The result is a supremely successful televisual hybrid.

I now want to argue that what is most distinctive about the new talent shows is their promise to change people. The reward is not to be a richer version of yourself, empowered with a cash prize to use as you will, nor enjoyment of commodities you have somehow earned. Rather, it is the exchange of your old self for a new one.

The older talent shows focused mostly on the moments of performance and their assessment by judges. In the new crop with their higher stakes, real job prizes, the central moral focus behind the ordinary contestant formats is the guarantee of a new life for the single winner. Reijinders, Rooijakkers and van Zoonen argue that *Idol* acts to place 'exemplary' members of the community on a pedestal so as to celebrate their ritual transformation. Comparing it to Dutch talent shows of the 1960s they find that whereas the older programmes offered brief weekly transformations of participants into stars, *Idol* extends the process over the entire series (2007, 287–9).

Whatever they are applied to, makeover narratives depict processes that may lead to a dramatic increase in value, whether use-value (newly loving the home or body you inhabit) or exchange-value (being able to sell that better home, impress others with that better body, etc.), which is presented in the final narrative resolution. They amount to a kind of interrogation of the person, mobilizing the evidence for their need to change, and figuring the solution (Palmer 2004, 183–5). In work-based programming, such as The Apprentice, a similar means/end logic is applied to job performance, and thus the final value of the worker who has been tested. Despite the light entertainment wrapping, talent shows also essentially involve participants learning to labour for success. The goal is to achieve a performance that brings the person to signify correctly as a subject in a given professional context, allowing them to access associated entitlements. However, the competitive reward structure determines that only a few can attain the extraordinary outcome of stardom.

The performances themselves have become embedded in an ever-increasing focus on the contestants' backgrounds, dreams, experiences, efforts, and their responses to their unfolding fates in light of their bids to transform themselves. From the very beginning to the very end participants are positioned as seekers of a better life, not simply wannabe performers. The hosts insistently use phrases like 'life-changing prize', and 'change your life forever' with reference to contestants, who duly supply their own aspirational sentiments.

Comments made around the performances in a single *X Factor* episode (of first-round auditions held in three cities) highlight how such claims constantly frame performances, and are part of programme structures, rather than being occasional asides:

[Judges travelling to auditions in an executive jet]

Louis (judge): Today I'm very optimistic because all we need is one person to walk into that room with star quality.

[At the Belfast public auditions]

Narrator: So as Simon, Sharon, Dannii and Louis take their seats, and the auditionees are all hoping they can leave their everyday life behind and hit the big time.

Auditionee 1: Instead of plastering I want to do singing well.

Auditionee 2: I can't go back to being a sales assistant.

Auditionee 3: I want to say goodbye to Tony the café owner.

[At the Newcastle public auditions]

Narrator: The *X Factor* is open to people of all ages; proving you are never too old to follow your dreams is 70-year-old shop worker, Maria.

Narrator: Next up and desperate for a "yes" is 20-year-old Sam. Growing up in a small corner of Newcastle he never thought he'd get his chance to follow his dream, until today.

[At the Birmingham public auditions]

Narrator: Outside the hopefuls continue to arrive, all hoping that the *X Factor* can change their life forever.

Narrator: The end of the day in Birmingham. One of the last contestants to see the judges is 28-year-old Natasha and her 7-year-old daughter Jasmine. Natasha needs her dream to come true more than most. ... Being a single mum means Natasha has no one to look after Jasmine, so they will be facing the judges together.

Natasha: It's really important for me to get through today, putting the past behind me and actually seeing for the future and helping myself and my daughter get a better life.

(*X Factor*, ITV1, 8 September 2007; Fremantle Media/Talkback Thames)

An important aspect of the shows is the ethos of the open talent search that will consider all comers. As the above illustrates, all kinds of ordinary folk that the nation has to offer are admitted for consideration. The one constant amid all the characters presented is that they want to live their dreams of success and leave their old lives behind. In some cases, such as Natasha's, this is presented as a pressing need.

At the beginning of series 3 the makers of *X Factor* proudly claimed their show to constitute the largest British talent search ever, with 100,000 people having auditioned. However, by series 4 the numbers had apparently doubled to 200,000 (ITV 2007). Arsenal Football Club's Emirates Stadium was used for the London auditions of 50,000.

Although the mass of have-a-go heroes are left in the audition halls, the discourse of opportunity is sustained throughout the series. It intensifies as contestant numbers reduce and the airtime given over to each personal story increases. In these later stages they have to learn and adapt to the professional requirements demanded of them in tasks. Various techniques track characters at multiple points through the overall process. They are shown in training; they are interviewed about the progress of themselves and others; they may be shown living and interacting with other contestants and mentors in the day-to-day of rehearsal, in partner and teamwork and in the social interaction between contestants that is constructed through recreational activities.

In the final of *Any Dream Will Do* (BBC1, 9 June 2007; BBC Entertainment) the three remaining contestants are still called upon to justify themselves: Why should they remain in, win the prize? They reiterate routine answers given throughout the shows and which articulate individualistic, achievement-oriented virtues liable to be approved by sections of the audience as grounds for worthiness (Reijnders et al. 2007, 289). They claim they should stay because they have a dream to fulfil, passion, self-belief, determination, faith of supporters to repay, abilities to work hard, learn from mistakes, etc. Such qualities are illustrated through footage taken from the series, charting their highs and lows. On top of the performances in the final itself, previous ones are recapped, strengths and weaknesses are assessed by judges, emotions are revisited, and intentions are renewed. In their final weekly trip (to Mallorca), the candidates reaffirm their own trajectories of life makeover. For Keith, 'It would mean everything for me to win this. From 10,000 people to be the one left standing; it's like a dream, a dream I always had when I was young, and a dream I've always had becoming a reality.' While for Lewis, 'To be in the West End. I've always said it ever since I was a little kid. ... That's what I was born to do. I worked so hard to get where I am. I feel like I am the right Joseph.' Host Graham Norton then interviews Connie Fisher, winner of the linked show, *How Do You Solve a Problem Like Maria?* His single question to her is: 'Last time you were on this stage you were a telesales girl, now you are an award-winning leading actress; in what ways has winning the role of Maria changed your life?' Both Keith and Lewis, incidentally, fail to take that final step.

It is not that previous talent shows did not express similar aspirational sentiments to some extent. Both the old and new versions revolve around the core activities of artistic performance by members of the public, followed by their rating by judges and audiences. However, different frameworks are built around these defining features. The extensive paraphernalia of person-watching and review was absent from the previous shows. Selection processes are also much more complex and sophisticated now. There has been a ratcheting up of the judging and voting aspects to the extent that they play a much more important role than in 1970s and 1980s classics like *New Faces* and *Opportunity Knocks*. In the latter (which ran with gaps from 1949 until 1990), studio audiences expressed their responses to acts through the loudness of their applause as captured in haphazard fashion by a 'clapometer'. Voting was by postcard. In the earlier series of *New Faces* (1973–88) panel judges exclusively dealt with scoring, telephone voting only being introduced towards the end of the show's life. Now, the intimate, interactive relationship between audience and the world of the show is centralized through rapidly-processed telephone and text voting, giving audience members power to help decide the destinies of contestants, while also earning huge sums for the producers to add to advertising revenue and profits made from contestants' singing and celebrity careers.

The consequences of the performance evaluation are heightened by the dramatic tearful rituals of 'selecting out'. This is the gradual elimination of candidates based on negative screening, isolating their relative failure/unpopularity and voting them off until the proverbial last person remains standing to live the dream. This is the inverse of the conventional competitive rounds of *New Faces*, in which the winners of weekly rounds (each a separate contest with assorted different contestants we hardly know) make it through to finals. Selecting out is crucial to the new shows. It emphasizes the 'all or nothing' nature of the goal, and allows for the week-to-week continuity of contestants, and thus elaboration of their fortunes in soap-opera-like through-narratives. Indeed, much of the overall airtime is chat about and with the people. This is not only an element of the main shows, but also spills over into dedicated supplementary programmes. For instance, *X Factor* is actually four programmes that are aired across ITV's channels: the main one, the results, and two chat/docusoap shows that track contestants: *The Xtra Factor* and *The X Factor 24/7*.

All this makes for a tenor distinct from the classic variety talent searches in which members of the public, or as yet undistinguished professionals, 'gave it a go', being uncoached and free to exhibit their talent as they saw fit. They often expressed irony and wit in light of audience preferences for novelty acts. The world in which singer and comedian Su Pollard was beaten by a singing dog in *Opportunity Knocks*, 1974 (BBC 2002) is a different one from that of *Idol* and *X Factor*. Although some (like 'Chico' in *X Factor*, series 2) play the joker, the new shows are concerned with professional standards in every aspect of being a performer. The tasks prescribed by judges constantly measure contestants' fitness for purpose.

The people's meritocracy

The talent show then depicts what it means to be successful in productive processes, and to earn a new kind of status as a result. The genre has grown to a point where consideration of matters of the suitability of the person that were previously implicit are now the focus of intense interest in discourses that endlessly evaluate their rightness for the role and the rewards that come with it. The narrative added value is in the processes of *lifestyling*, questions of how to be and act so as to fulfil a goal, in conforming to work demands made.

It is tempting to construe this kind of TV peopled by ordinary persons as being entertainment above all else. However, while lifestyle television in general may have muscled out some more sober kinds of factual viewing from the schedules, as Tania Lewis (2007, 292) has pointed out, it is an error to assume it has no educational rationale amid its pleasures. This is intensely pedagogic television which presents how people should act.

This returns us to the issue of the terms of participation of ordinary people in popular television and the matter of whether they can be conceptualized as democratizing. The critical questions that I would like to highlight revolve around the value of persons in a setting where they appear on condition that they must seek to change towards something better. Made over talent shows rely on a moralistic notion of enterprising selves who modify their behaviour towards an end that is invested with overriding value.

On the face of it the models of success in play are instantiations of the pervasive capitalist myth of 'making it'. Talent shows have always had a certain kind of democratizing power in that they effect social mobility. They have in quite literal ways provided mechanisms for talented but unknown performers, from Lenny

Henry to Victoria Wood, to launch careers. Although those who make the journey are few, talent shows may contribute to what Geoff Dench refers to as the 'people's meritocracy' of popular entertainment (2006, 9). As a cultural sector almost wholly responsive to demand, entertainment provides opportunities for ordinary people to earn fabulous sums irrespective of background and privileges afforded to them.

However, the intensity with which the new talent shows pitch the dream for life change, while offering high rewards to the best, would seem to articulate particular structures of feeling of an aspirational society. The discourses of success presented may be seen to advance a chronic anxiety about remaining ordinary. As Jo Littler (2003, 13) has noted the contemporary valorization of celebrity normalizes the idea that to be ordinary nowadays may actually involve the desire to become an extraordinary person, in particular, a celebrity.

The ethos of social inclusiveness claimed by *X Factor*, *Idol* and counterparts revolves around unrestricted, non-discriminatory access to opportunities, represented as democratization of life chances for those who audition. Yet there are fundamental contradictions in espousing the enfranchisement of all through *chances* to be successful, under conditions that ensure success and its entitlements remain scarce. Inevitably the shows cannot but dramatize 'how capitalism necessarily works for the few at the expense of the many' (Holmes 2004b, 158). Quite literally, what they turn into a spectacle is the commodification of labour, the selection, reward and performance management of workers on highly competitive terms. This is by definition a process in which the value of the person is instrumental. In the kind of market setting depicted, and which holds in the broader economy, people are worth not an inherent value, but the surplus value that can be derived from them by the parties that are providing and controlling the opportunities.

While the shows act as literal mechanisms of mobility, they legitimate, by their association with pleasure and optimism, a meritocratic sleight of hand: equality of opportunity amid inequality of reward. Their structures ensure that the mobility achieved is dependent upon hierarchy, as one winner takes all, monopolizing rewards and status gains. While all may give it a go, only a few make it, and they make it big. The structural corollary of the extraordinary success of the individual is mass relative failure of others. In a sense this is to be expected in a genre that depends upon the dramatic tension of competition, and which takes place in a society in which different rewards for labour are normal. However, the innovation of 'life-changing' prizes and their centrality to the shows articulates a more extreme rationality of neoliberalism. This is not just expressive of an unchanging competitive sociality of capitalism. It involves outlandish claims about the ability of markets to 'deliver' happy people.

Such rhetoric of opportunity pervades populist British political discourse. Eager to distance itself from a more brutal Thatcherism (with little sensitivity to the social consequences of markets), since its inception in 1997 the 'New' Labour government staked its progressive credentials on the claim that it will help all citizens to make the most of a market society, and create, in the electioneering words of minister Alan Milburn (2005), 'a nation based on merit, not on class' (cited in Lister 2006, 232). However, such a view of social justice favours equality of opportunity over actual material parity between citizens. The latter is the equality traditionally associated with social democratic labour and fiscal policies that effect greater social security and wider distribution of wealth than markets alone. In contrast, the main policy thrust of the supposed opportunity society of New Labour is to leave markets ('wealth creation') unhindered by regulation, while the state is considered the custodian of the human capital markets require ('education, education, education'). According to the OECD's flexibility index, the UK has the second least regulated labour market in the developed world, after the United States (Coats 2007, 132).

In her assessment of the egalitarianism expressed by the current British Labour government, Ruth Lister (2006) shows how the theories of meritocracy espoused have very little to do with equality. Businesses do not exist to deliver it. They provide employment only insofar as, and on terms that, they create profit. Meritocracy is not a 'principle of distribution of rewards' (232). Indeed, the ascription of merit is precisely a differential determination of value, such that different people putatively get 'what they are worth' in the narrow definitions of those with the power to judge and interests in doing so. In contexts where this is left to market logic (aided by the liberalization of employment laws to promote ease of hiring and firing), meritocracy promotes economic inequality (233). Indeed, a series of recent studies has suggested that inequality is increasing in the UK. A 2007 Joseph Rowntree Foundation report concludes that it is at its highest in 40 years (Dorling et al. 2007). A particular feature of modern Britain is its increasingly polarized labour market, with the dynamic knowledge economy (above all financial services) creating a wealthy elite, while the largest growth in jobs created – and related life chances – is in the low-skilled and low-paid service sector (Cruddas 2006, 205).

That is not to say the new talent shows are solely an epiphenomenon of such neoliberal social relations. There is no doubt that they combine dimensions of a range of pre-existing genres of television, including previous talent shows, and that in doing so they appeal to longstanding audience interests in spectacle, character and narrative. However, it would be equally banal to assign them the status of 'just entertainment'. The elements which make the new generation of talent TV most distinctive, principally those techniques which foreground the personal stories of success and failure, are very much embedded in a recognizable broader social world in which a great deal of moral responsibility for risk and welfare is assigned to private persons and agencies. As Couldry (2006, 8) notes, when discussing the affinities between *Big Brother* and the surveillance of worker performance in the contemporary workplace, the point is not that television simply reflects neoliberalism. Rather, the ritual expression of its norms may be thought of as a cultural fascination that enables societal reflection upon common forms of experience that are presented in displaced form.

In the new talent shows, the discourses about human potential that overlay the entertainment and provide the rationale for action are explicitly driven by the declarations of all involved that, above and beyond the joys of artistic performance, the overall meaning of participation lies in the life change to which it might lead. In this, the currency of makeover talent shows is dependent upon the kind of structural inequality that is symbolically maintained by their reward structures. The dream that is shown to come true, in spectacular, ecstatic fashion, somewhat akin to winning the lottery, is one of vaulting from one side of the hourglass economy to the other.

This is a confirmation that the myth of making it and the ethics of individual success and achievement upon which it depends, are imperatives of societies that provide many with a formal right to progress materially, but not necessarily the capacity to do so (Collinson 2003). The shows stand as a kind of magical intervention into social reality, whereby those without any of the forms of economic, educational and social capital that often determine levels of success enter a world where they are not necessary, and the dream becomes real.

Yet there is little doubt that the tears of failure that issue from other contestants' inability to live out hyped-up life chances are also very real. This counterpoint of symbolically legitimated joy and pain represents the kind of interplay between anxiety and hope that Frederic Jameson (1979) identifies in popular culture texts which contain and ultimately license social tensions of their historical moment. Having signed up to the project, unsuccessful participants have no grounds to blame the mechanism that gave them the chance.

But what of the 'rest' who have been implicitly separated out from the 'best'? While the opportunity afforded to the final lucky contestants who make something from the shows acts as a parable of social mobility, the new talent TV simultaneously represents working class life as something to be escaped from by individuals through the labour market, rather than something that can be developed by sharing the benefits of wealth creation more equitably. In pitching its dreams, it repeats the twin myths that the value of a person is purely what the market assigns to them and that they morally deserve the life that this buys them. It is the same structure of feeling articulated by a government that denies the existence of and politics of class, and instead overrides it with the high-blown rhetoric of aspiration, as though the telos of free market capitalism is to turn everyone into a millionaire. Meanwhile, social research shows that the principal goals of real ordinary people are good, stable jobs that allow them to live well in their existing communities and reference groups (Roberts 2006).

If in 'meritocracies, dignity and respect are no longer an automatic birthright', but are 'conditional and have to be earned and achieved' (Collinson 2003, 531), talent television, by commending those who can show themselves to be exceptional, provides a way of inscribing ordinary people and their lives as inferior. The new stars are valorized not for emerging as lucky representatives of 'our' pop culture (as I would argue the persons of the older talent shows were), but for their having passed over to an elite. Life transformation is not a developmental model of progress. It requires a rupture. It requires that in order to live a good life an ordinary person must break with their past, leave it behind to be their best self. Their existing life is not worth improving, only improving upon. In the midst of disparity of rewards, this beguiling, entertaining, apparently democratizing form of television consigns the 'meritless' majority to a position of no dignity and respect.

Bibliography

BBC (2002), 'Great Nottinghamians: Su Pollard', <http://www.bbc.co.uk/notting ham/features/2002/11/great_nottinghamians_su_pollard.shtml>, accessed 12 May 2008.

BBC (2004), '*Pop Idol* Mogul Sues Simon Cowell', <http://news.bbc.co.uk/go/pr/f/ r-/1/hi/entertainment/tv_and_radio/3645004.stm>, accessed 12 May 2008.

BBC (2007), '*X Factor* Copyright Case Settled', <http://news.bbc.co.uk/1/hi/ entertainment/4482216.stm>, accessed 12 May 2008.

Bell, D. and Hollows, J. (2005), 'From Television Lifestyle to Lifestyle Television', in D. Bell and J. Hollows (eds), *Ordinary Lifestyles: Popular Media, Consumption and Taste* (Maidenhead: Open University Press), pp. 1–18.

Biltereyst, D. (2004), 'The Controversy Around Reality TV in Europe', in S. Holmes and D. Jermyn (eds), *Understanding Reality Television* (London: Routledge), pp. 91–110.

Biressi, A. and Nunn, H. (2003), 'The Especially Remarkable: Celebrity and Social Mobility in Reality TV', *Mediactive* 2, 44–58.

Bonner, F. (2003), *Ordinary Television: Analyzing Popular TV* (London: Sage).

Coats, D. (2007), 'Hard Labour? The Future of Work and the Role of Public Policy', in G. Hassan (ed.), *After Blair: Politics after the New Labour Decade* (London: Lawrence and Wishart).

Collinson, D.L. (2003), 'Identities and Insecurities: Selves at Work', *Organization* 10:3, 527–47.

Couldry, N. (2002), '*Big Brother* as Ritual Event', *Television and New Media* 3:2, 283–93.

Couldry, N. (2006), 'Reality TV, or the Secret Theatre of Neo-liberalism', translation of 'La téléréauté ou le théâtre secret du néolibéralisme', *Hermès*, 44, available at <http://www.lse.ac.uk/collections/media@lse/pdf/HERMES_REALITY_TV_ ARTICLE.pdf>, accessed 12 May 2008.

Coutas, P. (2006), 'Fame, Fortune and Fantasi: *Indonesian Idol* and the New Celebrity', *Asian Journal of Communication* 16:4, 371–92.

Cowell, S. (2004), 'All Together Now! Publics and Participation in *American Idol*', *Invisible Culture* 6, 1–12.

CNN (2008), 'Football, *Idol* Lead to Historic Ratings Win', *CNN* (website), <http:// edition.cnn.com/2008/SHOWBIZ/TV/01/24/nielsens.ap/>, accessed 12 May 2008.

Cruddas, J. (2006), 'New Labour and the Withering Away of the Working Class?' in G. Dench (ed.), *The Rise and Rise of Meritocracy* (Oxford: Blackwell), pp. 205–13.

Dann, G. (2004) '*American Idol*: From the Selling of a Dream to the Selling of Nation', *Mediations* 1:1, 15–21.

Dench, G. (2006), 'Introduction: Reviewing Meritocracy', in G. Dench (ed.), *The Rise and Rise of Meritocracy* (Oxford: Blackwell), pp. 1–15.

Dorling, D., Rigby, J., Wheeler, B., Ballas, D., Thomas, B., Fahmy, E., Gordon, D. and Lupton, R. (2007), *Poverty, Wealth and Place in Britain, 1968 to 2005* (Bristol: Joseph Rowntree Foundation/Policy Press).

Dovey, J. (2000), *Freakshow: First Person Media and Factual Television* (London: Pluto Press).

Holmes, S. (2004a), '"But This Time *You* Choose!" Approaching the "Interactive" Audience in Reality TV', *International Journal of Cultural Studies* 7:2, 213–31.

Holmes, S. (2004b), 'Reality Goes Pop! Reality TV, Popular Music, and Narratives of Stardom in *Pop Idol*', *Television and New Media* 5:2, 147–72.

Holmes, S. (2007), '"The Question Is – Is it All Worth Knowing?" The Cultural Circulation of the Early British Quiz Show', *Media, Culture and Society* 29:1, 53–74.

Holmes, S. and Jermyn, D. (2004), 'Introduction: Understanding Reality TV', in S. Holmes and D. Jermyn (eds), *Understanding Reality Television* (London: Routledge), pp. 1–32.

ITV (2007), 'The Auditions Begin…', <http://www.xfactor.tv/news/article/?scid=24>, accessed 12 May 2008.

Jameson, F. (1979), 'Reification and Utopia in Mass Culture', *Social Text* 1, 130–48.

Lewis, T. (2007), '"He Needs to Face His Fears with These Five Queers!": *Queer Eye for the Straight Guy*, Makeover TV and the Lifestyle Expert', *Television & New Media* 8:4, 285–311.

Lister, R. (2006), 'Ladder of Opportunity or Engine of Inequality?', in G. Dench (ed.), *The Rise and Rise of Meritocracy* (Oxford: Blackwell), pp. 232–6.

Littler, J. (2003), 'Making Fame Ordinary: Intimacy, Reflexivity and "Keeping it Real"', *Mediactive* 2, 8–25.

Macdonald, M. (2003), *Exploring Media Discourse* (London: Arnold).

Morris, N. (2007), '"Old, New, Borrowed, Blue": Makeover Television in British Primetime', in D. Heller (ed.), *Makeover Television: Realities Remodelled* (London: I.B. Tauris), pp. 39–55.

Moseley, R. (2000), 'Makeover Takeover on British Television', *Screen* 41:3, 299–314.

Palmer, G. (2004), '"The New You": Class and Transformation in Lifestyle Television', in S. Holmes and D. Jermyn (eds), *Understanding Reality Television* (London: Routledge), pp. 173–90.

Reality TV World (2005), '*Strictly Come Dancing* Beats *X Factor* in British Finale Showdown', *Reality TV World* (website), <http://www.realitytvworld.com/news/strictly-come-dancing-beats-x-factor-in-british-finale-showdown-1006589.php>, accessed 12 May 2008.

Redden, G. (2007), 'Makeover Morality and Consumer Culture', in D. Heller (ed.), *Makeover Television: Realities Remodelled* (London: I.B. Tauris), pp. 150–64.

Reijnders, S., Rooijakkers, G. and van Zoonen, L. (2007), 'Community Spirit and Competition in *Idols*: Ritual Meanings of a TV Talent Quest', *European Journal of Communication* 22:3, 275–92.

Roberts, Y. (2006), 'Marginalised Young Men', in G. Dench (ed.), *The Rise and Rise of Meritocracy* (Oxford: Blackwell), pp. 97–104.

Scannell, P. (2002), '*Big Brother* as a Television Event', *Television and New Media* 3:3, 271–82.

Taylor, L. (2002), 'From Ways of Life to Lifestyle: The "Ordinari-ization" of British Gardening Lifestyle Television', *European Journal of Communication* 17:4, 479–93.

Whannel, G. (1990), 'Winner Takes All: Competition', in A. Goodwin and G. Whannel (eds), *Understanding Television* (London: Routledge), pp. 103–14.

Chapter 11

Masculine Makeovers: Lifestyle Television, Metrosexuals and Real Blokes

Buck Clifford Rosenberg

This chapter focuses on connections between lifestyle television and representations of masculinity. I argue that contemporary masculinity is in constant transformation and that makeover and lifestyle television play a role in redefining it. I examine and compare two case studies of makeover television which deal with questions of masculinity. The first is the American programme *Queer Eye for the Straight Guy* (hereafter *Queer Eye*), and the second is Scott Cam, a celebrity carpenter and host of numerous Australian makeover television programmes.

I believe that *Queer Eye* promotes a transformation of traditional masculinity. It transforms uncouth and unreflexive men into hip metrosexuals: 'new men' interested in their appearance and emotions. It promotes the 'new man' rhetoric in a period when traditional masculinity is thought to be in crisis. This perceived state of crisis, and the development of the 'new man', have resulted in a small programming backlash in which the aim is to reclaim traditional masculinity. The second case study examines this backlash through the figure of TV carpenter Scott Cam, star of Australian home makeover shows *Backyard Blitz* and *Renovation Rescue*. Indeed Cam represents what might be regarded as the 'backlash man'. He promotes Do-It-Yourself (DIY) home-improvement as men's work, as a means for men to reclaim their 'true' masculinity. Cam plays the role of the working class man whose masculinity is bound to physical labour, and a not yet redundant Australian national identity. This working class masculinity is the very masculinity which *Queer Eye* works upon, and seeks to transform, if not erase. Cam is aware of this threat of erasure. His response, contra *Queer Eye*, is to offer lessons in the performance of traditional masculinity that aim to maintain at least the appearance of this threatened identity. In short my intention is to examine the shifting nature of masculinity and the role played by lifestyle and makeover television – and those in its service – notably *Queer Eye*'s lifestyle specialists, and Australia's DIY guru, TV carpenter Scott Cam.

Masculine crises and the 'new man'

In recent decades, traditional masculinity can be understood as being if not in crisis, at least in transition. By traditional masculinity I mean a type of masculinity based on physical strength, resourcefulness, stoicism and pragmatism, and frequently, physical labour. In this way it overlaps with working class masculinity. But in recent decades, this traditional masculinity has been fractured by two key forces. The first was second wave feminism which triggered numerous social and political changes (see Caine and Pringle 1995). The second was the transformation of the labour market, both in response to second wave feminism, but more importantly, global capitalism (see Cohn 2000; Harvey 1990). The de-industrialization process since the 1970s has seen the manufacturing sector decline to be replaced by an increasingly feminized service sector. This reduction in traditional masculine employment has reduced the spaces in which traditional masculinity can be displayed and hence learned by the next generation of men.

James Heartfield (2002) offers three general views regarding the crisis of masculinity. The first characterizes masculinity as intrinsically pathological, a deviant identity, in constant need of management and correction. The second refers to elegiac accounts of masculine defeat, such as Susan Faludi's *Stiffed: The Betrayal of the Modern Man* (1999). These sympathetic accounts see men as victims of social forces out of their control such as the collapse of male dominated industries as mentioned above. Heartfield's third perspective might be described as the sceptical. This perspective calls into question the actuality of a masculinity crisis, notably by feminists who point out that men still have disproportionate wealth, authority and power (Heartfield 2002, 8–10). But Heartfield follows the second view, arguing that rather than men losing power to women, both men and women have lost power to capital. He writes: 'The cumulative defeats inflicted upon working class organisations in the 1980s and 90s have created a condition in which working class subjectivity has been diminished. The crisis is not one of masculinity, but one of the working class' (Heartfield 2002, 3). Whilst the working class has been fragmented and reconfigured in recent decades, masculinity – in particular the traditional working class variety – has been, and continues to be, transformed. These changes have led to new definitions of masculinity amongst which is the 'new man' or what is called in Australia, the 'SNAG': the Sensitive New Age Guy.

This 'SNAG' or 'new man' was seen as the lightning rod to transform gender relations or at least erase gender inequality. This new man was supposedly in touch with his feelings, and considerate of women: he cooked, cleaned and changed diapers (see Singleton and Maher 2004, 228). But does such a man exist? Singleton and Maher's project 'Generation X' focusing on heterosexual men born in 1965–79 suggests not. They write that 'Despite married women's increased labour force participation and the advent of second-wave feminism, domestic equality between men and women has not been achieved' (Singleton and Maher 2004, 228). Anthony McMahon agrees: 'In practice men have not assumed domestic responsibilities at a rate commensurate with women's entry into the paid workforce. The rhetoric has changed but a major social transition has not occurred. The way in which New Man rhetoric manages to mystify this fact is very revealing' (McMahon 1998, 148).

Recently the new man rhetoric has morphed into the image of the metrosexual. I now turn to examine *Queer Eye*'s role in promoting this newly aestheticized masculinity.

Becoming metrosexual: *Queer Eye* and the makeover of masculinity

Metrosexuality can be regarded as the next stage of 'transitional masculinity' developed within the Australian SNAG. Toby Miller notes the emergence of this shift in masculinity in the United States, which took similar form in Australia. He writes that by the 1990s, 'The variegated male body was up for grabs as both sexual icon and commodity consumer, in ways that borrowed from but also exceeded the longstanding commodification of the male form' (Miller 2006, 106). But whereas SNAGs emerged within the popular debates about gender equality in divisions of heterosexual domestic labour, the metrosexual is integrated into capitalism in a different way. He is fundamentally integrated into consumer culture. Whereas traditional men consumed given products, such as beer and cars, metrosexual men became *consumers*. They became targeted by marketers and advertisers, notably for grooming and fashion products, and other means to aestheticize their bodies in the same way women have for generations. Men are now 'subjected to new forms of governance and commodification' (Miller 2006, 106). The metrosexual constitutes 'a neoliberal subject who must govern himself as a new aesthete, generated from shifting relations of power and finance' (Miller 2006, 112). *Queer Eye* reflects and promotes this new type of neoliberal consumer man, and uses gay men as the template.

Queer Eye for the Straight Guy targeted the connection between personal and domestic style and traditional masculine behaviour and aimed to encourage men to transform their lives through aesthetic transformation and commodity consumption. In each episode five hip gay men, the 'Fab Five' – Carson (fashion savant), Kyan (grooming), Thom (design doctor), Jai (culture vulture) and Ted (food and wine connoisseur) (bravotv.com) – enter the life and home of a straight man. From here they proceed to mock his aesthetic choice of clothes and decor, and demonstrate horror at his lack of hygiene and personal care, before transforming him into a stylish metrosexual hipster and his home into a hip pad. The man is re-educated in how and where to shop, how to cook, and how to apply the correct moisturizer, all of which turn him into a 'better' person.

Queer Eye brought together three key ingredients in the reshaping of conventional or traditional masculinity: class, sexuality and consumer culture. The first relates to the reshaping of the relationship between traditional masculinity and the working class. The working classes, and any middle class 'slackers' who resembled them were key targets for metrosexualization. As Miller states, 'Cosmopolitan queers descend on these hapless bridge-and-tunnel people … [these] male losers in the suburban reaches of the tristate area (New York, New Jersey, and Connecticut) who are awaiting a transformation from ordinary men into hipsters' (Miller 2006, 115). It is generally upon the bodies and homes of such men that the *Queer Eye* team work. In many ways they seek to erase working class masculinity, seen as uncouth, potentially violent and most definitely vulgar, and replace it with a stylish metrosexual middle class masculinity (see also Allatson 2006, on *Queer Eye* and working class men). Such straight and frequently working class bodies used in the programme are, according to Dennis W. Allen, the 'unmarked male'. He writes, 'Here man's "natural" body is imagined literally, as a body seemingly untouched by civilization: badly groomed and unkempt, living in squalor' (2006, 19). The hosts heap scorn upon these uncivilized working class men. For example, when Carson, discussing a makeover recipient's belongings, states, 'Do you have bad credit or just bad taste?' (Hart 2004, 247), he is linking working class economic realities to poor aesthetic judgement. With the Fab Five's help, such men will be transformed, lifted out of this world of squalor and poor taste. *Queer Eye*, then, functions as a civilizing and colonizing mission, led by gay men in the service of consumer capitalism. Their aim is to teach traditional straight men – both uncooperative middle class slackers and the working class – how to be modern civilized neoliberal subjects, through implementing new forms of masculinities based upon the purchase of certain grooming and fashion products.

Queer Eye operates upon the tension and distinction between different sexualized and classed masculinities: the queer, urban, middle class masculinity of the presenters, and the traditional masculinity of the straight, often working class, makeover recipients. As Berila and Choudhuri write, it 'brings queerness into mainstream television space and into the homes of both straight and queer viewers, creating a kind of contact zone that potentially disrupts heteronormative assumptions' (Berila and Choudhuri 2005, 6). Yet it emits mixed messages about such masculinities. As Hart notes, the structure of the programme 'continues to remind viewers that straight guys and gay guys are classified into separate categories, even as the episodes attempt, at least on the surface, to eradicate such distinctions' (Hart 2004, 251).

This surface attempt at eradicating the straight/gay distinction, or more correctly its blurring, however, only serves heterosexual masculinity. Straight men's masculinity is allowed to be transformed through moisturizer and pinot noir, but for gay men, their identity remains static. They remain pinned to the stereotype that gay men innately possess knowledge about style, taste and culture, a stereotype firmly upheld by *Queer Eye*. Indeed Miller regards *Queer Eye* as signifying 'the professionalization of queerness as a form of management consultancy for conventional masculinity, brought in to improve efficiency and effectiveness' (Miller 2006, 116). Gay men, consequently, become typecast as aesthetic service providers in the new economy, guiding the mainstream (read heterosexual) in matters of taste, style and culture. And whilst Hart suggests that such representations of gay cultural capital can be read as 'implicitly suggesting that gay men are actually superior – rather than inferior – to heterosexuals' (Hart 2004, 246), their place within popular culture remains dependent upon providing advice on consumption and not upon their claims to any real difference from the mainstream.

Queer Eye aims not to turn straight men into gay men, but to transform traditional masculinity. It proposes cosmetic changes to the recipient's traditional masculinity, often with the aim of impressing the women in their lives. Wives and girlfriends are central to the programme; they provide the final arbitration regarding the makeover.

Far from 'queering' gender or sexuality, or significantly blurring the boundaries between straight and gay, Berila and Choudhuri write that 'the entire purpose of the show is to uphold the heteronormative imperative' (2005, 8). Hence the recreation of an aestheticized, and more 'sensitive', metrosexual man will make him more attractive to heterosexual women (and incidentally, gay men) and a better partner/ husband than before the makeover.

Such a transformation will then (magically) lead to better outcomes for both the men and women, in the form of 'happiness'. Happiness is the essence of makeover television programmes. They rely on the formula: happiness equals self-transformation through consumption (see Deery 2006, 160). Like most makeover programmes, *Queer Eye* functions to sell products and services (see Deery 2006; Palmer 2007; Redden 2007) but also promotes 'the beneficial effects of consumption itself' (Allen 2006, 7), whereby consumption is held in moral terms as 'a right action leading to improvement' (Redden 2007, 152). But for Hart, *Queer Eye* has an added component to this magical happiness elixir: gay men. He writes: 'it is only gay men who know what it really takes for straight men to be truly happy or to truly please the women they love' (Hart 2004, 251).

The centrality of consumption is presented as crucial to becoming a new objectified man. The show operates from the acknowledgement that gay masculinity is somehow already commodified, defined through particular cultural commodities. 'Gayness' itself is commodified as 'a lifestyle of practices that can be adopted, discarded, and redisposed promiscuously' (Miller 2006, 115), used for the purposes of making over one's masculinity for instrumental means, such as heterosexual dating or improving marital relations. Now it's the straight man's turn to be commodified. Allen argues that if *Queer Eye* can be read as a means by which straight men become more like gay men, it is because 'it submits the straight men to a logic of self-commodification with which gay men are already familiar' (2006, 15). The relentless emphasis on self-presentation, on grooming and clothing 'is to make him [the straight guy] fully conscious of himself as an object' (Allen 2006, 15).

Queer Eye demonstrates that being a commodified metrosexual man requires constant governance of actions, behaviour and consumption. It requires what Berila and Choudhuri refer to as 'daily maintenance rituals', which mirror those to which women have long been subjected. They write:

> According to *Queer Eye*, masculinity now requires similar expenditures of time and energy in order to produce docile bodies. Men on the show spend a great deal of time in front of mirrors, and in salons, malls, and kitchens. Being a 'successful' or 'attractive' man, in other words, means policing one's body through daily rituals, that require participating in conspicuous consumption, so that one has the right accessories and accoutrements to 'produce' and maintain this sensitive masculinity. (Berila and Choudhuri 2005, 25)

Labour, then, is crucial for this metrosexual masculinity. Yet it is a particularly gendered type of labour. Like the new man/SNAG of the 1980s and 1990s, who was defined by his (supposed) uptake of feminized domestic labour, so too the metrosexual. *Queer Eye* tells men that a new type of feminized labour must be incorporated into their understandings of masculinity. These include care of the self regimes, the constant maintenance of appearance through grooming techniques, and consuming and wearing appropriate (read: stylish) clothing. Such feminized aesthetic labour, like domestic labour, must be incorporated into men's constructions of self and masculinity, transforming them in the process. This feminized labour is one of the few forms of labour witnessed on *Queer Eye*. We see some labour required for self-presentation, such as advertorial scenes on how to apply face creams or correct shaving techniques, but others are missing. For example, unlike most home-renovation programmes, the home-makeover segment in *Queer Eye* never shows any form of labour. Time is compressed into a before shot of the usually messy homes, and the after shots of the now stylish decor. We do not see the Fab Five transforming the houses, nor the hidden labour of the off-screen *Queer Eye* staff that actually do the work (Berila and Choudhuri 2005, 27). *Queer Eye* makeovers appear as if by magic, a consumerist fantasy where even money, in the form of the price of goods, is removed. This is a modern day fairytale (Allen 2006, 9–10; Palmer 2007) that produces Prince Charming.

Whilst the *Queer Eye* referred to above was the original American show, it was screened across various parts of the globe, including Australia, where it averaged a prime time audience of 1.5 million viewers during 2003 (Dale 2004). These successful ratings figures for the American version did not translate into high ratings for the soon-to-follow Australian version, however. The Australian *Queer Eye* began reasonably strongly with 900,000 viewers but shrank to 725,000 by week two (Hornery 2005) then plummeted to 230,000 by the third week (Anon 2005) after which it was axed. But despite the relative success of the American *Queer Eye* on Australian screens, many examples of traditional masculinity remain. I will now turn to just such an example: Scott Cam.

Performing the bloke: Scott Cam and the traditional masculine backlash

Scott Cam is the Australian TV carpenter who seeks to repel the advances of SNAGs and *Queer Eye*'s middle class metrosexuality, by promoting DIY as a means through which men can reclaim their traditional masculinity. Anything but Prince Charming, Cam attempts to reignite this masculinity in an interesting way. Like *Queer Eye*, he draws upon a form of feminized labour mentioned above. He suggests men can reclaim their traditional masculinity through makeover and performance, by highlighting the importance of how 'real' men should look and what they should wear. But in so doing he calls into question his initial aims of a return to traditional masculinity.

The makeover has traditionally been regarded as a feminine practice, a fairy tale through which ordinary women can become Cinderellas. It has become fundamental to Western culture, in no small part due to its long history on television in programmes such as *Queen For a Day* (Watts 2006), *Glamour Girl* (Cassidy 2006) and *My Fair Lady* (Harrison 1994). But whereas makeovers of the past featured cosmetics, clothes and other commodities, today's versions go further. Not content with just working on the surface, they now cut into (mostly) women's bodies via plastic surgery, on programmes such as *Extreme Makeover* or *The Swan* (see Deery 2006). Moseley has written on the feminization of prime time and lifestyle television's focus upon the more 'feminine' concerns of the private and the personal (Moseley 2001). Makeovers were a prominent feature on daytime television, notably in segments on talk shows such as *Oprah*. With the transformation gendered as feminine, makeover television of any ilk, be it the male makeovers of *Queer Eye* or home-makeover programmes, all feature something of this Cinderella-esque fairy tale. Yet even within this feminized genre, traditional masculinity endures, notably in Australia, in figures such as Scott Cam.

Cam is a forty-something qualified carpenter-tradesman (or 'tradie'), and the star of numerous Australian lifestyle programmes. Cam got his first big break on *Burke's Backyard*, the first Australian 'lifestyle' programme, which as Bonner claims, replaced the more 'infotainment' programming of the 1970s (Bonner 2000). This programme was one of the longest running in Australian television history, holding down a prime time slot on Friday evenings for nearly two decades. Cam's onscreen charisma worked so well on *Burke's Backyard* that it led to his hosting three more lifestyle television programmes. He became co-host of *Backyard Blitz*, with former male-revue star Jamie Durie. This successful programme had the same format as *Ground Force*, which saw people's often underused backyards converted into lifestyle entertainment spaces. Incidentally, *Backyard Blitz* was regarded as having so close a format to the Australian version of *Ground Force* that legal action was undertaken (Bonner 2003, 82, 180–1). Cam was then lead host on *Renovation Rescue*. This programme combined both interior design and backyard makeovers for recipients deemed 'worthy', namely through their commitment to others such as volunteerism, or because of illness.

The success of these makeover television roles secured Cam a more unconventional position. This was as prime host of *Our Place*, a live-to-air variety cum home-lifestyle programme. It fused a studio audience, on-stage segments and a band with home-, pet- and self-related advice from experts, as well as lifestyle television's usual product placements. Unfortunately for Cam, this programme did not last a full season and was cancelled within a matter of weeks, leaving Cam to continue with *Backyard Blitz*. Despite *Our Place* failing to catch on, Cam had by now become acknowledged as a leading figure in Australian television. Indeed he became so ubiquitous that on an internet forum discussing Australian television one punter asked whether Scott Cam was the new Eddie McGuire: 'Seems like this guy is popping up more than Eddie Everywhere' ('Chock', Aussie Phorums 2005). This was in reference to Eddie 'Everywhere' McGuire, host of *Who Wants to be a Millionaire*, *The Footy Show*, Australian Rules Football TV commentator and just about any TV special Channel Nine has to offer.

Cam displays all the stereotypical characteristics of the traditional archetypal Australian man (see Ward 1958; White 1981). He is macho, white (Anglo-Celtic) and working class, demonstrated by his accent and impudent yet jocund manner. He is part 'larrikin' – a loud-mouthed, witty, performative risk taker – and part 'ocker' – unreflexive, boorish and bigoted (see Rickard 1998), two identities which have historically characterized Australian traditional/working class masculinity. Cam positions himself, and others position him, as a working class icon. For example, in the Archibald's – Australia's premier art prize for portraiture – Scott Cam was the subject of a category winner. Artist Michael Mucci's *Working Class Man*, a realist portrait of Cam, won the Packing Room Prize, awarded by those in the gallery storeroom who work setting up the annual exhibition. Mucci, a former high school classmate of Cam, claimed he wanted to capture the essence of a working class man. He claimed, 'I've titled the painting "A working class man" because that is exactly how Scott likes to be known so that is exactly how I painted him' (Mucci, quoted in Anon 2006).

His working class background as a 'tradie' positions Cam as an expert with the authority and legitimacy to dispense knowledge. The 'tradie' also possesses a unique form of working class identity. For 'tradies' like Cam are part of an 'elite', quasi-professional fragment of the working class distinguished by their high-earning potential, guild-like creative rights, skill and relative autonomy. Nonetheless, despite or perhaps because of these qualities, they abstain from climbing the social ladder. Their very freedom from the economic and employment constraints of Marx's more 'alienated' working class enables them simultaneously to be a central, albeit ambivalent, symbol of that class. This combination of creative freedom, relative autonomy and symbolic centrality has given them a certain privileged cultural freedom. Because they choose to remain within the working class culture, they become cultural heroes by abstaining from middle class pretension, for remaining 'real' people. Conversely, they gain a much cherished contempt from the middle classes, who deride them precisely because they choose to remain 'vulgar'. Yet, as Bourdieu would argue, these 'tradies' are not as free as their position within the capitalist economy might suggest, as their 'habitus' – their class-based enculturation – still impacts upon their cultural presents and futures (1984). Cam's 'tradie' background provides him with some 'working class honesty', or authenticity, where his on-screen persona appears unmediated and unconstructed. This functions to reduce the disjuncture between television's encodings and the viewers decoding practices. Nonetheless, despite Cam's unpretentious 'honest bloke' persona on screen, this becomes muddied within his DIY/masculinity manual where he reveals an interest in concepts of play and performance when it comes to DIY practice.

Class and masculinity are inextricably linked in Cam's DIY/masculinity manual, *Scott Cam's Home Maintenance for Knuckleheads* (2003). Against a back drop of de-industrialization and declining working class masculine spaces, Cam has developed this manual as a reaction against the 'new man'. It seeks to re-establish traditional (working class) masculinity, in opposition to the SNAGs and the middle class metrosexual agenda evident on *Queer Eye*. Cam's mission is to get men to reignite their traditional masculinity through learning DIY handyman skills. He writes:

> There really are too many sensitive New Age guys out there these days and too many girls looking after these blokes. The only place for a SNAG is between two bits of white bread with a pile of tommy [ketchup] and heaps of salt … Its time to stand up and be counted. Go back to the old days where blokes were blokes, when everyone had a shed with the full tool kit … As soon as there was a drama, Dad would go straight to the shed, sort the problem, and all the kids would look up at him with admiration. (Cam 2003, 6)

Cam laments the decline of traditional masculinity, and is openly nostalgic for a time when men were 'real' and knew how to take charge in any given situation. As he proclaims: 'This little book is going to be the start of the revolution … The SNAG is old news' (Cam 2003, 7). Scott Cam, then, is similar to the pre-makeover working class participants from *Queer Eye*. Yet unlike such men, who eventually succumb to their transformation, Cam positions himself as a beacon of resistance against the processes of metrosexualization.

Cam operates within a heteronormative and, unlike *Queer Eye*, homophobic framework. One of his co-hosts on *Renovation Rescue* was Peter Everett, a slightly camp yet 'unthreatening' host, far from the 'over-the-top' gay stereotype portrayed by Carson on *Queer Eye*. Throughout the programme Cam would subtly critique Everett's masculinity through what was meant to be fun and friendly sexual innuendo, but which had a homophobic subtext. The producers aided Cam in this process. For example, in one episode, we witness Everett, who also dabbles with design on the show, engaged in the production of a painting. As the programme goes into a commercial break we see a preview of the next scene. Cam is standing with a painter's palette and we hear a voice-over which claims that Cam 'gets in touch with his feminine side', in reference to Everett being engaged in an 'un-masculine', and hence 'queer' task. Cam then proceeds to destroy Everett's work by pouring paint over the canvas in what is supposedly a moment of hilarity, but is really a form of symbolic violence. In this very same episode, which has a musical theme, both Cam and Everett dress as the male members of ABBA. They are shown emerging in costume from two separate toilets, with Cam emerging from a clearly marked male toilet, and Everett from a clearly marked female toilet, making further links between Everett's 'queerness' and feminized behaviour. This homophobia was continued in Cam's DIY manual, in which he refers to gay men as 'rough putters', but where he also performs an unconvincing politically correct acceptance of their sexual choice. As he notes of gay men in his pub, a traditionally masculine space: 'The two fellas who putt out of the rough are great blokes who I get on with, no problem. Each to his own' (Cam 2003, 176).

As we saw in *Queer Eye* masculinity could be transformed through certain practices, notably consumption. The consumption of commodities, however, far from revealing an essential identity, illuminates the essential performativity of identity, including gender. In *Gender Trouble* (1999), Judith Butler argues that gender is a performative act, that gender:

> ought not be construed as a stable identity or locus of agency from which various acts follow: rather, gender is an identity tenuously constituted in time, instituted in an exterior space through a *stylized repetition of acts*. The effect of gender is produced through the stylization of the body and, hence, must be understood as the mundane way in which bodily gestures, movements, and styles of various kinds constitute the illusion of an abiding gendered self. (Butler 1999, 179)

This 'stylized repetition of acts' is crucial in understanding how Cam approaches the re-traditionalization of masculinity through teaching men DIY, whether through television or books. Cam is not so concerned with the actual teaching of traditional masculine practices, but with performative acts of traditional masculinity. This brings to mind Michael Herzfeld's anthropological account of the masculine performances of 'Glendiot' village men, from the mountains of Crete. For these villagers

> there is less focus on "being a good man" [a SNAG] than on "being *good at* being a
> man" – a stance that stresses *performative excellence*, the ability to foreground manhood
> by means of deeds that strikingly "speak for themselves" ... instead of noticing *what* men
> do, Glendiots focus their attention on *how* the act is performed. (Herzfeld 1985, 16)

Cam's task on his makeover television programmes, and especially in his DIY
manual, is to teach men how to be good at the performance of traditional masculinity,
a space where they can immerse themselves in Butler's 'stylized repetition of acts'.
Here they can reconnect with traditional masculinity, what Cam sees as 'true'
masculinity.

But whilst Cam may be unhappy with the increasing embourgeoisement of the
working and lower middle classes and its impact on Australian masculinity, this
does not mean he believes DIY is the ultimate solution. Scott Cam himself knows
DIY to be a performative, even hyper-performative practice by acknowledging that
it offers a space for theatrical performativity. He positions DIY in this theatricality
by outlining the importance of appearance. For Cam, the actual doing of DIY is not
the whole point. What is important is that one looks the part. Traditional masculinity
then, does not necessarily have to be reclaimed through action, but through *intended*
action, which requires an aesthetic makeover. One needs to wear a specific symbolic
costume, for in this performance one needs to pass, to be convincing in the role of
'handyman'. Cam says:

> If you're going to fix things around the house, you have to look the part. In summer wear
> a flanno [checkered flannelette] shirt (cut the sleeves off at the elbow), work shorts (make
> sure they've been washed 15 times before their first outing), one pair of footy socks ...
> and elastic-sided brown work boots. (2003, 10)

Hence the theatricality of the performance must be pursued to its full extent through
the adoption of this costume – the working class 'tradie' uniform – which possesses
transformative powers, to enable the SNAG to metamorphose into the traditional
male. This costume operates in similar ways to the 'magical transformation' inherent
within commodity consumption displayed on *Queer Eye*.

Costume work also plays an integral role within Cam's commodification of
his commercial self. Cam advertises for Bisley, a company that sells work-related
clothes, notably for working class manual labour occupations. It takes its name from
an English town which once hosted recreational shooting competitions, and employs
the image of the boar 'which symbolizes the strong resilient nature of the Workwear
we make' (bisleyworkwear.com). Cam is a perfect fit for this company, for he exudes
strength and resilience as evidenced by his well-built physique, his tradesman skills
and his resistance to middle class metrosexualization. Cam, however, does not just
put his name and face to the product. He reproduces and commodifies narratives of
himself, utilizing stories from his own experience. This mirrors the process used
in his DIY/masculinity manual where he re-tells stories of his own adventures and
people he has met and worked with throughout his life. For example, on a radio
advertisement to sell Bisley clothing, he states:

G'day Scott Cam here from Bisley. Now I've seen all sorts of things on the worksite. I've seen an apprentice build himself into a cupboard; I've seen an older bloke nail-gun his boot to the floor and I've seen a plumber ride a sheet of tin down a two-storey roof like a surfboard. I tell you what I cacked myself [laughed hard]! But I've never seen anyone complain about their Bisley workwear. It's good reliable stuff. (Bisleyworkwear.com)

Clearly wearing the right clothes helps the job get done. But whether or not such narratives are written or remembered, it is Cam's performance which is crucial. The character of 'Cam' – the hyper-masculine TV carpenter – is continuous, it remains constant, unchanging from television, to book, to advertisement. Such commodification sees 'Cam' forever reproducible, continually deployed to sell products which overlap with the lifestyle and working class masculinity he projects.

With the promotion of this traditional masculine costume (and where to get it), we can witness a reversal of the *Queer Eye* process. Rather than a makeover *from* working classness to metrosexuality, Cam plans to turn SNAG consumers *back* into 'real men'. The adoption of the working class 'tradie' costume enables middle class men to reclaim an historically determined Australian working class masculinity. But whilst consumption still underpins this transformation, the items crucial to this costume are far removed in terms of status and cost from the high-end fashion offered on *Queer Eye*, and are totally cosmetics-free. In this way they are not part of a 'makeover' but represent a return to an essential masculinity.

The need for men to engage in makeovers reflects the similarities between *Queer Eye* and Scott Cam. *Queer Eye* seeks to reconfigure masculinity through consumption which includes the purchase of stylish clothes. This emphasis on clothing and appearance in *Queer Eye*, I have noted, requires the employment of what has been traditionally termed feminine labour. And yet Cam too employs this 'feminine labour' by drawing attention to appearance in order to reclaim traditional masculinity. As a result Cam's reliance upon performativity unsettles and undermines his ambition to reignite traditional masculinity.

Both *Queer Eye* and Scott Cam demonstrate the instability of contemporary masculinity. Cultural and economic forces have produced a masculinity which is unsure of its future, but cannot return home. It constitutes a diasporic masculinity, where some men are forever unsettled in this new gender territory and seek a return to the traditional masculine 'homeland'. Yet, as Cam demonstrates in his emphasis on performativity, they are forever aware that despite visits 'home', a full return is impossible, for that 'homeland' no longer exists. To compound matters, men must increasingly submit themselves to the logic of consumer capitalism and self-governance which transforms them into commodified neoliberal middle class subjects.

Bibliography

Allatson, P. (2006), 'Making Queer for the United States of Empire', *Australian Humanities Review* 38 (April).

Allen, D.W. (2006), 'Making Over Masculinity: A Queer "I" for the Straight Guy', *Genders* 44.

Anon (2005), 'Queer Eye Axed', *The Age* [website] (25 February 2005), <http://www.theage.com.au/news/TV--Radio/Queer-Eye-axed/2005/02/25/1109180086381.html>, accessed 8 February 2008.

Anon (2006), 'Artist's "Working Class Man" Wins Packer's Prize', *ABC News Online* (updated 16 March 2006), <http://www.abc.net.au/news/newsitems/200603/s1593186.html>, accessed 18 January 2007.

Aussie Phorums (2005), 'Scott Cam – the New Eddie McGuire?', <http://phorums.com.au/showthread.php?t=101380>, sourced 18 December 2007.

Berila, B. and Choudhuri, D.D. (2005), 'Metrosexuality the Middle Class Way: Exploring Race, Class, and Gender in *Queer Eye for the Straight Guy*', *Genders* 42.

Bisley Workwear, 'About Us', <http://www.bisleyworkwear.com.au/www/188/1001127/displayarticle/1001239.html>, accessed 18 December 2007.

Bonner, F. (2000), 'Lifestyle Programs: "No Choice But to Choose"', in G. Turner and S. Cunningham (eds), *The Australian TV Book* (St Leonards, NSW: Allen & Unwin).

Bonner, F. (2003), *Ordinary Television: Analyzing Popular TV* (London: Sage).

Bourdieu, P. (1984), *Distinction: A Social Critique of the Judgement of Taste*, trans. R. Nice (London: Routledge).

Bravo TV (no date), <http://www.bravotv.com/Queer_Eye/bios>, accessed 28 January 2008.

Butler, J. (1999), *Gender Trouble: Feminism and the Subversion of Identity*, 10th Anniversary Edition (New York and London: Routledge).

Caine, B. and Pringle, R. (eds) (1995), *Transitions: New Australian Feminisms* (St Leonards, NSW: Allen & Unwin).

Cam, S. (2003), *Scott Cam's Home Maintenance for Knuckleheads* (Sydney: Murdoch Books).

Cassidy, M.F. (2006), 'The Cinderella Makeover: Glamour Girl, Television Misery Shows, and 1950s Femininity', in D. Heller (ed.), *The Great American Makeover: Television, History, Nation* (New York: Palgrave Macmillan).

Cohn, T.H. (2000), *Global Political Economy: Theory and Practice* (New York: Longman).

Dale, D. (2004), 'Viewers Turn a Queer Eye on Reality', *Sydney Morning Herald* [website] (4 February 2004), <http://www.smh.com.au/articles/2004/02/03/1075776062148.html>, accessed 8 February 2008.

Deery, J. (2006), 'Interior Design: Commodifying Self and Place in *Extreme Makeover*, *Extreme Makeover: Home Edition*, and *The Swan*', in D. Heller (ed.), *The Great American Makeover: Television, History, Nation* (New York: Palgrave Macmillan).

Faludi, S. (1999), *Stiffed: The Betrayal of the Modern Man* (London: Chatto & Windus).

Harrison, T. (1994), *The Australian Film and Television Companion* (East Roseville, NSW: Simon & Schuster).

Hart, K.-P.R. (2004), 'We're Here, We're Queer – and We're Better Than You: The Representational Superiority of Gay Men to Heterosexuals on *Queer Eye for the Straight Guy*', *The Journal of Men's Studies* 12:3, 241–53.

Harvey, D. (1990), *The Condition of Postmodernity* (Oxford: Blackwell).

Heartfield, J. (2002), 'There is No Masculinity Crisis', *Genders* 35.

Heller, D. (ed.) (2006), *The Great American Makeover: Television, History, Nation* (New York: Palgrave Macmillan).

Heller, D. (ed.) (2007), *Makeover Television: Realities Remodelled* (London and New York: I.B. Tauris).

Herzfeld, M. (1985), *The Poetics of Manhood: Contest and Identity in a Cretan Mountain Village* (Princeton: Princeton University Press).

Hoggart, R. (1957), *The Uses of Literacy: Aspects of Working-Class Life with Special Reference to Publications and Entertainments* (Harmondsworth: Penguin).

Hornery, A. (2005), 'Aussie Queer Eye a Big Turn-off for Advertisers', *Sydney Morning Herald* [website] (19 February 2005), <http://www.smh.com.au/news/TV--Radio/Aussie-Queer-Eye-a-big-turnoff-for-advertisers/2005/02/18/1108709437657.html>, accessed 8 February 2008.

McMahon, A. (1998), 'Blokus Domesticus: The Sensitive New Age Guy in Australia', *Journal of Australian Studies* 56, 147–57.

Miller, T. (2006), 'Metrosexuality: See the Bright Light of Commodification Shine! Watch Yanqui Masculinity Made Over', in D. Heller (ed.), *The Great American Makeover: Television, History, Nation* (New York: Palgrave Macmillan).

Moseley, R. (2001), 'Real Lads Do Cook … But Some Things are Still Hard to Talk About: The Gendering of 8–9', in C. Brunsdon, C. Johnson, R. Moseley and H. Wheatley, 'Factual Entertainment on British Television: The Midlands TV Research Group's "8–9 Project"', *European Journal of Cultural Studies*, 4:1, 29–62.

Palmer, G. (2007), 'Extreme Makeover: Home Edition: An American Fairytale', in D. Heller (ed.), *Makeover Television: Realities Remodelled* (London and New York: I.B. Tauris).

Redden, G. (2007), 'Makeover Morality and Consumer Culture', in D. Heller (ed.), *Makeover Television: Realities Remodelled* (London and New York: I.B. Tauris).

Rickard, J. (1998), 'Lovable Larrikins and Awful Ockers', *Journal of Australian Studies* 56, 78–85.

Singleton, A. and Maher, J.-M. (2004), 'The "New Man" Is in the House: Young Men, Social Change, and Housework', *The Journal of Men's Studies* 12:3, 227–40.

Turner, G. and Cunningham, S. (eds) (2000), *The Australian TV Book* (St Leonards, NSW: Allen & Unwin).

Ward, R. (1958), *The Australian Legend* (Melbourne: Oxford University Press).

Watts, A. (2006), 'Queen for a Day: Remaking Consumer Culture, One Woman at a Time', in D. Heller (ed.), *The Great American Makeover: Television, History, Nation* (New York: Palgrave Macmillan).

White, R. (1981), *Inventing Australia: Images and Identity 1688–1980* (Sydney: Allen & Unwin).

Chapter 12

A Nation of Cocooners? Explanations of the Home Improvement TV Boom in the United States

Madeleine Shufeldt Esch

Home-focused lifestyle television now constitutes a major segment of the cable television schedule. Programs on which homes are redecorated inside and out, renovated, toured, bought, sold and flipped comprise a distinct sub-genre of lifestyle programming. In the USA, factual entertainment forms emphasizing home improvement have been present at least since the 1980s, but the transformation from the venerable public service programs such as *This Old House* (PBS) to celebrity-driven how-to shows and the later proliferation of reality makeover formats is a 1990s phenomenon. The trend had really developed by 2000 when the mega-hit *Trading Spaces* (TLC) based on the British *Changing Rooms* first aired and began drawing record high ratings for its network. In the American context, this programming category has been little studied by media scholars, but it has been widely noted in the popular press. TV critics and cultural observers discuss the trend with some amazement, noting, for example, how 'home improvement has spread like mildew under the sink' (White 2004). A crucial tipping point in this development might be identified as the 1994 launch of America's first dedicated home improvement cable network, Home and Garden Television (HGTV). This debut brought shelter-themed lifestyle programming to the airwaves 24 hours a day, seven days a week.

No longer relegated to daytime broadcasts and public broadcasting, home improvement television seemed to have arrived. Quickly viewership increased and formats multiplied. HGTV has since been joined by home-themed lifestyle programming blocks on the basic cable networks Discovery, TLC, Lifetime, A&E, and selected programs on a variety of other networks; the digital cable offerings are even more varied. On HGTV alone, viewers can choose from surprise makeover shows, gardening themes, property shows, how-to and travelogue formats, to name a few. With its 'tidal wave of hearth-and-home programming', HGTV 'is to home and garden what ESPN is to sports and MTV is to pop music' (Rogers 2002). To casual observers, this national 'fix-it fixation' (Foege 2002) seemed both a surprising development *and* an apt reflection of the cultural zeitgeist. In this chapter, I explore how the rise of this category of programming and the success of HGTV have been made sense of in the popular press and ask what portrait these explanations paint of the sub-genre of home improvement television.

In 1997, *The Washington Post* took note of this curious boom in home-themed programming. Reporter Megan Rosenfeld (1997) marveled:

> No longer is daytime the sole province of soap operas and talk shows. Dozens of these "lifestyle" shows focused on the domestic arts – home repair, decorating, cooking, gardening, crafts, hobbies, pets and remodeling – are drawing millions of viewers, a new audience made up of not only traditional housewives but also telecommuters and home business proprietors. (Rosenfeld 1997)

Rosenfeld's trend story and others like it, appearing in papers across the country since the mid-1990s, identify a number of possible motivations for this apparent shelter boom. These occasionally include reference to shifting dynamics in the television industry, enthusiastic advertiser support, or the appeal of low production costs, but far more often, the explanations promoted emphasize American values and a curious phenomenon called 'cocooning', that is, a purportedly widespread urge to curl up in the comfort and safety of our own homes. The frequent appearance of these two themes, cocooning and American-ness, is the focus of this chapter. I argue that neither the cocooning explanation nor the linkage to timeless American values hold up well under scrutiny, but I want to take seriously the appeal of these explanations. I suggest that the idea of cocooning was particularly salient for reporters because it resonated with other popular cultural themes and trends at the time; meanwhile an emphasis on 'timeless' American values displaces political and economic perspectives on the television trend. The characterization of home improvement lifestyle television that emerges from this popular press discourse is significantly different from that which is being sketched out in academic analyses of these texts where the focus is more often on issues of discipline, taste cultures and class aesthetics. I do not question the utility of these readings, but I suggest that the competing discourses I discuss here are also important to consider. Recent work in television genre theory suggests that in addition to textual characteristics, audience reception, industrial practices, and popular press discourses are also influential in the development and characterization of new television genres. How, then, do the discourses of cocooning and American-ness shape our understanding of the genre of lifestyle television?

Despite their seeming ubiquity, ordinary television formats and lifestyle programming have been marginalized within television studies (Bell and Hollows 2005; Bonner 2003), and this is especially true in US scholarship. Martha Stewart has, of course, been the subject of a growing body of literature, but beyond this there are very few studies that address popular American domestic advice lifestyle television programs. One rare attempt to illuminate the contours and popularity of this category of programming is Anna Everett's (2004) exploration of HGTV and TLC's success with 'transformation TV', so named for the makeover format that these networks have come to specialize in. Everett draws some observations about the rise of HGTV as a result of factors such as the expansion of cable narrowcasting, attitudinal changes of baby boomers, and government-sponsored urban renewal programs, but a full theorization of these connections is not the focal point of her article. In Britain, Charlotte Brunsdon and her colleagues in the Midlands TV Research Group have addressed the rise of lifestyle television as prime time programming.

Brunsdon (2004) noted three of the cultural contexts in British society out of which lifestyle television emerged in the 1990s including increased home ownership, the rise of female participation in the workforce, and postponed motherhood among British women. Although this work has been a great contribution to the study of home improvement and other lifestyle programming in Britain, much work remains to be done in the American context. Because of vast differences between the two nations in television structure, housing patterns, class dynamics and social policy, for example, we cannot rely on international studies to explain American television trends.

Various historical methods might be employed to trace the development of home-themed television in America, perhaps focusing on the diversification of cable networks or the dramatic shifts in the housing stock in the post-war era. However, here I wish to begin the project of understanding the emergence of this new television category by drawing on genre theory and considering how the generic definition of home-themed television contains its own stories about the category's origins. Although home improvement television might best be understood as a sub-genre within lifestyle television, we can apply insights from genre theory to interrogate its emergence. While traditional approaches to genre in literary and film studies have focused on textual characteristics and identifying a corpus of works that illustrate the formal features of a genre, this is not the only way of employing the concept. Recent trends in genre studies encourage conceiving genre as *process*, or what Gary Edgerton and Brian Rose (2005) describe as 'part of a much broader system of signification that derives its deeper meanings from the interrelationship between an assortment of creative, technological, industrial, institutional, and reception-related practices' (2005, 7). Film scholar Rick Altman (1999) has argued forcefully that genres are not simply the products of textual or formal features but are strongly shaped by industrial practices of promotion and distribution and the assessments of professional critics, among other influences. He argues for a pragmatic view of genre – that is, a consideration of how genres are functional for an industry or a society.

Drawing on this work, Jason Mittell (2004) has argued for a television-specific genre theory that is attentive to the discourses surrounding television texts. Recognizing that television has a distinct institutional and promotional structure from that of Hollywood, Mittell expands upon Altman's pragmatic approach to include the influence of fan discussions, TV reviews, political debates about the morals or value of certain program categories and so forth. Ultimately, for Mittell, genre identification results from popularly circulating ideas about genres such that industry labels, audience practices and critical assessments may be in tension, but through this discursive contestation, the cultural category of the genre emerges. For example, while 'lifestyle television' is a term used by scholars and some television networks to identify the niche that includes home improvement, cooking, fashion, travel and other topics, this label is notably absent from American news coverage about HGTV and its rivals. The articles on HGTV that I analyse here do not compare home improvement shows to other 'lifestyle' types such as cooking shows or fashion makeovers. These are implicitly understood as distinct categories; consequently lifestyle television as a generic label is contested. On the other hand, to the extent that producers, television critics and audiences basically agree that home improvement programs are 'useful' television, that label becomes part of the generic identity – whether or not these programs are on balance demonstrably helpful. Furthermore, the themes of cocooning and American-ness that I highlight in this chapter are *not* defining features of the programs themselves, so a strictly textual reading of genre would not recognize these as themes at all. And yet, these discourses shape our general sense of the genre.

Mittell (2004) asks us to problematize one-dimensional genre histories and consider more carefully other discourses surrounding the group of texts we aim to study. 'The history of a genre would thus explore how particular definitions, interpretations, and evaluations became associated or disassociated with the cultural category and trace out how these discursive practices play out within the various realms of industry, audience, text, critics, policy makers, and broader social context' (Mittell 2004, 30). In the present case, how is it that the cocooning trend and Americana became associated with the sub-genre of home improvement television?

Mittell frames this project in terms of Foucauldian genealogy, rejecting any search for deeper meaning and aiming for breadth over depth; 'We should not attempt to interpret generic discourses by suggesting what statements "really mean" or how they express meanings beneath the cultural surface' (Mittell 2004, 13). This approach works well to understand how certain generic labels come to prominence and how certain characteristics are articulated to the genre through discourse. However, this focus on 'how' tends to neglect questions of 'why.' In my view, this position problematically discounts material conditions and ignores the possibility that new generic forms may strategically reflect or elide contemporary social tensions.

For instance, when new genres emerge or existing ones seem to evolve, it is not necessarily simply in response to audience demands, interests or felt 'needs'. Rather, as Jane Feuer (1987) explains in a much earlier article on television genre: 'The concept of audience "need" is a substitute for an explanation of shifts in a culture, in an industry, and in a narrative form; in itself it does not explain anything' (Feuer 1987, 152). Feuer's approach seeks to integrate the concepts of genre and ideology. She asks, 'What caused the industry to redefine the audience at certain points, and to what extent did this really correspond to material changes in the culture?' (Feuer 1987, 152). The phrasing of this sort of research question is attuned to the possibility that explanations for generic success might naturalize certain ways of looking at the world.

Inspired by Mittell's approach, I take popular press discourses about HGTV programming as at least partially constitutive of the genre identification for home-themed lifestyle television. However, drawing from Feuer's stance, I am also interested in to what extent these discourses correspond to identifiable cultural shifts and material evidence. It is beyond the scope of this chapter to examine fully the industrial practices, audience reception and textual characteristics that also contribute to genre identity; this chapter begins the process by examining popular press discourse. Here, I focus on how journalists offer explanations for the trend by drawing on messages from HGTV executives, as well as expert sources, audience feedback and their own viewing experiences. In considering journalistic coverage of the trend, I take a position informed by sociology of news studies (for an overview, see Berkowitz 1997), recognizing that journalists are subject to numerous pragmatic constraints including reliance on credentialed sources with whom they have established relationships and working within time pressures which might encourage the use of standard narrative frames. For instance, journalists are likely to give voice to and privilege the rhetoric of network executives because these executives are expert sources with whom journalists strive to maintain good working relationships. This framework also suggests that journalists are likely to draw on dominant ideological themes in order to shape their coverage of events and trends; by extension then, these discourses also shape evolving generic definitions for home-themed lifestyle television in ways that might not give the fullest picture of this type of programming.

The remainder of this chapter is an analysis of popular press coverage of the home-themed lifestyle boom on US television. To provide focus, I selected articles from US newspapers focusing on HGTV during a time span from its launch in 1994 to the present.[1] Of the many articles on HGTV programs or personalities, surprisingly few made any attempt to explain the apparent 'fix-it fixation'. Although few in number, these articles are potentially powerful shapers of how the American public thinks about home improvement television. That is, readers who have never watched HGTV will form their opinions of the network and its offerings, in part, in response to these trend stories. Furthermore, fans glean from these stories a sense of what cultural place is held by the programs they love. As reporters convey the expert opinions of network executives, professors or interior designers, these analyses judge the merits and motivations of home-themed lifestyle TV in ways that define the genre. In these articles two prominent ideas about the factors behind the success of this category emerged clearly: the cocooning trend and a uniquely American love of home.

It's the cocooning trend

The idea for HGTV was born in the early 1990s, the brainchild of Kenneth Lowe, a television executive and weekend do-it-yourselfer. Lowe pitched the idea for an all-home cable channel to E.W. Scripps Company 'by drawing a house in which every room from attic to wine cellar was its own TV show' (Fact Sheet 2002). According to company lore, the inspiration came from Lowe's own experiences with frequent moves, home improvements and frustration with inadequate sources of advice for his home projects. With an initial investment of $25 million from Scripps, Lowe developed original programming, some of which continues to air today (Krueger

---

1   The articles that are the subject of this analysis have been collected over the course of several years of paying attention to this topic. The bulk of this sample, however, was culled from a targeted Lexis-Nexis search for articles on HGTV since its 1994 launch. To make analysis of the hundreds of articles more feasible, only those published in US-based newspapers and articles over 500 words in length were considered. Of the approximately 120 articles that met the initial criteria, those that provided some attempt at explanation or contextualization of the home improvement trend were most carefully considered. Roughly two dozen articles comprise this final set.

2004). The network now reaches over 80 million households in the United States and Lowe is now CEO of Scripps (Fact Sheet 2002). In the ten years since HGTV's launch E.W. Scripps' profit has more than doubled, and in 2004, 49 per cent of Scripps' total profit was generated by HGTV and its sister networks (Food Network, Fine Living, DIY Network and the lesser-known Great American Country) (E.W. Scripps 2004). Today his network is 'must-see TV for the home obsessed' (Rogers 2002). The official house history of HGTV, published on the network's tenth anniversary, recognizes that 'the path to HGTV's launch is marked with fortuitous coincidences and good timing' including concurrent growth of the cable industry and the winning attitudes of the network executives (Krueger 2004, 4). Lowe, however, at least in speaking with the press, has been more likely to ignore the strong support of home improvement retailers and structural changes in cable television; he ties the phenomenal success of HGTV to the overwhelming interest of Americans in their dwelling spaces. As he told the Associated Press,

> Some people live in an apartment, some in a half-million dollar home. Yet their common interest is that sanctuary where they live. ... The passion is the same, and the sensibility is the same – improving your home. *There is nothing new here. It is the cocooning trend.* (quoted in Mansfield 1995, emphasis added)

A programming executive at the rival network, Discovery Channel, offered to the *Washington Post* a startlingly similar explanation for the category's success: 'We are feathering our nests more; home and hearth means more to us. ... We're cocooning, as the demographers say, returning to a different set of values' (quoted in Rosenfeld 1997).

Despite scant demographic evidence of any such trend, the cocooning thesis has survived largely unchallenged and the idea is implicit in much coverage of the home improvement television boom. One reporter explained, 'People who study these things have been warning us for years that once the baby boomers settled down and got serious about taking care of houses and yards, it would ignite an interest in the topics such as we've never seen before' (Blundo 1996). 'American cocooners' are regularly presented as a de facto demographic category, as in one reporter's assessment that 'In 2004, America's cocooners devoted to their homes and gardens made the Knoxville, Tenn-based network the 17th most popular among the 59 ad-based cable channels Nieslen Media Research rates' (Lubenski 2005).

When exactly this category emerged is rarely questioned but its longevity and durability are marveled at. For example HGTV's senior vice president of programming, Burton Jablin, explained to the *Boston Globe*, 'The economy is good and people are still spending money on their homes – the whole cocooning phenomenon just doesn't seem to be abating' (quoted in Doten 1998). The creator of *This Old House*, the public television mainstay of home improvement, suggested to the *Washington Post* that the interest in home is inflation-proof, recession-proof and generally unshakable (Winslow 1999). As I will discuss below, this tension between cocooning as a trend and some deeper timeless interest in home flows through the coverage of HGTV's success. However, whether or not the interest in feathering our nests is new, we can pinpoint the moment when the label 'cocooning' was attached to it.

The 'trend' has its origins as a marketing buzzword coined by 'futurist' Faith Popcorn sometime in the late 1970s, although the trend became popularized in the 1980s and was formalized in Popcorn's 1991 book, *The Popcorn Report*. She describes it as 'the impulse to go *inside* when it just gets too tough and scary *outside* … [It's] about insulation and avoidance, peace and protection, coziness and control – a sort of hyper-nesting' (Popcorn 1991, 27–8). She predicted that companies who tapped into a homebody sensibility focusing on home entertainment (privatized leisure) and domestic creature comforts would do well in the 1990s. As an example, she too links cocooning to the success of HGTV and a new crop of home and garden magazines appearing on newsstands around the same time (Popcorn and Marigold 1996).

Susan Faludi (1991) has been among the leading critics of the idea that any such impulse was actually being acted upon. Positioning the purported trend as an aspect of the anti-feminist backlash of the 1980s, Faludi characterizes the introduction of the cocooning 'trend' in this way:

> In 1986, Faith Popcorn managed to please the media trend writers and her corporate clients at the same time with the coining of a single world, "cocooning". The word "just popped into my head" in the middle of an interview with the Wall Street Journal, Popcorn recalls. "It was a prediction … It hadn't happened". But that wasn't quite how she marketed it to the media at the time. (Faludi 1991, 83)

Faludi continues, 'Popcorn defined cocooning not as people coming home but as women abandoning the office' (Faludi 1991, 84).

Federal records on employment trends during this period indicate this exodus did not happen. According to the US Bureau of Labor Statistics, in 1970, 40.8 per cent of women were employed in some capacity. This figure steadily increased through the 1980s and 1990s with a few exceptions – years in which the percentage of employed men declined at a similar rate, indicating economic downturns, not a gendered trend of dropping out. In 2000, 57.5 per cent of women were employed. 'Along with rising labor force participation, women also made substantial inroads into higher paying occupations. In 2004, half of all management, professional, and related occupations were held by women' (Women in the Labor Force 2005, 1). Neither is it the case that women were increasingly moving to part-time work, as one of Popcorn's related trends labeled 'cashing out' might suggest. The Bureau of Labor Statistics reports that over the past 35 years, women's participation in part-time employment has remained relatively constant while men's part-time work has increased. Furthermore, the percentage of working mothers rose even more sharply, from 47 per cent in 1975 to a remarkable 73 per cent in 2000. Of course, this is not to say that the employment picture for women was entirely rosy, but rather to indicate as Faludi surmised in 1991, that there were not significant demographic shifts to support Popcorn's 'trends'. Of course, government statistics cannot clue us in to how many women would have preferred to 'cash out' and head home to the cocoon if that were a realistic possibility.

But Popcorn's formulations of the trend have been remarkably flexible, helping the idea of cocooning to significantly outlive the ten-year lifespan she normally forecasts for cultural trends. In the earliest formulation, as Faludi describes, it was about women leaving careers and the workplace. By the publication of the *Popcorn Report*, Popcorn had apparently downplayed the rejection of the workplace, arguing instead that working women (*and* men) were being drawn to 'cushy comfort' and 'an almost '50s sense of domesticity – even if working matriarchs had to rush home from the office every day to simulate it' (Popcorn 1991, 29). Even if it came at the end of the workday, it was a 'retreat' – 'away from the cold, sterile, alienating office and back to the welcoming warmth of the cocoon' (ibid. 51).

This language has been picked up quite directly by designer Chris Casson Madden, often described as one of the leading pretenders to Martha Stewart's throne. Madden has made cocoon-crafting her design niche, launched with the publication of her coffee table book, *A Room of her Own*. She explained to a *New York Times* reporter, 'There wasn't anyone speaking to women's personal needs for a sanctuary. … Nor were there affordable, durable, stylish home furnishings available to make their homes a haven' (quoted in Mason 2002). Madden credits women's craving for a place to relax, to balance their many roles, for the growing interest in interior design and home-themed lifestyle television.

This emphasis on retreat (as both verb and noun), however, coexists with an emphasis on 'empowerment' that permeates the do-it-yourself rhetoric of home improvement media. This sensibility is also evident in many of the articles covering home-themed lifestyle programming and is particularly clearly expressed by some of the leading female domestic advisors, at least as reporters choose to quote them. Lynette Jennings, host of *Lynette Jennings Design* (Discovery Network), states it plainly in a *New York Times* article: 'It's empowerment. That's what the shows are about' (quoted in Tomashoff 2000). Likewise, TV personality and designer of a line of tools specially designed for women do-it-yourselfers, Barbara Kavovit – known by her television moniker Barbara K – recognizes the tremendous strides women have made: 'They've taken on so many roles in the twenty-first century: They're career-oriented, they're heads of households', and now, she adds in an interview with the *Washington Post*, 'Women really want to be able to fix things around the house', which she sees as a 'natural extension' (quoted in Coombes 2004). Here Kavovit taps into the sensibilities of a 'modern' woman who seeks to balance her workplace accomplishments with a more powerful domestic femininity.

Kavovit's description also characterizes well a postfeminist sensibility that permeated American culture in the 1990s. More complex than a straightforward anti-feminist backlash, the position labeled 'postfeminist' appreciates and recognizes the gains of second-wave liberal feminism but dismisses political organization as no longer necessary. Yvonne Tasker and Diane Negra (2005) characterize postfeminism as 'simultaneously assuming the achievement and desirability of gender equality on the one hand while repeatedly associating such equality with loss on the other' (Tasker and Negra 2005, 108). What has been lost is often understood to be a sense of domestic femininity. Thus, Tasker and Negra continue, 'one of the most persistent themes in postfeminist representation is that of "retreatism" or "downsizing"' (ibid. 108). Presumably balance can be restored in cozy homefront havens. The idea of cocooning fits easily within a postfeminist sensibility that was prominent in American popular culture in the 1990s. Because of this convergence, cocooning may have been a more attractive causal trend for home improvement television than other possible explanations – including other trends posited by Popcorn that seem on the surface to be just as relevant.

In the same 1991 book where Popcorn elucidated the cocooning trend and the impulse to 'cash out', she also predicted that successful marketing strategies would be attuned to the paired trends of 'small indulgences' and 'egonomics'. I want to suggest that these purported trends are eschewed as explanations because they point too directly to the hyper-commercial and 'aspirational' nature of home improvement programming. Small indulgences is a straightforward idea that consumers want a little luxury but not to be too ostentatious; at least two of the examples Popcorn provides for the phenomenon are tied to the cocoon – we'll choose a new red chair instead of the new red car and perhaps a new pool instead of a new house. Meanwhile, egonomics 'is about individuating, differentiating, customizing' (Popcorn 1991, 43). Among the examples Popcorn links to this trend is the rise of niche market magazines and television networks. It would seem, then, that small indulgences and egonomics are just as likely explanations for the success of HGTV as cocooning and cashing out. In fact, personalization and affordable luxury are more frequent themes of HGTV programs themselves than any explicit reference to cocooning. While particular episodes may focus on creating inviting havens or romantic escapes (as in cocooning), more often programs highlight self-expression through color and furnishing choices (as in egonomics) or designing stylish rooms on a budget (as in small indulgences). However, Popcorn's other trends are never summoned by programming executives and journalists trying to contextualize the trend.

By 1996, Popcorn is able to fuse cocooning, small indulgences and egonomics in a description that sounds as if she could be chronicling an episode of an HGTV home tour: 'We're four-postering and four-pillowing our beds with Italian linen sheets, cashmere throws, pleated silk dust ruffles. And changing our utilitarian bathrooms into luxurious spas with RainStorm showerheads that spray 127 separate streams of water, automatic hand dryers, heated towel racks for our three-initialed monogrammed towel sets' (Popcorn and Marigold 1996, 60). If we are sprucing up our nests as much as these trend forecasts suggest, we might expect to see a marked increase in spending on the home, but again, statistics do not bear this trend out.

Anecdotally, the phenomenal success in the late 1990s of 'big box' home improvement retailers Home Depot and Lowe's seem to support this thesis and their healthy sales figures are occasionally cited in trend stories about home improvement television. Home Depot became the second largest US retailer in 2001 and its profits have quadrupled in the past decade; in 2006, the company netted $29,783 million from its 2,147 stores. Lowe's, its closest competitor in the category, had a gross profit of $16,198 million in 2006 from sales at its 1,385 stores nationwide. This strong growth is frequently taken as evidence that Americans are spending more on sprucing up their abodes. However, the federal Bureau of Labor Statistics (BLS) annual Consumer Expenditure Survey reflects no astronomical increases. While overall spending on home furnishing and housekeeping has been increasing in terms of raw non-inflation-adjusted dollars, spending on the home as a percentage of total expenditure has remained relatively constant over the past 20 years, hovering around 5 per cent of annual expenditure (Consumer Expenditure Survey 2005). Furthermore this proportion is constant across all income levels so it is not the case, as one might hypothesize, that increased spending among the upper middle class is balanced by decreased spending among the lower classes. The brisk sales at Home Depot and Lowe's, then, seem to come primarily from luring shoppers away from smaller independent home improvement retailers – an explicitly stated goal in Lowe's year 2000 annual report. Whether we buy at the big box stores or from local hardware shops, as a nation, we seem to have a ceiling on the proportion of our income that we allocate for feathering our nests. It is, of course, possible that the nature of our spending has changed, perhaps as consumers focus more on achieving a coherent style in their furnishings. Again, the fact that little measurable change can be identified does not, of course, rule out the possibility that cashing out/cocooning and nest-feathering were powerful fantasies in American culture in the years when HGTV was getting off the ground. The sense that cocooning might have been more about domestic fantasy and escape than DIY improvements actually becomes clear in the newspaper articles covering the trend. Rather than sprucing up our cocoons, we may just be hiding out from the world in them. And, crucially, home improvement television provides relaxing fare to watch while we zone out.

In news coverage of the trend, there are numerous references to the 'stress-free' nature of this kind of programming. These programs are apparently exactly the sort of television you want to watch when you're hiding from the world – no matter if you are hiding in a well-appointed nest or a shabby studio apartment. Whereas cocooning is largely interpreted to emphasize home and hearth, Popcorn's formulation also speaks of 'insulation and avoidance' (Popcorn 1991, 28). Reporters and network executives affirm how HGTV shows and similar programs provide an avenue for escapism and relaxation – paradoxically even as the on-screen hosts encourage viewers to tackle new projects around the house. One reporter explains that viewers use this 'no-stress programming' as 'background noise while doing housework, reading, or talking on the phone. It's a quiet, uncomplicated relationship with a 'friend' that doesn't make demands on one's emotional or intellectual inner life.' HGTV's Burton Jablin explains, 'There's nothing offensive, nothing disturbing. Watch HGTV, and you'll never find anything to upset you' (quoted in Strum 1999). A *Boston Globe* reporter calls it 'a *Mister Rogers Neighborhood* for adults', adding, 'no one is shouting at you. No guns are fired. No bodies are flying through the air' (Doten 1998). The shows offer what columnist Charles Strum calls 'G-rated fantasies', referring to the all-ages ratings code for family friendly films. The G-rating is echoed by Megan Rosenfeld (1997) and described again by Jablin as 'useful escapism', contrasting the feel-good nature of these shows with his past experience working in television news where the audience 'blamed us for all the ills of society' (quoted in Rosenfeld 1997). HGTV and its ilk are presented as more calming than other television fare and, more importantly, than the world outside the cocoon.

Pursuing this line of thought further to interrogate why such soothing fare would be particularly relevant in the 1990s raises complex issues better suited to the front page of the paper than the entertainment section. Here is the limit of the cocooning trend's utility as an explanation for this genre's development. What is it that we are supposed to be retreating *from*? Probing this might lead journalists to connect a surging interest in the home to fears that our cities and communities were in decline.

We might draw links between sprucing up the home and increased crime and urban decay; focusing on home upkeep might be related to economic recession and an increasing strain on the middle class. Or perhaps this sort of inward focus might be pegged as part and parcel of a decline in civic participation. Sociologists noted that fewer Americans in the 1980s and 1990s were joining community organizations and voluntary associations than in past decades. This trend was most notably captured by Robert Putnam, Dean of Harvard University's Kennedy School of Government in his 'bowling alone' thesis. Putnam quotably articulated this social withdrawal with the memorable factoid that although more Americans enjoyed the pastime of bowling in the 1990s, fewer and fewer of us were joining bowling leagues, that traditional bastion of fraternal feeling. In the richly researched book *Bowling Alone* (2000), Putnam lays out thousands of statistics that paint a picture of a nation increasingly staying home, dining in, watching TV, commuting from the suburbs rather than participating in our communities. Although the precision and causality of his argument were called into question from some quarters at the time, this idea was influential and widely discussed. President Bill Clinton invited Putnam to a prestigious planning summit and incorporated a call for a return to communitarian values in his 1995 state of the union address (Devroy and Harris 1995). Clinton explained in an interview: 'There are all these pressures that will tend to let us be alone more ... But in the end, unless we are citizens, unless we have certain networks in our community, it's going to be very difficult for what we do here in Washington to explode in a positive way across the country' (quoted in Powers 1995). With such ideas circulating so widely at least among pundits at the time, the mid-1990s surge in home improvement television and nest-feathering could certainly have been tied to a wider decline in community involvement and labeled as a symptom of the 'bowling alone' culture. That is to say, cocooning was not the only potentially applicable theme circulating in the culture; the 'bowling alone' thesis and other more critical perspectives were also available to reporters seeking context for the television trend. However, the cocooning thesis, whether in its 'sprucing up' or 'zoning out' strains, keeps the focus on an independent demographic trend and affirms the beneficial – even therapeutic – nature of these programs without problematizing the felt need for this form of 'therapy' or its possible effects.

I suggest that instead of probing this sort of implication, the journalistic frame shifted to supplement the idea of cocooning with a characterization of home-themed lifestyle television as just the latest incarnation of an enduring American love of home. As advertising guru Jack Myers explained to an *Atlanta Journal-Constitution* reporter, 'This is a long-term business, not a trend.' He said, 'They've tapped into a sensibility in America, toward do-it-yourself and middle American home life that appeals to everyone' (quoted in Wilbert 2003). The American-ness of this trend is a theme that is seen clearly, often in the same sentence with cocooning. This idea is particularly supported by the most frequently quoted expert source journalists seem to consult on the topic: Dr Robert J. Thompson, director of the Center for the Study of Popular Television at Syracuse University. Thompson affirms both an American interest in transformations, domestic and otherwise, and the American dream of home ownership. He is quoted in one article explaining that the theme of transformation 'is one of the deepest myths in American culture' (Wilbert 2003). And in another article, he suggests, 'The history of the United States is one big makeover show' (Lubenski 2005). Discussing the HGTV spin-off, DIY Network, more recently, Thompson has suggested that these programs 'are tapping into something that runs deep, deep in the American mindset' and suggested the theme could be traced 'at least as far back as the pilgrims' (quoted in Rayworth 2007).

Statistics are sometimes offered to back up this theme of national interest. For example, one report describes HGTV as 'the first 24-hour cable channel to capitalize on the interests of the 75 per cent of Americans who consider themselves home enthusiasts' (Cassidy 1996). In a single example such as this, the identification of an *American* interest may seem just a convenient word choice, but the repetition of this theme is striking. Another article offers, 'The popularity of these shows speaks to the American love affair with home, reflected most clearly in the $587 billion that Americans spend on home improvement, crafts, decorating and gardening every year (Rosenfeld 1997). Reporters suggest that home improvement television programs' 'good fortunes are directly linked to Americans' new obsession with improving their lives by improving their homes' (Tomashoff 2000). In interviews with the press, Burton Jablin and HGTV founder Kenneth Lowe both emphasize how their programs reflect and speak to a broad swath of 'middle America'. In fact, a few HGTV programs explicitly call up national feeling with titles such as *Homes Across America* or *Restore America*, but these few examples hardly represent the category as a whole.

This articulation of feeling for home and American-ness does indeed tap into a long history of myth, in the Barthesian ideological sense; whether or not this is the sort of myth Dr Thompson has in mind is unclear in his platitudes. Home and hearth are repeatedly held up as values that are as American as apple pie. The project of associating home ownership and improvement with American values has been a theme of domestic advisors since the birth of the nation (Leavitt 2002) and in sometimes very overt ways by the federal government itself. For example, Karen Altman (1990) describes a post-World War I economic development program called the 'Better Homes in America' campaign based on federally sponsored public relations efforts to promote home ownership and increased attention to beautifying and maintaining houses. Altman argues that, through this long-running campaign, 'buying a home, furnishing it with standardized commodities, and doing its labor by following expert advice were patriotic acts that supported an historically formed political, economic and social order in the postwar expansion of capital' (Altman 1990, 291). Altman positions this explicitly as a project of naturalization, which 'occurs in discourse that claims historical conditions are natural, instinctual, innate or inborn' (ibid. 288). In this way, we might similarly understand the emphatic characterization of home-themed lifestyle programming as American to be a naturalizing discourse. Aspirational domestic consumption is constructed as a national impulse and perhaps even a patriotic activity. Meanwhile, it may be worthwhile considering what this emphasis on a *national* trend ignores – namely the global nature of the home improvement boom.

The idea that a home-themed lifestyle television boom might extend beyond the borders of the US is almost completely absent in American popular press coverage of the television trend. A few articles mention the development of HGTV sister networks in Canada and Japan and the *export* of HGTV programming, but the fact that many of our most successful programs are based on formats licensed or borrowed from abroad is almost never mentioned. The rare exception is an occasional reference to *Trading Spaces'* roots in England as *Changing Rooms*. While popular television scholars and journalists may not be fully aware of the scope of this home improvement boom in other national contexts, certainly those closely associated with the television industry must recognize the increasing global trade in programs and format licenses. This phenomenon has been explored by Albert Moran (Moran 1998) who argues that format-adaptation is so attractive because it 'offers some insurance and security to broadcasters and in an industry so beset with uncertainty, such a promise is worth having' (ibid. 20).

Network executives who minimize the global phenomenon of home improvement television may be wary of opening up an exploration of the production environment for the home shows audiences love. In addition to a global trade in low-risk formats, the production circumstances for home improvement television include low-cost production, tremendous support from advertisers eager to have their products featured in instructional segments, copycat formats, and a dependence on makeover participants to donate their own labor and sometimes construction expenses (Shufeldt and Gale 2007). The absence of this understanding allows the characterization of these programs as having a 'public service' inclination to go unchallenged; instead, as HGTV executive Burton Jablin often repeats, these shows are affirmed as being about 'ideas, inspiration and information'. Of course, it is hardly surprising that popular coverage does not take a critical perspective on global television production (it is reasonable to expect such issues to be overlooked in entertainment section reporting), but it is interesting to note the willingness of journalists to support an alternative narrative emphasizing the American-ness of the trend – in light of what would seem to be clear evidence to the contrary.

Already solidly in place as the primary characterizations of the boom in home improvement lifestyle television, the paired themes of cocooning and American-ness took on new relevance in the immediate aftermath of the September 11th attacks. Many commentators at the time noted the tendency for Americans to seek solace at home and with family. For instance, a trend story in the *Atlanta Journal-Constitution* reported that, 'Craft experts say perhaps the most successful endorsement for sewing and quilting followed Sept. 11. People stayed close to home and family, and cocooning impulses sent people in search of silk and cotton and wool' (Lewis 2002). This time, reporters did offer some sales figures to support the claim of a renewed attention to feathering our nests, but often evidence remained vague. Craft stores fared significantly better in the period after the attacks than they had in the same period the previous year (Lewis 2002); *USA Today* reported that electronics retailers were stunned by unusually brisk sales of large-screen TVs and other home electronics in the fall of 2001 leading up to the Christmas season (Snider 2001). However, during this period, there is no notable increase in annual revenue reported by Home Depot and Lowe's, nor is there a spike in the federal data from the consumer expenditures survey. Still, in the post-9/11 climate, as an *Atlanta Journal-Constitution* reporter put it, 'home emerged as *the* safe, comfortable place to beat a retreat to. For every canceled airline reservation and empty restaurant or theater seat, there was a modern-day hermit sitting at home, jacking into the Net, tuning in to CNN, or picking up the phone to check on relatives and friends' (Snider 2001). When people sought a break from the news, HGTV was there with its now well-established brand of 'useful escapism'.

By now, a cocooning urge was not the explanation of some other trend but an old familiar habit to which we eagerly returned. Steve Thomas, host of *Ask This Old House*, explained to the *New York Daily News*, 'The trend that used to be called "cocooning" was in place before 9/11, but that [event] helped sharpen people's focus' (quoted in Huff 1999). In the post-9/11 version of cocooning, the gender politics of the early 1990s are almost completely absent, but the distinctly *American* nature of this instinct has taken on a new importance. Television scholar Robert Thompson updated his analysis, noting in a *Washington Post* interview that 'we still revere the notion of home in this country, even more since 9/11'; he added that it's an 'old-fashioned vision of home as a place where your family has lived for generations. The idea is, that if you can in fact fix the drain on your sink or make your own grapevine centerpiece' you can recreate that classic notion of the all-American home (quoted in Rogers 2002).

Conclusion

Finally, I want to return to the idea of the development of a *genre* of lifestyle television and the particular sub-genre of home improvement television. Rather than being flummoxed by the vast number of shows that might fit within this category and the many types (reality, how-to, travelogue, etc.), a cultural theory of genre as a process calls our attention to the discourses that work to unite the field. Following this view of genre shaped by the discursive constructions of producerly and critical assessments alongside the reception of audiences, we can see that the idea of American cocooning has been important in shaping conceptions of the category of home-themed lifestyle television. What this means, then, is that the understanding of the sub-genre for much of the 1990s has been particularly attuned to its psycho-spiritual benefits for men and women (indeed for American families) to the exclusion of emphasis on other possible themes that contradict this notion. The brief analysis presented here raises a string of related questions for further studies. To what extent has this characterization informed how HGTV's many fans interpret its offerings? To what extent is the idea of cocooning prominent in the programs themselves? How do networks such as HGTV negotiate the tension between encouraging viewers to relax on the couch and inspiring viewers to work at sprucing up their cocoons? What are the further implications of a generic discourse that naturalizes spectacular domestic consumption as a spiritually nourishing activity with deep American roots? Like other types of ordinary television, the lifestyle genre and home improvement programs in particular are not transparent, nor are the discourses surrounding them.

Bibliography

Allen, R. (ed.) (1992), *Channels of Discourse, Reassembled* (Chapel Hill, NC: University of North Carolina).

Altman, K. (1990), 'Consuming Ideology: The Better Homes in America Campaign', *Critical Studies in Mass Communication* 7:3, 286–307.

Altman, R. (1999), *Film/Genre* (London: BFI).

Bell, D. and Hollows, J. (eds) (2005), *Ordinary Lifestyles: Popular Media, Consumption and Taste* (Buckingham: Open University Press).

Berkowitz, D. (1997), *Social Meanings of News: A Text-reader* (Thousand Oaks, CA: Sage).

Blundo, J. (1996), 'Yet Another House Magazine Inspired by TV is on the Stands', *The Columbus Dispatch*, 5 May, 9L.

Bonner, F. (2003), *Ordinary TV* (Thousand Oaks, CA: Sage).

Brunsdon, C. (2004), 'Lifestyling Britain: The 8–9 Slot in British Television,' in L. Spigel and J. Olsson (eds), *Television after TV: Essays on a Medium in Transition* (Durham, NC: Duke).

Cassidy, T. (1996), 'HGTV: Where Martha Stewart Meets "Home Improvement"', *Boston Globe*, 30 May, At Home, 89.

Consumer Expenditure Survey (2005), Bureau of Labor Statistics, <http://www.bls.gov/cex/home.htm>, accessed 10 May 2008.

Coombes, A. (2004), 'Hardware Shows its Feminine Side: Home-improvement Industry Discovers Women's Buying Power', *Washington Post*, 31 July, G02.

Devroy, A. and Harris, J. (1995), 'At Clinton Dinner, Ideas Were on the Menu', *Washington Post*, 20 January, A8.

Doten, P. (1998), 'Tuning in to Cocoon: Cable Channel Whets Appetites with its 24-hour Menu of Home Shows', *Boston Globe*, 19 November, At Home, A1.

Edgerton, G.R. and Rose, B.E. (eds) (2005), *Thinking Outside the Box: A Contemporary Television Genre Reader* (Lexington, KY: University of Kentucky).

Everett, A. (2004), 'Trading Private and Public Spaces @ HGTV and TLC: On New Genre Formations in Transformation TV', *Journal of Visual Culture* 3:2, 157–81.

E.W. Scripps, Inc.: Annual Reports (1999–2006), <http://phx.corporate-ir.net/phoenix.zhtml?c=98686&p=irol-IRHome>, accessed 9 October 2007.

Fact Sheet (2002), Home and Garden Television, <http://www.hgtv.com/hgtv/about_us/article/0,1783,HGTV_3080_1420107,00.html>, accessed 2 December 2005.

Faludi, S. (1991), *Backlash: The Undeclared War against American Women* (New York: Crown Publishers).

Feuer, J. (1987), 'Genre Study and Television', in R. Allen (ed.), *Channels of Discourse, Reassembled* (Chapel Hill, NC: University of North Carolina).

Foege, A. (2002), 'Fix-it Fixation', *Mediaweek*, 15 July.

Home Depot: Annual Reports (1999–2006), <http://ir.homedepot.com/reports.cfm>, accessed 9 October 2007.

Huff, R. (2002), 'TV's New Subdivision: Fixer-uppers,' *New York Daily News*, 30 September, TV, 87.

Krueger, A. (2004), *HGTV: The First 10 Years* (Knoxville, TN: Scripps Networks).

Leavitt, S. (2002), *From Catharine Beecher to Martha Stewart: A Cultural History of Domestic Advice* (Chapel Hill, NC: UNC Press).

Lewis, S. (2002), 'An Emerging Pattern: The Popularity of Interior Design TV Shows Has a New Generation of Hobbyists Embracing the Benefits of Sewing and Quilting', *Atlanta Journal-Constitution*, 25 September, 1F.

Lowe's Companies, Inc.: Annual Reports (1999–2006), <http://www.shareholder.com/lowes/index2.cfm>, accessed 9 October 2007.

Lubenski, C. (2005), 'Home Improvement Network Has Built Quite a Following in 10 Years', *San Diego Union Tribune*, 8 May, I23.

Mansfield, D. (1995), 'Cable Network Hopes Tap Big Nesting Niche,' *Associated Press*, 30 January.

Mason, B. (2002), 'An Empire, Yes, but More Serene than Martha's', *New York Times*, 28 April, 13:4.

Mittell, J. (2004), *Genre and Television: From Cop Shows to Cartoons in American Culture* (New York: Routledge).

Moran, A. (1998), *Copycat TV: Globalisation, Program Formats and Cultural Identity* (Luton: University of Luton).

Popcorn, F. (1991), *The Popcorn Report* (New York: HarperCollins).

Popcorn, F. and Marigold, L. (1996), *Clicking: 16 Trends to Future Fit Your Life, Your Work, and Your Business* (New York: HarperCollins).

Powers, W.F. (1995), 'The Lane Less Traveled; Can a Nation of Individuals Give Community a Sporting Chance?', *Washington Post*, 3 February, D01.

Putnam, R. (2000), *Bowling Alone: The Collapse and Revival of American Community* (New York: Touchstone).

Rayworth, M. (2007), 'Show Adds Drama to DIY Format', *New Orleans Times-Picayune*, 18 August, Inside Out, 8.

Rogers, P.D. (2002), 'Channeling Home Shows: HGTV, a Network Devoted to View-it-youselfers', *Washington Post*, 5 December, H01.

Rosenfeld, M. (1997), 'Do-it-yourself TV: Daytime Home Shows Cater to the Nation's Urge to Cocoon,' *Washington Post*, 22 October, D01.

Shufeldt, M. and Gale, K. (2007), 'Under the (Glue) Gun: Containing and Constructing Reality in Home Makeover TV', *Popular Communication* 5:4, 1–20.

Snider, M. (2001), '"Cocoon" Is Where the Electronics Are', *USA Today*, 1 October, 3D.

Spigel, L. and Olsson J. (eds) (2004), *Television after TV: Essays on a Medium in Transition* (Durham, NC: Duke).

Strum, C. (1999), 'A-frames and Other G-rated Fantasies', *New York Times*, 25 April, 13:4.

Tasker, Y. and Negra, D. (2005), 'In Focus: Postfeminism and Contemporary Media Studies', *Cinema Journal* 44:2, 107–10.

Tomashoff, C. (2000), 'Wowing 'em with Rakes and Power Saws', *New York Times*, 4 June, 13:4.

White, G. (2004), 'Blame Bob Vila: Makeover Junkies Find Comfy Home with Decade-old HGTV', *New York Times*, 30 December, 1D.

Wilbert, C. (2003), 'Home is Where the Showbiz is; Trendy Television: Slicker-than-ever House Improvement Shows Popular with Viewers, Advertisers', *Atlanta Journal-Constitution*, 16 October, 1G.

Winslow, H. (1999), 'The Do-it-yourself Boom: From This Old House to HGTV, It's Hammer Time,' *Washington Post*, 3 October, Y06.

Women in the Labor Force: A Databook (2005), <http://www.bls.gov> (home page), accessed 2 December 2005.

Chapter 13

'Ecoreality': The Politics and Aesthetics of 'Green' Television

Lyn Thomas

Introduction: Alternative hedonism on TV

This chapter will discuss what might be characterized as an ecological turn in contemporary British lifestyle television: the appearance of programmes on our screens at prime time aiming to improve not the participants' fashion sense, diet or relationships, but the ecological impact of their everyday practices. I will explore the politics and aesthetics of this new development from the perspective of 'alternative hedonism', a concept developed by my colleague, Kate Soper, in our research project on this theme.[1] In her elaboration of the concept of 'alternative hedonism', Soper argues that the apparent beneficiaries of a society and economy premised on ever increasing levels of consumer spending and productivity are in fact beginning to suffer significant disadvantages resulting from this mode of living: stress, congestion, health problems, pollution and so on. From the alternative hedonist perspective, this mode of social and economic organization is not only substantially responsible for these sources of dissatisfaction, but may also be pre-empting important pleasures, such as leisureliness, slowness, silence and even conviviality. We would go on to argue that these dissatisfactions and immanent desires for lost or obscured pleasures might be effectively mobilized in environmental politics, and that the appeal to 'save the planet' may need to be accompanied by more self-centred motivations (Soper 2007). This has a particular relevance to the discussion of television, and leads directly to my consideration of the aesthetics, as well as the politics of 'green' television. The political significance of alternative hedonism lies in its suggestion that the politics of convincing consumers to adopt less ecologically destructive practices needs to emphasize gains and pleasures, perhaps rather than, and certainly as well as, losses and sacrifices.

One of the project's aims was to explore the extent to which a sense of dissatisfaction with affluent lifestyles and of desires for other pleasures might be colouring media representations in contemporary Britain. Its focus on the consumer and on the pleasures and problems of individual lives made lifestyle television and magazines the natural choice for this research, which aimed to consider self-oriented, as opposed to altruistic motivations for the adoption of more environmentally

1   Funded by the ESRC/AHRC Cultures of Consumption Programme; Grant number: RES-154-25-005.

responsible behaviour. Lifestyle television's concern with 'the good life' and how to achieve it also made it a suitable focus for exploration of our sense that conceptions of this may be changing. We wanted to research a cultural site that was not produced or accessed mainly by those already converted to the environmental cause (such as the websites of campaigning groups and organizations). Despite the problematic nature of the term 'mainstream', it captures something of the area we hoped to research: broadcasts on terrestrial channels accessible to almost the whole British population at peak viewing time (8–10pm). In this time slot, we identified four relevant genres of lifestyle programming: 'heritage cookery', 'relocation' (to a rural or exotic home), 'spiritual journey' and 'ecoreality'. The first three are structured around a quest narrative, whether for local, high quality food, the rural idyll, or spiritual peace (see Thomas 2008) but it is the fourth, where environmental concerns are directly addressed, that I will discuss here.

In the programmes I will mainly focus on – *No Waste like Home* (Celador for BBC2, 2005), *It's Not Easy Being Green* (BBC Bristol for BBC2, 2006, 2007) and *The Real Good Life*, (Granada London for ITV, 2005) – the narrative is driven not by desires for village life, wild food or peaceful contemplation, but by the adoption of lifestyle changes designed to reduce destructive consumption. Like the other genres we identified as resonant with 'alternative hedonist' desires and dissatisfactions, and indeed most lifestyle television, these programmes rely on 'ordinary participants' who are not actors or media professionals. The term 'ecoreality' was coined to encapsulate these two defining characteristics. The programmes also form part of the moral landscape, or it could be argued, moralizing tendency, of much lifestyle television, where participants, and by extension and identification, viewers, are cajoled and even, in some cases, bullied into changing their way of living. If reality television proper simply observes and makes dramatic viewing out of the participants' eccentricities and foibles, many lifestyle programmes, through the good offices of the teacher-presenter, criticize behaviour and guide towards change and improvement. Palmer has commented on the ideology of class that underpins programmes where participants are made aware of the inadequacy of their ways of dressing, eating or living more generally, in scenarios of shame and guilt (Palmer 2004). Palmer points to the shared emphasis on individual achievements in the 'personal development movement' (PDM) and its literature, and in lifestyle TV, which both seem to be premised on the view that if our lives are not perfect, we are entirely and personally responsible. Skeggs and Wood identify an academic version of this 'PDM' literature in some contemporary social theory, primarily the work of Giddens and Beck, where 'older structures of belonging are replaced by the biographical project of the reflexive self'; they, like Palmer, argue that in reality these forms of lifestyle television reinforce the oppressive structures of gender and class and demonstrate the problematic nature of such theory (Skeggs and Wood 2004, 205). The 'ecoreality' programmes discussed here share this drive towards self-improvement and emphasis on individual solutions, but in a context where the advice proffered has a broader social and political relevance than is usually the case, and where the changes brought about are relevant to human and ecological survival rather than individual identity and appearance. Despite this, the programmes may be complicit with, or indeed actively participating in, the construction of acceptable middle class identities, which both Palmer and Skeggs and Wood identify in lifestyle TV generally. Indeed, my aim here is to discuss the significance and role of the 'ecorealities': do they represent the 'greening' of lifestyle television, or can they be seen as another dimension of lifestyle's reinforcement of the culture of surface identities analysed by Palmer? What kinds of 'green' politics are mobilized here? How do these agendas intersect with the politics of gender, class, 'race' and ethnicity?

The 'ecoreality' formats

The first of the three 'ecorealities' discussed here – *The Real Good Life* (Granada London for ITV) – was launched on 31 May 2005, at 8pm. The 'good life' here was a suburban affair, with three households giving up their paid employment for one year in order to experiment with self-sufficiency. The theme music and title of the programme refer to the highly successful 1970s sitcom, *The Good Life* (BBC 1975–78), whose stars, Tom and Barbara Good, played by Richard Briers and Felicity Kendal, also give up paid employment and live off the vegetables and meat they can produce in their suburban back garden. This seems to be an apposite example of a trend in British terrestrial TV observed by Brunsdon et al. where documentary, current affairs, light entertainment and sitcoms have to a great extent been replaced in prime time slots by 'factual entertainment', that is, lifestyle and reality TV and 'docusoap' (Brunsdon et al. 2001). In this case, the reworking of the 'quality' sitcom (with well-known actors and received pronunciation) as a reality show (with video diaries and ordinary people 'playing Tom and Barbara'), takes place alongside the consecration of the original text, which is occasionally repeated as a comedy classic. The commercial imperatives driving this shift are clear; production costs will vary across the broad range of lifestyle and reality programmes and production contexts, but the possibility of selling and /or replicating a format and of 'revisit' programmes which repackage the same material, along with sponsorship and spin-off products, make lifestyle programmes an attractive option to broadcasters and production companies struggling to survive in a deregulated market.

The aim of the 'real good life' experiment is ostensibly to see what happens when three families are deprived of their normal income and lifestyles. In this sense, *The Real Good Life* is generically close to other reality shows where ordinary people are placed in new and strange situations, such as living in another family home for two weeks (*Wife Swap* RDF Media for Channel 4, 2003 onwards). Annette Hill has characterized this sub-genre as 'life experiment TV' (Hill 2005, 36); it shares with reality television the 'fly on the wall' observation of the participants in a stressful situation, but also, like lifestyle programmes, it addresses the question of how to live well, with each example of the sub-genre presenting a new and specific challenge. Here, as is the case in many of these 'experiment' style programmes, drama is generated by the contrasting and conflicting motivations of the protagonists: two of the households (the Aldridges and the Smiths) appear motivated more by slightly vague desires to spend more time together and to have a common project, than by commitment to the ecological cause, while for the third, a couple (Lisa and Steve Attfield) the principles of self-sufficiency and of leading a less environmentally damaging life are presented as significant factors in their decision to participate. When all three families meet on a field trip to a self-sufficient community in Wales, conflict inevitably ensues.

The BBC's *No Waste like Home* (Celador for BBC2, 2005) ran for eight weeks between 18 August and 6 October in the same year. In this programme, the format of most lifestyle television, where an 'expert' presenter guides participants to an improvement in a specific aspect of their way of living, is adopted. The participants of lifestyle are 'ordinary people', but they are also people defined by a problem, which might be poor relationships with their children, dogs, own bodies, clothes or money. The lifestyle presenter has a mission to sort this, and them, out, with varying degrees of evangelism and domination. In *No Waste like Home*, the presenter, Penney Poyzer, an 'eco-expert' or 'self-styled queen of green' as the voice-over commentary describes her, confronts families whose problem – wasting precious resources – is shared by much of the Western, affluent world. In a pre-title sequence, Poyzer introduces the main theme of the programme, speaking to camera in relevant locations such as power stations, landfill sites or reservoirs. The next section introduces the household under scrutiny and demonstrates its wasteful practices, focusing strongly on the theme of the week, be it waste of water, electricity or food. Poyzer talks the family through a new regime designed to address the problem, and visits to assess progress after one week. The second visit involves not only assessment of progress so far, but the issuing of a further challenge, a raising of the stakes. Frequently, the initial quite rational demands of the regime are replaced by an extreme measure, such as cutting off the electricity supply to the house completely for 24 hours. The next section of the programme shows this second phase of eco-improvement, or eco-challenge, and is followed by Poyzer's third and final visit – the 'reveal' – where she shows how the participants fared, and even gives them back the sum of money they have saved.[2] In the middle of the programme there may also be a visit by Poyzer to a site of good practice, such as the Alternative Technology Centre in Wales.

It's Not Easy Being Green was broadcast on BBC2 less than one year later, from 28 March 2006, when it was launched with a one-hour first episode, and ran in six further half-hour shows till 16 May. Here there are some elements of the 'life experiment' sub-genre in that the programme follows the Strawbridge family who move to a farmhouse in Cornwall not just to live off the land, but also to create an eco-friendly house by installing full insulation, composting toilets and generating their own electricity and producing biofuel. However, unlike some of the life experiments, the participants are fully committed to the enterprise, and one of them, Dick Strawbridge, the father of the family, also presents the programme. In this sense the participants are not the objects of the gaze in the same way as most reality or lifestyle TV protagonists. Dick Strawbridge observes as well as being observed, and his commentary structures and frames the narrative. The high level of commitment to the project manifested by the whole family means that they

---

2   The 'reveal' is a term coined by Rachel Moseley in her discussion of the makeover genre of lifestyle TV which culminates in a moment of spectacle when the newly made-over room, garden or person is revealed to the audience within and beyond the text (Moseley 2000).

are not 'set up to fail' in the same way as the life experimenters, and in general convey a sense of agency. The shared commitment also means that conflict is not the driving force of the narrative. In these ways, this programme can be seen as an innovative contribution to reality/lifestyle TV, not only in its subject matter, but also in its form. A second series was commissioned and broadcast in spring 2007; here the format was different and the programmes featured only the male members of the family, Dick Strawbridge and his son James, who travel round the country helping other committed 'greens' to realize schemes ranging from the installation of a solar panel to the construction of a wind turbine. The programmes contain a revisit element so that there is a sense of continuity rather than completely separate episodes; here we return to a modified version of the expert presenter format, but with the significant difference that the knowledge gap between the presenters and participants is less marked (the Strawbridges have only recently converted the eco-house in Cornwall and their 'subjects' are equally committed to the environmental cause). The programme is about improving practices that are already ecologically aware rather than demonstrating the participants' inadequacy and shame.

Production and reception contexts

The balance of commercial and 'public service' motivations in the production and broadcasting of programmes with an environmental agenda is likely to vary in the different programmes/contexts discussed here. In the case of *The Real Good Life*, the fate of the programme suggests that commercial pressures may have been dominant. The programme was dropped from the prime time schedules after only two programmes had been broadcast, having achieved a first night audience of 2.7 million viewers, in competition with an England football match broadcast on BBC1 to an audience of 6.4 million. The simultaneous axing of other ITV shows suggests that the decision results more from a generalized panic within ITV over ratings and audience share than from concerns about the reception of this programme's specific content. The speed with which the decision was taken also supports this thesis. *The Guardian* reports that Simon Shaps, Chief Executive of Granada, shared the view that the programme, along with others, may have been the victim of ITV's overall scheduling strategy, and that ITV may have launched too many new shows within a short time frame.[3] From all of this we can conclude that the programme was not successful in a highly competitive market and at a sensitive moment in ITV's struggle to achieve a 20 per cent plus audience share. Given the fact that the subject matter, if not the reality format, was innovative in televisual terms, an audience of 2.7 million can be viewed as a cultural, if not commercial, success. This is supported by the fact that it was transferred to a Sunday afternoon slot on ITV, rather than axed completely, and later sold to the Australian 'lifestyle' channel and TVNZ in New Zealand. Nevertheless, the fact that it was withdrawn from prime time suggests that in this case the broadcaster's priority was commercial viability, rather than a commitment to environmentally responsible television.

---

3   <http://media.guardian.co.uk/site/story/0,14173,1505306,00.html>.

Although certainly no more successful in audience size terms than *The Real Good Life*, *No Waste like Home* ran for the full length of the planned eight programme series. The audience figures show a steady decline, from 2.91 million on the first night, to 1.67 million at the end (BBC Audience Research).[4] The fact that this did not result in the programme's withdrawal suggests that the public service broadcasting ethos of the BBC is not completely lost, despite the very real pressures of the market. Celador's website explains that the series and the format have been sold to Australia's 9 Network. The possibility of international sales (perhaps to 'greener' countries than the UK), a spin-off book and the suggestion of discussions with DIY stores and energy and water suppliers about the promotion of a licensed range of 'white goods' indicate that, for production companies, if not broadcasters, national audience figures are not the only factor defining viability.[5] However, even if the BBC broadcast the whole series, to date no further series have been commissioned, so that *No Waste like Home* cannot be considered an unmitigated success.

It's Not Easy Being Green, in contrast, has generated a second series with a different format, as well as a book, independent website and BBC web page; the first series has also been sold to a US cable channel, 'Sundance', which specializes in film, arts programmes and ecological topics. The independent *It's Not Easy Being Green* website is linked to the January 2008 Channel 4 campaign on the inhumane treatment of battery-farmed chickens by chefs Hugh Fearnley-Whittingstall and Jamie Oliver, and offers the opportunity to sign up to the campaign. This connection with other successful programmes and celebrity chefs whose personas include a social conscience establishes *It's Not Easy Being Green* as a significant feature of the landscape of 'green' politics on TV.

In the domain of reality and lifestyle TV, the BBC thus seems to have the strongest track record of broadcasting programmes that directly address environmental issues, and the commercial channels do indeed seem to be more strongly influenced by the requirement to win audience share. For the BBC, the need to justify the licence fee in terms of audience value and public service seems to mitigate the commercial imperatives, which of course the corporation is also subject to. In order to provide a comprehensive assessment of environmental coverage, it would, of course, be necessary to look at other types of programming such as documentary and news. My focus here, however, is on the integration of environmental issues in a dominant area of popular programming, broadcast at prime time, and in this context, the BBC has demonstrated more commitment to the topic and has characteristically found a reasonably successful format with some claims to 'quality' credentials. During the main period of this research (2004–6), the fact that Channel 4 was significantly absent from this area, despite its substantial investment in lifestyle and reality, and its original mission to cater for minority interests, reinforced this point.[6]

However, in early September 2007, after a major advertising campaign, Channel 4 launched a new reality show where 11 participants were taken to live

---

4   BBC Audience and Consumer Research email to the author, 23 December 2005.

5   <http://www.celador.co.uk>.

6   The broadcast of Jamie Oliver's campaign to improve school dinners in 2005, though not 'ecoreality' can, however, be seen as a step in this direction.

on an artificially constructed rubbish dump near a landfill site in Croydon. *Dumped* (Outline Productions for Channel 4, 2007) aired nightly in four one-hour segments. *Dumped* resembled Channel 4's ground-breaking reality TV success, *Big Brother*, in its technique of placing a large number of mainly young participants in an artificially created environment, and shows such as *I'm a Celebrity Get Me Out of Here* in its theme of survival in an extreme environment. The programme was billed as an 'eco-challenge', which involved the participants in building a camp for themselves and making money from salvaged waste. There were regular visits by an 'eco-design expert', Rob Holdway, and sustainable gardener, Steve Jones. Holdway played the role of expert presenter and provided much of the ecological content of the programme through his commentaries on national statistics relating to waste and energy use. Through this programme, and the related web page devoted to green issues, Channel 4 entered the ecoreality field, albeit two years later than BBC2. The commercial underpinning of this activity in Channel 4's case is highlighted by the EDF advertisement on the web page, which uses the original 'Kermit the Frog' song that inspired the title of *It's Not Easy Being Green*. The presence of an advertisement for a large energy multinational on the page must at the very least raise questions about Channel 4's green credentials.

The politics of the programme itself do little to counteract these doubts. The format, unlike that of the other ecorealities considered here, does not address the issue of introducing environmental practice in everyday life, and relates far more to the 'extreme challenge' genre of reality television. The situation is artificially constructed, and the participants build luxury items such as a sauna and hot tub; they are mostly young and attractive, and have different levels of commitment to green politics and practices, so that the stage is set for conflict and drama. The prioritization of the latter is demonstrated by the producers' decision to keep the nature of the challenge secret from the participants until they arrive at the dump: 'The production team felt that it was important that the group came to terms with the scale of Britain's waste problem on camera. Had they known in advance, they might have done research beforehand and this might have diluted the impact of the experience'.[7]

It is clear that motivations for the production and broadcasting of popular TV formats on environmental issues are complex and intertwined with commercial considerations, in part because of the requirements of corporate responsibility, and in part because green is arguably 'the new black'. In the following sections I will consider in more detail the politics of the three programmes I have selected, in order to establish how effective they might be in terms of the promotion of environmental awareness, regardless of the ambiguities of the contexts of production.

The politics and aesthetics of ecoreality

In this part of my discussion of these representations of the 'green' agenda, I will consider both the politics of the programmes and their aesthetic qualities, on the

---

7   <http://www.channel4.com/lifestyle/green/dumped/day-by-day/index.html>.

grounds that unless the programmes succeed as television, viewers are unlikely to be engaged by the subject matter, however worthy. My analysis is also grounded in an alternative hedonist approach – a belief that the potential for pleasure needs to be foregrounded in any appeal to the public to change their everyday practices for the sake of humanity's and the planet's survival. I will therefore discuss not only the extent to which the programmes are making such an appeal, and its precise nature, but I will also discuss them in relation to the seductive qualities found in some other sub-genres of lifestyle: cookery, 'relocation' and 'spiritual journey'. In almost all of these, alternative hedonist pleasures are invoked both through the narratives based on quests for peace and tranquillity, delicious local food or community life, but also visually, through shots of beautiful rural landscapes, convivial gatherings and community events.

In the first two programmes of *The Real Good Life* series, broadcast in a prime time slot, the emphasis is on struggle and difficulty, even for the most committed participants (Steve and Lisa Attfield). Perhaps more than the less engaged but more cheerful participants, they experience conflict and even misery in relation to the experience, so that commitment to environmentally friendly practices is here associated with negativity and sacrifice. The only family who experience pleasure in the early stages of the project are the Aldridges, who take time out to go skiing! *The Real Good Life* does not set out a coherent green politics: there is no expert presenter and the voice-over merely comments on the narrative of struggle and conflict within and between the households. The project itself – of becoming self-sufficient in food in suburban gardens – although more based in everyday life than *Dumped*, is clearly designed far more to make interesting television than to make viable suggestions to viewers about how to develop less environmentally destructive ways of living. An alternative hedonist sense that 'being green' might involve pleasure rather than pain seemed mostly absent from the series. This may go some way to explaining the broadcasters lack of faith and reluctance to invest further.

In *No Waste like Home* the emphasis is on the small everyday changes that can be made to diminish negative environmental impact which the presenter, Poyzer, argues forcefully can make 'a difference'. The changes suggested, in relation to food, waste, use of electricity, water and cars, are accessible to all. However, the narrative is structured around shame, punishment and reward like other lifestyle programmes, and it is no surprise to learn that the programme's producers, Celador, also make the highly successful *You Are What You Eat* for Channel 4. Here presenter Gillian McKeith goes through a similar sequence of visiting – in this case overweight – participants in their homes, demonstrating to them how badly they are eating and setting them targets for recovery. Although *No Waste like Home* shares with *You Are What You Eat* a highly didactic approach and a dominant female expert 'naming and shaming' the participants, the narrative is upbeat in tone, and some of the participants find pleasure in their new ways of living, in the peace and quiet of a home with no electricity, or in walking or cycling to work. In some of the programmes the participants become proactive, rather than merely achieving the targets set. In programme five, for example, one of the members of the student household featured extends his newly adopted recycling practice to his place of employment, a restaurant, while in programme four, two gay men living in a luxury block in London transform not only their own practices but those of other residents in the block. Nonetheless, the programme's focus on domestic life and its repeated, rigid format offer only limited pleasures to viewers.

In *It's Not Easy Being Green*, the structure of punishment and reward of *No Waste like Home*, and the conflicts and struggles of *The Real Good Life* are replaced by the representation of a team effort in which all participants are committed and engaged. In this sense environmental politics are not merged with the moral landscapes of lifestyle based on hierarchies of knowledge and power, or the *Schadenfreude* dimension of reality TV. The presenter, Dick Strawbridge, is less didactic and evangelical than Penny Poyzer or even *Dumped*'s Rob Holdway, and his approach seems to have something of the alternative hedonist appeal to an environmentally aware practice which is not solely based on sacrifice and 'giving things up': 'I don't want a hemp shirt and hairy knickers, I want a 21st century lifestyle with a coffee machine' (programme one, transmitted 28 March, 2006). In the first series the narrative conveys a strong sense that the project of converting a semi-ruined farmhouse into an 'eco-house' is fun: the younger Strawbridges invite friends to help, and there are also various experts in residence – so that instead of *The Real Good Life*'s and *No Waste*'s isolated households or *Dumped*'s bizarre mix of individuals we have the impression of a united and dynamic community. Strawbridge himself is expansive and positive, and the whole family is full of confidence, energy and joy. There are many scenes of laughter, play and convivial meals, so that this programme is the most consonant of the three with the alternative hedonist version of 'green' politics. It may be no coincidence that it is also the most successful so far. However, this project is on a grand scale, and relies on Strawbridge's skills and background as an engineer. Building a waterwheel to generate electricity is clearly beyond the capacity of most people, and the considerable amounts of time which all family members devote to the project are simply not available to most. If *No Waste like Home* offers a more quotidian and accessible version of environmentalism, the first series of *It's Not Easy Being Green* provides little practical enlightenment, but does succeed in making 'being green' seem, if not easy, certainly great fun. The second series features smaller scale and more accessible projects, and the atmosphere of positive enjoyment of the activities is retained, though the episodic structure means that some of the narrative cohesion is lost.

Diverse shades of green?

The discussion of the 'green' politics of the programmes must be accompanied by analysis of the politics of representation in play here in a broader sense. Just as the association of ecologically responsible practices with misery and sacrifice is detrimental to the cause, a focus on a narrow section of society, or the reinforcement of existing social inequalities would also be counterproductive.

Gender seems to be one of the reefs on which *The Real Good Life* flounders. From the outset, gender difference seems to be a factor in the motivation of some of the participants in the experiment: it is Veronica, the mother, who is presented as the most committed member of the Aldridge family and her willingness to participate is presented as based more on her desire to improve relationships between family members than in environmental politics per se. Neil Aldridge, on the other hand, does not seem to share even this commitment, so that the notion of the mother's responsibility for relational work in the family goes unquestioned. In the other two households, giving up paid work and taking on the self-sufficiency challenge has the effect of reinstating gender differentiated roles, with the women more confined to 'light' work, and chasms opening up within the couples. Lisa Attfield, who has left a middle class professional job, finds it difficult to play the supportive wife role to her ex-plumber partner, while the Smiths feel separate and isolated in their work. There is no discussion of the interesting question of why relinquishing paid work triggers this adoption of rigid gender roles and boundaries, so that the programme merely reinforces a rather depressing status quo. If we connect the politics of gender to those of the environment, then women here are represented, at least at the discursive level, as most responsible, and as labouring under a heavy burden.

This feminization of 'green' issues also seems to occur in *No Waste like Home*, through the double-edged choice of a female presenter who appears as both guardian of the environment and finger-wagging teacher figure. The association of women with the domestic sphere through the female presenter and subject matter is reinforced by the fact that of the seven households represented, only two diverge from the overwhelmingly heterosexual family structure. It is a pity that the feminization of prime time identified by Moseley leads to versions of femininity which conform to, rather than question, stereotypes (Moseley 2001, 33). However, perhaps *No Waste like Home*'s high point, in terms of both gender and 'green' politics is the 'reveal' scene in the programme featuring the gay couple, Andrew and Philip. The two men have exceeded Poyzer's expectations in every way, and there have been some amusingly camp moments en route, where they look with horror at the unstylish 'green' garments she offers them (perhaps Strawbridge's dreaded hemp shirt …) and wonder if they can survive on less than three showers and changes of clothing a day. In the 'reveal', the power relationship between participants and presenter and an unwritten rule of lifestyle (presenters don't cry) are overturned when Poyzer is so moved by the men's achievements that tears flow down her cheeks. It is a moment of high emotion, in which, unusually, all participate, and the low affective engagement offered by scenes of nappy changing and filling washing machines in some of the other programmes of the series is surpassed. It is also one of the queerest moments of ecoreality, perhaps of lifestyle TV as a whole.

It's Not Easy Being Green could be seen as redressing the balance of responsibility for the environment in gender terms in that here we see men who are equally, if not more, active and committed. However, gender stereotypes are again at work here; the mother of the family, Brigit, is a matriarchal figure who takes a lead in planning meals and in 'feminine' activities such as making dolls out of scraps of material. She is described by Dick Strawbridge both in the programme and on the website as more spiritual than himself or 'definitely away with the fairies', and she expresses a new age, 'connection with the earth', style of 'green' politics. She works mainly on the gardening side of the project, thus reinforcing this nurturing, mother earth role. Strawbridge, on the other hand, makes and fixes things, in a *Boy's Own* fun kind of way, often with the help of his son James. In the representation of the Strawbridge family in the first series of *It's Not Easy Being Green*, gender polarization seems almost complete, and is mitigated only slightly by the fact that some of the male student helpers cook meals for the temporary community. *The Independent* commented on the first series: 'Somehow, this hunting, fishing soldier has managed to stay married to a slightly hippie chick, draped in scarves and dangly jewellery, who would be quite happy in a hairy shirt and hemp underwear' (O'Connell 2006).[8] Femininity is marginalized by the dominance of Strawbridge as presenter and of the big projects the men work on. In the second series this partnership of male strength and conventionally masculine skills is consolidated, since the female family members are absent. Even though some of the projects the Strawbridges assist with are led by women, there is an emphasis on gadgetry and DIY, which gives the programme a masculine tone. This seems to imply, not the rather hopeful gender hybridity found elsewhere in lifestyle by Moseley, but a 're-masculinization', at least of the ecoreality.

In all three programmes discussed here the white, middle class, heterosexual couple and family remain dominant structures. The participants in *The Real Good Life* are all white, and with the exception of Steve Attfield who is in skilled manual work, in middle class professions. In the first series of *It's Not Easy Being Green*, as we have seen, the focus is on a white, upper middle class family, though the representation of whiteness here is not confined to Englishness, since Strawbridge is from Northern Ireland and invites an Irish eco-expert, Donnachadh McCarthy, to advise the project. The student helpers also bring some ethnic and racial diversity to the programme. This dilution of the English ambiance of the programmes' rural setting is important given the danger that the programmes might appear irrelevant to multicultural urban Britain. In the second series, commitment to the environment is again associated with whiteness, even if a broader range of locations is included. Programme five (transmitted 19 April 2007) shows East London resident Andrew Martin trying to convince his sceptical black female neighbour that a heap of pipes designed to catch solar energy will not be an eyesore, and on arrival at Martin's terraced house in Stratford, Strawbridge comments that 'there aren't too many eco projects going on around here'. This gives the unfortunate impression of middle class white eco-warriors, in Strawbridge's case fresh from life on a Cornish farm, bringing the message to the ethnic minorities of the urban wasteland. However, greater diversity is achieved in one significant area. Unlike the first series of *The Real Good Life* or *No Waste like Home*, the programme features single person households as well as couples and families. Of the three programmes, *No Waste like Home* features more non-white participants and is not homogeneously middle class and heterosexual, but the family is still the most common household featured, and the focus is on suburban living. We can conclude that the 'ecorealities' are less successful in terms of the representation of diversity than some other areas of lifestyle; gardening programmes such as *The City Gardener* (Twofour for Channel 4, 2003–4), for example, avoid the association of environmentally friendly activity with whiteness and rural or suburban contexts.

---

8   O'Connell, S. (2006), 'Living the Eco-life in Cornwall', <http://news.independent. co.uk/environment/article352304.ece>.

The politics underpinning these representations of class, gender, 'race' and ethnicity clearly need to be addressed, if this new and important subject for lifestyle television is to appear convincing and relevant to all, rather than another opportunity for certain sections of the middle classes to display their eco-capital and green identities. Delights other than those of rural living, inaccessible to most, need to be invoked, if ecologically friendly practice is to be associated not only with mundane aspects of existence (important as these are) but with pleasures, such as quieter streets, green spaces and work-free time.

Bibliography

Brunsdon, C., Johnson, C., Moseley, R. and Wheatley, H. (2001), 'Factual Entertainment on British Television: The Midlands TV Research Group's 8–9 Project', *European Journal of Cultural Studies* 4:1, 29–62.

Hill, A. (2005), *Reality TV: Audiences and Popular Factual Television* (London and New York: Routledge).

Holmes, S. and Jermyn, D. (eds) (2004), *Understanding Reality TV* (London and New York: Routledge).

Moseley, R. (2000), 'Makeover Takeover on British Television', *Screen* 41:3, 299–314.

Moseley, R. (2001), '"Real Lads Do Cook … But Some Things are Still Hard to Talk About": The Gendering of 8–9', in C. Brunsdon, C. Johnson, R. Moseley and H. Wheatley, 'Factual Eentertainment on British Television: The Midlands TV Research Group's 8–9 Project', *European Journal of Cultural Studies* 4:1, 29–62.

Palmer, G. (2004), 'The New You … Class and Transformation in Lifestyle Television', in S. Holmes and D. Jermyn (eds), *Understanding Reality TV* (London and New York: Routledge).

Skeggs, B. and Wood, H. (2004), 'Notes on Ethical Scenarios of Self on British Reality TV', *Feminist Media Studies* 4:2, 205–8.

Soper, K. (2007), 'Re-thinking the "Good Life": The Citizenship Dimension of Consumer Disaffection with Consumerism', *Journal of Consumer Culture* 7:2, 205–230.

Thomas, L. (2008), 'Alternative Realities: Downshifting Narratives in Contemporary Lifestyle Television', *Cultural Studies* 22, 5–6.

Index